Lost Narratives

POPULAR FICTION SERIES

Series Editors:

Tony Bennett
Associate Professor
School of Humanities
Griffith University

Graham Martin
Professor of English Literature
Open University

Books in the series: all available in paperback:

Popular Fiction,
Technology, ideology, production, reading
edited by Tony Bennett
Contributors to this text include: Dana Brand, Catherine
Belsey, John Ellis, Raymond Williams, Stephen Heath, Tania
Modleski, Annette Kuhn and Jacqueline Rose.

Cover Stories
Narrative and ideology in the British spy thriller
by Michael Denning
Combining cultural history with narrative analysis, Michael
Denning tracks the spy thriller from John Buchan to Eric
Ambler, Ian Fleming and John Le Carré, and shows how these
tales tell a history of our times, and attempt to resolve crises
and contradictions in ideologies of nation and empire, of class
and gender.

Lost Narratives
Popular fictions, politics and recent history
by Roger Bromley
Explores the ways in which certain popular cultural forms:
narrative fictions, autobiographical writings, television
productions, contribute to the social production of memory.

Forthcoming in the series:
Steve Neale and Frank Krupnik on **Popular Film and TV Comedy**
John Caughie on **Television Drama**
Colin Mercer on **Popular Narratives**

POPULAR FICTION SERIES

Lost Narratives

Popular fictions, politics and recent history

Roger Bromley

Routledge: LONDON AND NEW YORK

First published in 1988 by
Routledge
11 New Fetter Lane, London EC4P 4EE
29 West 35th Street, New York NY 10001

Typeset in 10/11pt Sabon Linotron 202 by Input Typesetting
Ltd, London

Printed in the British Isles by The Guernsey Press Co Ltd,
Channel Islands.

British Library Cataloguing in Publication Data

Bromley, Roger
  Lost narratives : popular fictions,
  politics and recent history. – (Popular
  fiction series).
  1. English literature, 1945–. Special
  themes. Great Britain. Social conditions,
  1918–1945. Critical studies
  820'.9'355

ISBN   0 415 01873 0

Library of Congress CIP Data also available

For Anita

Series editors' preface

There are many good reasons for studying popular fiction. The best, though, is that it matters. In the many and varied forms in which they are produced and circulated – by the cinema, broadcasting institutions and the publishing industry – popular fictions saturate the rhythms of everyday life. In doing so, they help to define our sense of our selves, shaping our desires, fantasies, imagined pasts and projected futures. An understanding of such fictions – of how they are produced and circulated, organized and received – is thus central to an understanding of our selves; of how these selves have been shaped and of how they might be changed.

This series is intended to contribute to such an understanding by providing a context in which different traditions and directions in the study of popular fiction might be brought into contact so as to interanimate one another. It will thus range across the institutions of cinema, broadcasting and publishing, seeking to illuminate both their respective specificities as well as the relations between them with a view to identifying the ways in which popular film, television and writing interact as parts of developed cultural technologies for the formation of subjectivities. Consideration of the generic properties of popular fiction will thus be situated within an analysis of their historical and institutional conditions of production and reception.

Similarly, the series will represent, and coordinate a debate between, the diverse political perspectives through which the study of popular fiction has been shaped and defined in recent years. Feminist studies of the part popular fictions play in the production of gendered subjectivities and relations; Marxist perspectives on the relations between popular fictions and class formations; popular fiction as a site for the reproduction and contestation of subordinate racial and national identities: in encompassing contributions from these often sharply contrasting traditions of thought the series will explore the complex and intertwining web of political relations in which the production and reception of popular fictions are involved.

It should be clear, though, that in all this our aim is not to transform popular fiction into something else – into literature, say, or art cinema. If the study of popular fiction matters it is because what is ultimately at stake in such analysis is the production of a better popular fiction as well as of better, politically more productive ways of reading it.

Tony Bennett
Graham Martin

Contents

Bibliographical note

In dealing with primary sources (novels, autobiographies, diaries etc.) I have cited the original date of publication, the year of any significant reprint, and the date of the paperback (pb) where relevant. The dates for secondary sources are those of their original English publication, unless otherwise stated. Books or articles first published in a foreign language have been listed in the following way: Roland Barthes, *Mythologies*, trans. Annette Lavers (1957; Paladin, 1973), with the first date indicating original publication. Abbreviations, where used, are explained at the time of their initial introduction in the text or notes. NLB refers throughout to New Left Books.

Acknowledgments

The substance of this book was presented as a thesis for the Doctor of Philosophy degree at the University of Sussex. To Stuart Laing, my supervisor, I am particularly grateful for support, ideas and guidance. Geoff Hemstedt and Peter Brooker also offered invaluable insights in connection with this thesis which I have taken account of in the process of revision. My former colleagues at Portsmouth Polytechnic were also very helpful throughout. Over the years Sue Harper, Robbie Gray, Betty Owen, Brendan Kenny, Phil Jenkins, Judy Morey, Ken Lunn, Graham Davies, and, above all, John Oakley have shaped and influenced my own ideas and I am indebted to them.

A work of this nature inevitably owes debts to many sources and many people. *Making Histories*, produced by the Centre for Contemporary Cultural Studies at Birmingham, was a particular source of inspiration. Like so many others in the field I have been deeply influenced by the work of Stuart Hall and the numerous references to him throughout this work testify to this. Tony Bennett and Graham Martin both read the manuscript, made extensive suggestions and offered invaluable advice and support throughout. The staff at both Portsmouth Polytechnic and Sussex University libraries have been very supportive in providing information. Les Roworth, London Weekend Television executive, very kindly gave me access to all the episodes of *People Like Us*. Hannah Collins, community photographer in Bethnal Green, generously provided me with access to proofs of her writings.

Special thanks are due to Pam Miller-Burkett, Helen Kirton, Eileen Robinson and Nicolee Gubbins for all their efforts in typing the manuscript with great skill, speed and accuracy.

To my family I owe the greatest debt of all for their patience, good humour and healthy scepticism about the likelihood of this ever being finished! I hope that Carl and Catherine will consider this book as sufficient justification for all the disruption and neglect it may have caused. No words are adequate to convey the extent of my gratitude to Anita for all her support at every stage and at every level, often at the expense of her own work; to her this book is dedicated.

All faults, errors of interpretation, and other inadequacies remain my responsibility but, hopefully, events will soon make the findings of this book obsolete and its political implications part of a distant memory.

Preface

The origins of this book can be traced to a period shortly after the General Election of June 1983 which returned the Conservative party to power for a second term of office with a substantial majority. I had been working for some time on a study of politics and popular cultural forms in the inter-war period and the Conservative victory prompted me to think about the ways in which a particular moral rhetoric, an explicit nostalgia for 'eternal values', and common sense ideas about a national past all seemed to be predicated upon an image of the 1930s and the second world war, and had come to be articulated with Conservative ideology. The need to examine the ways in which we experience and perceive the present with cultural resources constructed from an imagined past of common memories (in fact, an active appropriation of selected and preferred recall) presented itself as an urgent task. Over the past decade conservative ideology has set up a series of categories through which the past is remembered and the present understood, limiting and constraining the ways in which we are able to 'think' both past and present. Above all, the Falklands war of 1982 both enabled and defined the forms in which the renovation and restoration of particular modes of common sense have taken place.

This book is concerned, therefore, with the ways in

which certain popular cultural forms – narrative fictions, autobiographical writings, and television productions – contribute to the social production of memory. Particular attention is paid to the ways in which the period 1918–1945 has been actively reconstructed in a number of cultural representations over the past decade. The main focus is upon constructions of working-class and lower middle-class experience which generate a sense of representativeness by the use of a number of recurring features.

These features enclose the particular period in a series of retrospectives which render it as *the* definitive zone of memory for an understanding of today. The zone is identified with a particular moral rhetoric and an explicit nostalgia. There is specific concentration in the book upon 'conservative' retrospects as symbol-making processes which stress the imagery of a usable national past. The past is seen as being constantly reconstituted as a means of lining up present economic and social imperatives with certain dominant ideological preoccupations. This is linked, at certain points, with 'Thatcherism' and its attempts to construct a 'national allegory' sedimented in common sense: the past as a set of narratable codes.

The introduction outlines the theoretical concerns of the book and briefly summarizes some of the main ideological features of popular Conservatism over the past decade. Chapter 1 examines a number of specific signifying practices, autobiographical in form and commercially published. The second chapter concentrates upon 'biofictions' – fictional narratives based upon biographical models – each of which has a strong, independent female subject at its centre. The main subject of Chapter 3 is R. F. Delderfield's fictions and the construction of national allegories in the form of lower middle class appropriations of particular symbolic activities. The final chapter looks at the ways in which the Second World War has been articulated to a specific form of 'generational transaction' and suggests ways in which the seemingly random selective procedures of popularized memory are subject to a range of organizing strategies. The conclusion examines a number of challenges to the constructions of social memory focussed upon in the main part of the book.

The book was completed shortly after 11 June 1987 when the Conservative government was re-elected for a third successive term of office. The Queen's Speech which followed the election (25 June) made it clear that Thatcherism was confirmed in its intentions of restructuring and transforming British society by displacing the whole post-war formation. The Speech contained proposals for the heaviest programme of legislation in a Parliamentary session since 1945, much of it directed against democratic institutions (education authorities and local councils) which represented possible opposition to the moral authority of Thatcherism. Support for this undertaking cannot simply be seen in terms of the naked self-interest of voters in the South East of England, because Thatcherism addresses a more complex 'constituency' of fears, anxieties and 'nostalgia for a lost narrative'. 'Narrative' (in the sense of offering coherences and continuities) is a crucial aspect of popular consciousness and part of Thatcherism's continuing success is that it 'invites us to think about politics in images'.[1] Its cultural power depends upon the coining and circulating of a new vernacular for *imagining* Britain as a unitary community, a carefully crafted idiom which has *textualized* at many levels a particular moral rhetoric (freedom, nation, family) which is the colloquial and axiomatic basis of much popular discourse[2]

West Ashling, Chichester
June 1987

'I wouldn't ask too much of her,' I ventured.
'You can't repeat the past.'
'Can't repeat the past?' he cried incredulously.
'Why of course you can!'
F. Scott Fitzgerald, *The Great Gatsby*, 1926

'Those who cannot remember the past are condemned to repeat it.'
George Santayana, *Life of Reason*, 1905

'Those who control the present control the past . . . those who control the past control the present.'
George Orwell, *Nineteen Eighty-four*, 1948

Introduction: organized forgetting?

'The first step in liquidating a people', said Hubl, 'is to erase its memory. Destroy its books, its culture, its history. Then have somebody write new books, manufacture a new culture, invent a new history. Before long the nation will begin to forget what it is and what it was. The world around it will forget even faster.'

'What about language?'

'Why should anyone bother to take it from us? It will soon be a matter of folklore and die a natural death.'

Was that hyperbole dictated by utter despair?

Or is it true that a nation cannot cross a desert of organized forgetting?

Milan Kundera, *The Book of Laughter and Forgetting,*
1978[1]

Popular cultural forms and politics are fundamentally linked. Narratives, particularly, represent our ideas about everyday life by producing cultural images and stereotypes of it. They thus have an important function in representing the past, because they provide crucial forms in which memories are made. Memory is not simply the property of individuals, nor just a matter of psychological processes, but a complex cultural and historical phenomenon constantly subject to revision, amplification and 'forgetting'. Memory is, therefore, a construction. Memories are actively invented and reinvented by cultural interventions. There are many ways in which the past is made sense of, constructed, in any society. My concerns are mainly autobiographical writings and narrative fictions and their contribution to the 'social production of memory'.[2] I shall concentrate on their social function in styling, not only modes of relationship, but also ways of seeing and remembering.

I have chosen writing whose theme is working-class and lower middle-class experience, often of a specific, perhaps unrepresentative, nature but produced in such a way as to generate a sense of representativeness by the use of a number of recurring features, which create a sense of 'habituation' and of familiarization. Since the images which shape our memory of the past define its 'reality', the issue of who decides what is remembered is crucial. Memory always involves a past-present relation. 'It is because "the past" has this living active existence in the present that it matters so much politically.'[3] This *past-present relation* forms the basis of this study. I have taken my bearings on 'popular memory' from Foucault,[4] Gramsci[5] (especially on 'common sense'), Agnes Heller,[6] Patrick Wright,[7] and *Making Histories*.

For Foucault, 'popular memory' only exists within the realm of discourse. It has no abstract, non-discursive mode of existence. It 'exists in the world rather than in people's heads, finding its basis in conversations, cultural forms, personal relations, the structure and appearance of places and, most fundamentally . . . in relation to ideologies which work to establish a consensus view of both the past and the forms of personal experience which are significant and memorable'.[8] My work was largely completed when Patrick Wright's *On Living in an Old Country* (1985) was published, but there are obvious overlaps between the types of thinking involved in our different projects. He is more concerned with the construction of memory within public forms and by public spaces, evidenced particularly in 'A Blue Plaque for the Labour Movement',[9] and though we share concepts of past-present alignments, especially in relation to, what I would call, the cultural-ideological project of Thatcherism and its discursive mobilizations of the past, we offer contrasting assessments of it. Wright argues basically that Thatcherism projects the past as something completed and finished, which does not and must not be allowed to infect the present except in 'memorial' form – e.g. the Mary Rose project.[10] I would argue, on the other hand, that such discourses are multi-accented, capable of diverse and contradictory articulations which see the past as a constantly renewable and 'rewritable' phenomenon. The past may be constructed as 'another country' but it is one which, it is suggested, it is still desirable for us to inhabit.

In this study certain forms of recall will be seen as having priority over others, both as a defence against anxiety and as an instrument of social power. The battle over memory among contending discourses will be examiend as part of a struggle over political consciousness, with the main emphasis falling on 'conservative' retrospects. Other, possibly oppositional, ways of making memory will be considered in the conclusion.

The question of recall will be explored as a matter of cultural mediation – the positing of an imaginary unity grounded in common sense and based on the past, but capable of deployment in contemporary debates. Cultural mediation works through images, symbols, styles as 'stock shots' which collectively 'editorialize' the process of memory making. In times of social stress this framework helps in the selection of 'preferred memories' – certain territorial or national prejudices, tendencies and continuities, re-inscriptions and prescriptions. For example, in a period of recession, like the one which began in Britain in 1974–5 and subsequently deepened, the resulting echoes of the 1930s were seen by the Right as needing to be challenged by another kind of retrospect framed in icons and images which suggested recuperation through symbolic activity. This is a main theme of the book, most sharply focussed in Chapters 2 and 3. A party and a government dedicated to refurbishing British capitalism in

terms of an American dominated world economy, has had
frequent recourse to symbol making processes which stress
a compensating national imagery. As Andrew Gamble says
in *Britain in Decline* 'One of the main achievements of
the Thatcher government has been to underline again and
again the sovereignty of the world market over the British
economy and the small room for discretionary national
economic management which that leaves.'[11] So, to re-
imagine the 'national' in the face of this contradiction,
involves drawing on 'popular memories' of the unified
nation during World War Two symbolized in numerous
national allegories. This forms the basis of the analysis in
Chapters 3 and 4.

The most prominent method for 'remembering' the past
in this way is what, in French, is called 'la mode retro' –
retrospective styling. Particular *forms* of re-articulation
have come to dominate popular cultural 'space'.
Outgrown or outworn tendencies are nostalgically reaffirmed by a 'coded sentimentality',[12] which seems direct
and unmediated, but derives from a mode of producing
memories using certain conventions and synthesizing
different discourses. Such preferred memories, whereby
the past becomes an event to be pictured, styled, and
filmed, have a stabilizing and conciliating function. Even
the most prominent modes of remembering are subject to
implicit social direction based on the power exercised by
existing dominant/popular cultural forms. So there are
'preferred' forms as well as simply 'preferred' memories.
The colonizing of memory by popularized imagery is a
complex process which is not simply a matter of personal
recall.

There is, of course, a generational aspect to 'popular
conservatism', marked by a strong reaction to the
'permissive' sixties (repeatedly stressed in Norman
Tebbit's speeches against those who are seen as the first
beneficiaries of the welfare consensus). But nostalgia is
never simply a passive reflection of 'the good old days'. It
is an active process of styling and 'making' the past. The
dominant versions of what *is* remembered construct

significance by means of cultural images which undergo considerable simplification of detail in the course of time. As Ruth Levitas shows in 'New Right Utopias', Mannheim pointed to the tendency of conservatives to project utopias into the past, rather than the future, which then becomes a way of seeing, self-validating and actively recruited for the present.[13] Elements of an original complex, a particular period for example, are selected out (e.g. 'Victorian Values' so often invoked by Margaret Thatcher and others) and come to stand for all the rest. A pool, or repository, of codes comes into existence.

It is not self-evident that specific generic strategies have to be the 'property' of the dominant culture. However, much of my analysis identifies those codings and representations which compose a particular *genre* of remembering, and whose effect is to dehistoricize and depoliticize the poverty and deprivation of the 1930s, aestheticizing them in the stylized sentimentality of 'sepia-tinted victims'. Poverty in this mode becomes a genre subject, a set of enclosed and detached images. They exist on their own, discontinuous with and estranged from 'our time', but narratively continuous with 'their time'.

The inter-war period is particularly problematic. So much of 'popular memory' about this period has emphasized its *pastness*, concentrating on the personal and the familial, constructing it as unitary, non-contradictory, and *closed*. Representations of the Second World War have been more interrogative, but even here, in the last decade, a 'genre' quality has begun to emerge, a specialized diction, imagery and system of metaphors increasingly 'unitary' in its structure. The repeated insistence on the whole period in question (1918–45) in novel, autobiography, television drama and documentary in recent years may even suggest that an attempt is being made to transform it into the total cultural form of our present and future life.

Condensation and distancing are the most frequent strategies for remembering the period. A complex of selected icons simultaneously 'memorializes' the time and insists upon its discontinuities with the present. They are all seen as 'period' symptoms – 'hard times'. Selected values *are* conserved as continuous, however. The passivity of a 'class' is contrasted, time and again, with the activity of the *mobile* individual. The process turns everything innto spectacle and gives priority to a 'synchronic grasp'. Particular events are 'fixed', removed from the complex flow of their constitutive elements. The narrative strategies and 'anecdotal' imagery compose specific rhetorical figu-rations which generate their own *coherence* for the period.

This process was thrown into relief by many issues raised by the 1984–5 miners' strike. A useful starting point is the concluding section of an article written by Peter Jenkins in the *Guardian* entitled 'Mrs Thatcher's Vision of Good':[14]

> For both government and opposition the miners' strike, when eventually it ends, will signify what is going out in our politics and not what is coming in. For the Labour Party it signifies the last spasm of a class politics which can no longer serve as a basis for future advance. It has revived the ghosts of 1926. For the government a victory over Mr Scargill may signify the triumph of the Thatcherite counter-revolution, a symbolic liberation from the past and departure from the road to collectivism. It will lay to rest the ghosts of 1974. If good is really to emerge from what the Prime Minister at Guildhall called 'this tragic strike' perhaps it will take the form of a much needed political catharsis.

In the past twelve years or so there has been a widespread attempt to achieve a symbolic liberation from the past by using the popularly dominant symbols *of the past* – especially of the inter-war period. This period has been signified as British capitalism's symbolic crisis in a series of cultural interventions, which have been partly effective *because of* a 'crisis' in popular socialist conceptions of the past, especially the 'Left decade' of the 1930s. We can say that by returning to the sites of the Left's imagery, the Right has taken them over for, what Peter Golding has called, 'contemporary neo-liberalism'.[15]

There has, in the past deccade, been a vast amount of

visual and verbal *schemata* of the inter-war period, part of a larger cultural anamnesia which while it corresponds in its forms to the structures of memory and remembering is, arguably, actually part of a process of *forgetting*. It can be regarded as part of a larger attempt, not to marginalize the conditions of working-class existence from history as such, but to signify the ending of class politics *per se*. A commonsensical image of a past working class is constructed in order to demonstrate that that was *the* working class, and it no longer exists. In many recent representations of the period, the stress is placed on the past as 'another country' – a strange place – where things were very different. The emphasis is on the degree to which things have changed *at the material level*. Television has played an active part in organizing this 'script' by the ways in which it repeatedly confers meaning through a range of signifiers of the period. The past is domesticated, made part of memory lane, an album of snapshots preserved in an archive. Above all, it is *THEN*. The high visibility of the past, and of poverty as codified in these forms, suggests a shared positioning in the present and a low visibility of poverty now, or of any other negative markers from the past, for that matter. There has recently developed a genre of 'poverty as landscape', a *coherent* narrative based upon a carefully selected range of highly visual imagery relating to housing, sleeping accommodation, pawnbrokers, clothing, hairstyles, faces, all framed in sepia-tinted stills. A surfeit of images 'uses up' the period and exempts us from any involvement in it.

If inter-war poverty is seen *iconically* then this helps to fix it, seal and secure it within a definitive version of poverty – i.e. four in a bed, bugs, tuberculosis, poor relief, raggedness, stylized forms of the unemployed. Contemporary claims of poverty can thus be dismissed as lacking the authenticating data – the stock shots of *the* poverty reference system, the validating signifiers, visual condensations. This is a particular problem for autobiography, as the ways in which 'authentic' experience is linguistically coded runs into the dominant mediations of already existing cultural narratives. A parodic version of this problem was produced in *The Secret Policeman's Ball* – a kind of poverty-capping sketch, drawing upon the heavily preconstructed discursive field that any 'account' of the period has to negotiate. It is this very *excess* – an over-realism always based on the same extreme material signifiers so that they can be discounted *now* – at the level of detail and style which helps to subvvert the politics of 'welfarism'. A significantly different kind of contemporary poverty cannot be validated because it doesn't fulfil the iconic requirements. The retrospective mode is part of a cultural testimony to the fact that *once* times were hard and poverty was real, and there was *then* a case for 'welfarism' but not now. At the same time, most of the autobiographies bear witness to the fact that survival and mobility were the result of enterprise, independence and self-determination.

The constant stress on the inter-war period is part of a revisionist project designed to show, not that poverty is a class myth, but that an 'authentic' class memory of *real* poverty has now 'vanished into the footnotes'. In other words, the re-discovery of extensive poverty in our own time has been ideologically blocked by a corresponding re-discovery of that *real poverty* at a time when it was nobody's fault if they were poor.

An interesting part documentary/part fiction exception to this was the television programme *Shebbear* (1984) where the icons yield to, and supplement, an experiencing, articulating subject who is not simply remembering, but building a verbal and visual script around the problematic of memory, the dialectic of then and now.[16] This is achieved structurally at one point when the observing, remembering narrator stands on the beach at Shebbear (in Devon) and becomes part of a dramatic reconstruction of that beach forty years ago with 'himself' acted by a small boy. The dramatization then blends with the presenting moment and the narrator interrogates both the scenario and his memory. It is precisely this interrogative mode which is absent from the widely circulated, popularized 'childhood' memories.

What seems to have happened is that the rhetoric and framework of oral history have been appropriated in ways designed to take the 'history' out of the interwar period and substitute for it a series of images which *stand in* for history and which condense, conflate and profess to sum up the period. These images transfix us by their insistent realism of detail and, as Barthes noted, 'any fashion so detailed becomes unreal'. This is, in other words, a way of using retrospect to *obscure*, a mode of cultural opportunism which turns everything – poverty, history, class struggle – into the costume drama of 'good television'. Memories are constructed so that poverty becomes distanced, specialized, part of a genre. By constantly working at the level of *cultural* signification, the terms of the debates about welfare and poverty are being constantly, and ingeniously, shifted and the agenda continuously revised. This insistence on particular iconic and discursive forms, sealed off from their historically specific complexity, leads to a media-specific approach to the past. Television versions of the period (and of the war) particularly encourage this conventionalization. Poverty is recalled in its purely *visual* dimension. In this form it is seen as belonging to a time, and not a system – a time, which in re-scripting is seen as an accidental, and temporary, *interruption* of the smooth path of capitalist development.

The versions of the past I am referring to draw extensively upon the period's own forms and styles. They 'quote' the imagery, tone, and textures of the pictures and films, but in such a way that the past becomes a *slide*, torn out of context, open to any arbitrary use. Is there a danger of our seeing each image, or set of images, as yet another 'view' or landscape? Has the past become so knowable, and known, that we can no longer look at it meaningfully? The tonal quality of many of the images presented on television, the sets and the impedimenta, draw extensively on the photographs of the time, so much so that they are perceived as 'objets d'art' and enjoyed as images of the time. We participate in a kind of recognition game which comes to dominate that which is being mediated. The textures, the blurs and fuzziness (an effect of technique) help to reinforce the visual quality of the past, and enhance its *pastness*. We become tourists in other people's reality. The appearance of an event, or item, is fixed and removed from the flow of which it was a part, yet made to look as if they 'are stencilled off the real'.[17] A specific 'look' or 'atmosphere' has been developed which helps to make sense of *our* crisis in the terms of the last one and, most importantly, *its* recovery. A process of elision, omission, and mythizing simplification has relieved us of the burden of remembering. It is 'history brushed with the grain'. The injuries of class, war, race, and gender are anaesthetized by the 'tokenism' of specific cultural imagery.

For many of us, and for a whole generation that has grown up since that time, the whole period is only remembered through cultural mediations – we see it in terms of specific inventories, *anthropologically* – segmented into specific rhetorical figurations which confer their own meanings and generate their own coherence. Even those for whom the period is part of 'living memory' must bear in mind Vernon Scannell's words: 'I realize that I do not remember it [World War Two] so clearly after all. History remembers it, and I remember it as history.'[19] It is tempting to substitute television for history in that quotation. It is certainly worth considering whether an attempt is being made to transform the interwar period into the total cultural form of our present life by sealing off and framing the poverty, and by mobilizing the housebuilding, the consumer durables, the mortgages, and the spirit of enterprise and neighbourliness – the revisionist version offered, for instance, by Stevenson and Cook in *The Slump*, the 'sunrise' aspect of the thirties; or, what might be called, the route to *now*.[19] Is it a symptom of the failure of a system that is not able to reproduce itself in forms other than those of a recessive symbolism?

The analogy with the last crisis is not only iconic then, but also a politically conservative act of memory, i.e. that crisis was temporary, so will this one be. The 'replay' is not simply unhistoricized nostalgia. It is a way of confronting the insecurity of the present with the already known *constructs* of the past – history, as Barthes said, slips into myth by a process of elision, omission and simplification.[20]

It will be shown, therefore, that although the 'selling point' of these works of popularized 'memory' is a nostalgia in which the personal and the familial tend to stand in for everything else, the political-cultural effect has a much deeper resonance than the term 'nostalgia' conveys.

In all societies the past is the subject of continuing debate. This intensifies at certain times and the struggle over the forms which this debate takes becomes part of a wider cultural politics – the site of national-popular memory. Arguably, since the breakdown of 'consensus politics' in this country, we live in such an 'intensified' time with images of the inter-war period (significantly conceived as that moment prior to the 'welfare state') which are frequently re-constituted as the concerns of the present. In some forms this becomes a process of retrieval with a method which 'blots out' everything that is known about later history. The method turns away from the complex images of the actual historical process towards the 'victors', or those who were upwardly mobile and were regarded as the successes of the system – *the enterprising individuals*. This mode of retrieval (in fact and fiction) documents the history of society's winners as they *choose* it should be remembered. It is a romanticization of the *present* and a legitimation of its current political forma-tions. This is why the specified period (1918 to 1945) has been chosen for emphasis because of its 'crisis' image and the commonsensical view of it as *exceptional* and sealed off for ever by the 'age of affluence' and the welfare state. In some versions of 'memory' (as in some 'revisionist' histories of the period) the depression was a temporary reversal which is not allowed to obscure the fact that the working class is moving with the current.

These particular narratives work because they appear to ground themselves in the surface appearance of things. They *style what we know* through the textual organization of recall by means of repetition, redundancy, clusters of signifiers, and formulary expressions. A series of retrospective life histories leads to a cell-like rendering of the past, with each cell hermetically sealed and with a particular kind of *social accenting* tending to prevail and win credibility. The naturalizing of historical conditions – part of the *interface* of fact and fiction – Marx called a *forgetting*. It reproduces the categories of bourgeois common sense by articulating the past 'as it really was' without its conditional character – without an inventory, in Gramsci's terms. Stripped of its contingency and its conditionality, history becomes a matter of common-sense knowledge, something which is always already there.

Forgetting is as important as remembering. Part of the struggle against cultural power is the challenge to forgetting posed by memory. What is 'forgotten' may represent more threatening aspects of popular 'memory' and have been carefully and consciously, not casually and unconsciously, omitted from the narrative economy of remembering. Part of this structure of amnesia is the recurring ideological sense that the representative individual replicates the essence of the society's experience. This is offered as the 'logic' of the period – its unvarnished truth – rather than a comment on cultural hegemony. Collective experiences are lightly sketched 'back projections' for the individual – they are de-mobilized. They do not seek to make the past part of the process of people making their own history, by putting it back into time, but establish a context which lends itself to arbitrary use by assembling a series of 'stills' through which we come to 'know' the period and its consequences.

Another recurring characteristic is the way in which the local experience mediates national identity and memory, although often there is a sense that the images of local particularity are 'fictioned' mosaics drawn from 'official' memories of the past diffused through press, literature, and broadcasting. A *surrogate* for social and political memory is created, a subtle in-folding of public with personal images takes place in any revisiting of the past. The eye witness is never a simple 'I'; individual testimony is always social, even more so when the unreliability of memory is considered: 'The memories that permeate the present are subsumed within a hierarchy of habit, recall, and memento.'[21] Recall is necessarily selective; selectivity is a matter of social and political determinations which is why the *forms*, the habits of phrasing, and the use of formulaic repertoires in these writings will be a central part of the study.

An interesting example of the cultural determination of specific modes of writing, from Raymond Williams' *Politics and Letters*, will serve as a useful summary of some of the concerns of my analysis of the *styles* of popular memory.[22] Williams refers to Orwell and the ways in which certain literary conventions dictate modes of observation in such a manner that what is taken as vivid and convincing and truthful is actually prescribed. In Orwell's Lancashire, he says, it is always raining, not because it often does or doesn't, but it has to do so as a condition of convincing local detail of the north. In similar fashion, the current popularity of 'social history' themes in television drama is marked by a painstaking concern for authenticity in terms of locale and period. Accurate historical reconstruction, however, becomes a matter of drawing from a repertoire of lighting techniques, camera angles, stock shots, costume and physiological 'typing' – in other words, what mobilizes these productions is not the historical resources but the idioms and iconography of television practice. In analysing the writings of popular memory no cynicism will be implied about the 'authenticity' of specific experience, but questions will be raised about what 'writes' these memories, what formal conventions are operating on the highly particularized details of the narratives. As with any form of writing one of the

problems is that of finding a language. One of my tasks
will be to try and trace the resources and conventions of
the range of styles used.

There are several difficulties involved in any discussion
of the 'politics' of popular writings in the form of popular
memories. At first glance much of the material to be
analysed looks as though it could be classified into
'conformist' or 'consensual', 'radical' or 'dissonant', but
the superficiality of such distinctions is revealed by two
extracts from writings about 'popular consciousness' by
Peter Townsend and Stephen Yeo. In *Poverty in the United
Kingdom*, Townsend says:

> [although many of the poor recognize they are relatively
> deprived, these feelings are] largely sealed off from more
> general or abstract perceptions of society. Some of the
> poor have come to conclude that poverty does not exist.
> Many of these who recognize that it exists have come to
> conclude that it is individually caused, attributed to a
> mixture of ill-luck, indolence and mismanagement. . . . In
> this they share the perceptions of the better-off. Divided,
> they blame individual behaviour and motivation and
> unwittingly lend support to the existing institutional
> order.[23]

The reference to 'divided' indicates an important feature
of the biofictional and autobiographical mode, namely the
category of the individual as a central structuring element,
the sealing off of an *ideology* of the 'personal' from more
complex notions of the personal-social dialectic. At root
is the idea of the personal testimony of individual women
and men as a category of historical (therefore, true)
discourse. Colin McArthur explores this in *Television and
History* and shows how the rhetoric of narration is used
as a guarantee of truth.[24]

A further aspect of such discourses has been pinpointed
by Stephen Yeo in 'The Politics of Community
Publications':

> One of the strong messages I get from many of these
> writings is how little the authors, whatever their level of

consciousness or position may be, have bought of the present system. In the face of all the long cultural revolution from above, it is remarkable how 'unsocialized' we remain, how little of our humanity we have collapsed into our social roles. . . . There is a lot of space for creative production and politics to work within. Even the nostalgia – 'those were the days' – given the sharp characteristics of the starvations etc. of those days – is, in my view, a rejection of these days, or at least a quite specific critique of Now, running through a channel of Then.[25]

The particular mode of popular writings which will form the centre of this theoretical and textual analysis will be mediations, or channels, of *Then* (1918–45). How far it will be possible to see these as critiques *or* confirmations of *Now*, or uneasy expressions of the tensions between the two approaches, I would see as the main purpose of the study of the interface between Popular Writing and Popular Memory.

It has been argued so far that memory undergoes a process of material *popularization*, is subject to reorganization and reconstruction, and is constantly reworked in the imagery of contemporary concerns. A brief sketch will be offered, in this introduction, of the political context of the concerns in terms of recession, the social market, neo-liberalism, authoritarian populism and, seen by some as synonymous with most of these, Thatcherism. First of all, however, we need further to consider the ways in which images of the past are deployed, manipulated and appropriated for sectional interests.

Something remembered, is not, in Berger's phrase, 'like a terminus at the end of a line'.[26] Numerous approaches or stimuli converge upon any process of remembering. However, popularized imagery seeks to close these approaches, work within a snapshot version of memory and produce a simple retrospect organized through emblematic fragments. Susan Sontag has made this point well. Texts are like cultural quotations which 'turn the past into an object of tender regard, scrambling moral distinctions and disarming historical judgements by the

generated pathos of looking at time past'.[27] This form of
cultural appropriation, this soft, abstract pastness she links
with other ways of *distancing:* 'A photograph of 1900 that
was affecting then because of the subject would, today, be
more likely to move us because it is a photograph taken
in 1900. The particular qualities and intentions of photographs tend to be swallowed up in the generalized pathos
of time past'.[28]

Equally useful is Judith Williamson's work on advertisements in *Decoding Advertisements.*[29] She talks of an
'iconographic past' given meaning only through the idea
of an individual's story (the past *personal* time of autobiography), while at the same time 'Real events, or objects
connected with real events, are hollowed out, as with other
referent systems leaving only the interiority of the subject,
an inside without an outside denying "objective" historicity'.[30] The notion of 'objective historicity' of course raises
problems of its own, but the comment does suggest links
with the ways in which autobiographies and 'biofictions'
(those narratives which take their shape from the
biographical mode) tend to 'swallow up' and 'hollow out'
history in a particular form of subjectivized appropriation
and misrepresentation. History becomes a narrative code
or visual item in an iconographic system – an Oxo tin, a
steam engine, Woodbines, or an endlessly repeated still of
an unemployed march. The past is commodified, made
secure, seen as 'a *moment, static* time rather than changing
time'.[31] The past, in this analysis, is seen as something
which 'must be stopped; caught and processed into something that can no longer slip away – in other words it is
made into a product. Time is a commodity, bought and
sold.'[32] The past is not simply used as a nostalgia for a
completed time, however, as it is constantly being reconstructed as a means of lining up present economic and
social imperatives with certain dominant ideological
preoccupations – the past – present alignment is never
allowed to settle.

Turning the clock back

> This path is still blocked, however, by the most fatuous of all fashionable arguments, namely, that 'we cannot turn the clock back'. One cannot help wondering whether those who habitually use this cliché are aware that it expresses the fatalistic belief that we cannot learn from our mistakes . . . Nothing less than a rededication of current policy to principles already abandoned will enable us to avert the threatening danger to freedom.[33]
>
> F. A. Hayek, *A Tiger by the Tail,* 1972

In describing the recent period since 1979 the term 'Thatcherism' and the 'politics of Thatcherism' have had extensive currency.[34] It is not the place of this study to add to these analyses, but it will be necessary to draw upon many of their findings.

Thatcherism was initially thought to have brought to an end the post-war period of consensus in politics, as the earlier economic crisis beginning in 1973 had ended the post-war boom. Neo-liberalism based on the so-called social market was to be the new policy which would restore Britain's place in the world economy, a policy usually described as monetarist. The consensus theory of post-war politics has been challenged,[35] but the term 'consensus' does indicate, at least, a *symbol* of what were held to be shared values, acquiesced in, if only passively, by many people. As far as Thatcherism is concerned that consensus, real or imagined, is identified inextricably with the politics of the post-war settlement which is seen as the root cause of current ills, needing to be radically altered. In order to effect this in a cultural form Thatcherism has set out to generate a set of affirmative images based upon the selective revival of particular symbols of person and nation, constructed specifically from 'stories' of war and the interwar period. This relegitimation of 'vanished' values is a complex and diffuse process and cannot be reduced to any simple notion of dominant ideology or manipulation. It is an activity which is not confined to Downing Street or even to Thatcherism exclusively, as it has a far wider purchase. In the process, not only has the 'consensus' been broken up by the Right, but many of the problems involved in the post-war 'settlement' have become part of a Left analysis. Some of the cultural forms of this questioning will be examined in the conclusion.

The new Conservatism with its allegiance to economic liberalism has roots which long precede the emergence of Margaret Thatcher as an influential politician. Such policies were theorized by F. A. Hayek, as well as by Enoch Powell and Keith Joseph with their attacks on Keynesian economics in the 1960s. The advocacy of a social market economy was only part of a wider political ideological definition of Conservatism which included attacks upon State intervention, social democracy, the trade unions, social security, and, in the case of Powell, black immigration. Defence, the family, individual enterprise and moral responsibility, freedom, and law and order have become the central forms upon which 'Thatcherism' is based. This involves a practice which is economically multi-national and rhetorically nationalist. The discredited, displaced 'consensus' had to be succeeded by a refurbished *national* consensus to guarantee a medium of exchange based upon a social market strategy. Keynesian economic management, it is claimed, and its accompanying inflation threaten 'to disrupt the elaborate mechanisms of exchange between individuals'.[36]

The slow down in the rate of growth, two recessions, unemployment (which first reached a million under a Labour government), corporatist strategies of the Wilson-Callaghan government, and the public sector strikes in 1978–9 all helped to provide a context in which the Conservatives came to power in May 1979. Initially, the government was by no means composed of adherents of the New Right, but in the past nine years many of the so-called 'Wets' have been shed and a more coherent 'Right' policy has emerged, buttressed by an ideological repertoire of symbols which seek 'to put the clock back', construct the 'permissive' sixties as alien and profligate, and argue for a sense of personal and cultural feeling of belonging to a nation in which 'welfarism' is seen as a dereliction of moral responsibility.

Andrew Gamble argues persuasively that Thatcher's governments are not as innovative as their rhetoric claims, but have added a more doctrinal and ideological inflection to a process which began to move away from Keynesianism with the Labour government in 1975 with its cash limits to control public expenditure, the doubling of unemployment from 1975 to 1977, and its commitment to the IMF. In fact, Thatcherism is more consistent and coherent ideologically than it is in practice. Milton Friedman has justly accused Mrs Thatcher of failing to deliver claims to control the money supply, while so-called 'moral authoritarians' like Roger Scruton and Peregrine Worsthorne feel that Thatcherism has fallen far short of its rhetoric in areas of social and moral responsibility. Others have not been satisfied by the 'piecemeal' approach to privatization and trade union legislation.

Moral revivalism and romantic nationalism have formed part of the means by which Thatcherism has sought not only to break the parameters of the post-war consensus, but also to rewrite the ideological scripts of modern British society. In many ways, Thatcherism should be seen as a response, or reaction, to a number of complex and contradictory forces in contention over this 'ideological landscape', rather than having an originating or generating function. A larger cultural appropriation of symbolic activity – the main concern of this study – has helped to establish a popular cultural profile to which some features of Thatcherism may be articulated. This profile has been both constitutive of, as well as constituted by, a process of 'making sense' in which popular conservatism, with its siege mentality, has constructed the dominant form of defences to 'challenges to the national way of life'.[37]

Stuart Hall has called the most characteristic tendency of this 'defence' of the nation 'authoritarian populism',[38] a response to the 'politics of recession',[39] and what Geoffrey Pearson, in *Hooligan*, has described in the following way:

Nor did it need riots to provoke these swan-songs for the old traditions. Throughout the 1970's, in a gathering storm of discontent, the same accusations had become a dominant feature of the social landscape. The decline of family life, the lowering of standards in schools, the 'permissive' worm within, the irresponsibility of working mothers and their delinquent 'latch-key' children, the excessive leniency of the law, and the unwarranted interference of the 'softly-softly, namby-pamby pussyfooting' of the so-called experts' – these were well trodden avenues of complaint by 'law and order' enthusiasts and 'anti-permissive' moralists, warning of a vast historical degeneration among the British people.[40]

Put in this synoptic way it sounds very much like a caricature, but many of the issues referred to did form part of an 'agenda' which carved the way for the moral content of 'Authoritarian Populism'. The concept has been challenged by Bob Jessop *et al.* for ignoring some of the potential sources of contradiction and tension within Thatcherism and for over-estimating its general strength and resilience.[41] One crucial aspect of 'Authoritarian Populism' was the implied convergence between those in positions of power and authority and 'popular' imagery of the type described above by Geoffrey Pearson. Jessop *et al.* are particularly critical of the way in which Hall conflates a number of contradictory theoretical positions to arrive at the notion, and also of his reliance on 'hegemony' and discourse theory which they consider reinforces the danger of 'ideologism'. They claim that 'Authoritarian Populism' tends to accept Thatcher's rewriting of post-war history which marks 1979 as a decisive break. Like Gamble, they indicate how breaks with Keynesianism came from within the social-democratic consensus (1975–9) and that Thatcherism gave the 'break' a specific ideological inflection by finding a social base in the petty bourgeoisie and small capital.

There is always the danger of simplifying Thatcherism to a point where it seems more substantial, unique and monolithic than it is. In reconstructing a 'national allegory', sedimented in common sense, Thatcherism is contradictory, uneven and inconsistent at the level of political practice, but the concept of 'Authoritarian Populism' *is* a useful analytical tool for describing its image-making, style-generating capacity – its *ideological* marketing. It does not account for complex class forces or the ambiguities of the social market economy, as it is more concerned with addressing matters of style and performance – the area in which Thatcherism's effectivity is secured. Its success depends, in cultural terms, on its *narrative commonsense* – its discursive forms – remaining unchallenged. In using the concept of 'Authoritarian Populism' myself I have confined it to a dimension of analysis which concentrates upon political-ideological forms and their articulation in cultural practices. Hall defends his own use in similar terms, convinced that an understanding of populist consent – what I would call furnishing the 'emotional household' in Agnes Heller's phrase – requires concepts drawn from discourse analysis as well as Poulantzas and Gramsci. Thatcherism is a generalizing strategy which demands analysis on many levels, not excluding the ideological dimension and the construction of subjectivities.

One of my purposes here will be to contribute to an analysis of the complex phenomenon of Thatcherism, which recognizes its many-accented character and which also acknowledges that the active reconstruction of popular social memory over the past decade is a cultural-ideological process in which Thatcherism is only one among many contributing tendencies. I say this in order to avoid any simplifying notion which assumes that the electoral defeat of the present Conservative government would leave a space free from the 'retro mode' of conceiving the future in terms of a carefully edited past.

At one point in his *New Left Review* reply, Stuart Hall indicates how he has tried to show how 'Thatcherism has managed to stitch up or "unify" the contradictory strands in its discourse – "the resonant themes of organic Toryism – nation, family, duty, authority, standards, patriar-

chalism with the aggressive themes of a revived neo liberalism — self interest, competitive individualism, anti-
statism".'[42] This 'stitching' process, part of what, if not
challenged, could become an 'organized forgetting', forms
the main thrust of my work.

A number of popular cultural forms have emerged in
'the service of the past' at a time when this has been
urgently needed for ideological purposes, but how they
have been appropriate is as impossible to determine as it
is to write a history of common sense, as Gramsci said;
one can only point to tendencies. The struggle for political
authority has been accompanied by a search for an *authorized*, secure and usable past. Time and time again, 1945
has been selected as the marker and terminus. The present,
and its anxieties, is being relieved by narratives of a carefully edited past which justify particular claims ('Britain
has not changed'), create confidence and offer symbols of
stability. The narratives strengthened the purpose of those
who possessed, or sought, power and reconciled those
who lacked it by recruiting them — 'ordinary people' — to
an honoured place in the cultural scripting of the past.

The popular cultural re-discovery of 1918–45 is
designed not only to justify, but also to educate. The post-
1945 settlement has been used as a scapegoat — it has been
used 'to explain, and therefore assuage, social frustration
and personal disaster, to lift the burden of personal
failure.'[43] This addiction to the past, expressed in *personal*
terms, most appropriately takes the form of popular narratives which can construct representations of 'living entities'
as symbols of situations which 'our people' were all
involved in. The past in this scenario is composed of a set
of 'narratable' codes, not a complex historical process; its
very 'narrativity' guaranteed its unfolding purpose.
Margaret Thatcher's Cheltenham speech after the
Falklands War (quoted in full on p.151) talks about 'the
re-discovery of ourselves', how 'Britain found herself again
in the South Atlantic' and the 'recovery of our self-respect.'
Re-discovery and recovery are both dominant themes in
the works I am examining, and it is not surprising that

Thatcher directly quotes Churchill: ('a little known speech . . . made just after the last war.')

> We must find the means and the method of working toge-
> ther not only in times of war, and mortal anguish, but in
> times of peace, with all its bewilderments and clamour and
> clatter of tongues.[44]

What Thatcherism has achieved is a classic synthesis of class/party/nation/past/people which is symbolically inaccessible to the Left. The political 'recidivism' is only one manifestation of a wider cultural recidivism – the 'return to the traditionalist reference points of the past has been one of the main lynch-pins of Thatcherism's ideological project.'[45] The populist connection is preoccupied with 'traditional values', 'true values', 'fundamental values', 'the tried and trusted values of common sense'. The repetitions, like the constant relay of cultural reiterations on the same theme, have a mesmeric effect.

Thatcherism is a contradictory ideological exercise, and it has required the *cultural* construction of narratives which resolve the contradictions and synthesize the competing images, symbols and meanings into a 'popular' and unitary form of consciousness.[46] This ideological unity does not depend upon logical consistency, but a process of symbolic transference in which a narrative of the past 'stands in' for the present and sediments itself in 'popular memories'.

I have divided my analysis of these cultural mobilizations into three separate chapters. Each one is, in a sense, discrete and self-contained, although many of the themes addressed in Chapter 1 recur, in different narrative form, in Chapter 2, while Chapters 3 and 4 are linked by a concern with the ways in which different media have invented and imagined the 'nation'. All the chapters are conceived, in a way, as sharing a common stock of interests and preoccupations which have been outlined in this introduction.

1

In those days

This chapter is concerned with the commercial popularization of particular forms of autobiography, based on working-class experience. I hope to show that their circulation within a market economy has the effect of explaining the current crisis as the result of a lengthy diversion from past values. How that past is mediated cannot simply be determined by examining political speeches or 'serious' news analysis. It is also necessary to trace the active role of cultural practices and processes in constituting the ways in which we come to understand the 'popular' and 'social reality'.

It is difficult to place a precise date on the origins of the commercial interest in publishing the autobiographies of working-class people, but the republication in 1973 of Flora Thompson's *Lark Rise to Candleford* by Penguin undoubtedly helped to establish this mode of writing as a popular genre. *Lark Rise* was first published by Oxford University Press in 1939, *Over to Candleford* in 1941, and *Candleford Green* in 1943. All three were published under the current title in 1945. At another level, and addressing another range of experience, the re-issue of Vera Brittain's *Testament of Youth* (1933) and subsequent television version also contributed to the same effect. The extensive marketing of *The Country Diary of an Edwardian Lady* (1977) is another such example.

The reasons for this growth of activity cannot be seen simply as a quest for origins, or as an indulgence of an uncomplicated 'nostalgia'. Although the different discourses may share common forms and refer to similar periods, they address very different experiences and articulate a complex, varied, and contradictory range of positions and attitudes. They have also been actively recruited and co-opted for radically different purposes.

Some of the texts most readily associated with the renewal of, and definition of, nostalgia in recent times have also become part of the profitable exploitation of what Fraser Harrison calls 'corrupt grief'.[1] A classic instance is Edith Holden's *The Country Diary of an Edwardian Lady*, (1977), published in fourteen countries, selling more than three million copies in hardback, and marketed in the form of over 900 products in Britain and the USA. A televised version in twelve half-hour episodes appeared in 1984. Fraser Harrison's excellent analysis in *Strange Land* makes a key point about the illustrations. The plants sketched are shown with, 'their roots . . . excised, their original earthiness has been scrubbed away and only their formal, abstract qualities are shown. These sketches have the lifeless, eerie look of pressed flowers, whose flesh withers to paper, but whose colours remain vibrant.'[2] Each page of *The Illustrated Lark Rise*, in similar vein, is decorated with a pressed flower.

It is this 'pressed flower' approach to the past which characterizes many recent television versions of the interwar period. The 'original' colours are lovingly restored, while the 'flesh' is stylized in its formal, abstract qualities. These versions are active agencies of symbolization through *style*.

Selectivity, conscious or unconscious, repression, interference, decay of memory and distortions, all form part of the limitations of recollection. The *time of remembering* (personal, cultural, social, political) is a crucial part of the process. In other words, there may well be current a number of explanatory frames which condition how and what is remembered. This applies equally to forgetting, which may also be cultural in some cases. Remembering is quite obviously an interpretive process. Bartlett showed that remembering is a reconstructive activity, and that the moment of remembering is as important as the time being remembered.[3] However suppressed, or excised, from the discursive representation, the present always intervenes significantly on constructions of the past. If the 'past' is widely thought of in abstract terms, and the present is dehistoricized, then the past could be liable to a 'remembering' of it in 'pressed flower' terms — torn from its roots and simply invoked as a witness for contemporary, dominant values. Bartlett also used the concept of *conventionalization* in his discussions of memory, by which he meant that people express their recall in terms of particular *conventions*. From this the question arises as to how and where these conventions are formed, and to whether it is possible to talk of dominant cultural conventions for recall. The currency and circulation of particular ideological assumptions and beliefs at the time of remembering may well have a critical role to play in the shaping of the past in the autobiographical mode. The fact also that many of the writers were living, at the time of writing, completely different lives (in terms of class position, status, and location) from those evoked and recalled, is a significant determination on the selective perceptions and evaluations, and the appropriation of the genre as part of the creating of ideology.

In other words, what is marketed and made available as the representation of popular experience is the result of a complex process of selection, appropriation, and cultural negotiation which has gone on in contemporary political processes even if, as is so often the case, no space is found within the specific published representations for those processes, except in attentuated, personalized, and dispersed forms.

Unsurprisingly, working-class autobiographies which focus on the inter-war period are dominated by references to poverty and deprivation. Interestingly enough, although I use the term 'working class', many of the autobiographies which have found commercial outlets concentrate upon 'lumpenproletarian' experiences, which perhaps helps to marginalize the specific details of the 'memory', while prioritizing the resourcefulness of the survivors. I will offer some specific analysis of particular texts in order to demonstrate the different ways in which these conditions are described. My broader concern, however, is with the generic characteristics of these writings, in particular their tendency to sideline the political, distance the poverty by means of discursive filters (linguistic, cultural), and their use as a distillation, or displacement of, memory. This is not to condemn any particular work as 'reactionary', or merely 'ideological', but to indicate the instability of any text and its potential cultural-political use. The intention of the individual writer is not in question, nor the integrity of the 'memory'. It is a matter of the proliferation of a particular genre of writing at a critical conjuncture (the past decade), and the possible use of this genre (with its potential for commercial 'spin-offs') as an instrument for foregrounding 'preferred' images of the past in a struggle over political memories.

By stressing the *physical* conditions of poverty – debt, overcrowding, hunger, raggedness – the genre produces an effect of exaggeration, of extremity, given that it is circulated in a political context of 'the invisibility of structural poverty.' Golding and Middleton analyse this context in which poverty is 'an enemy who has vanished into the footnotes', quoting a Conservative politician speaking in the 1950s:

> For primary poverty has now almost disappeared. . . . The Beveridge assumptions have governed our national outlook for a decade and a half. But there is nothing sacred or immutable about them. They postulate a Britain in which the great majority of citizens are too poor to provide for themselves. It is the business of Toryism to thrust that Britain into the history books, and to thrust the politics of poverty into the dustbin.[4]

What I am arguing is that in order to demonstrate, in absolute terms, that there is no poverty now and therefore no need for such a vast welfare apparatus, an ideology is being generated which seeks to recall 'that Britain' from the history books and to exhibit the 'refuse' of 'real' poverty rescued from the dustbin. The stress is on past/present disjunction, the need to conduct discussions about the past which emphasize its *absolute* discontinuities at the level of current 'comfort' and 'security'. Some need for welfare is acknowledged, but on a scale fitted to those 'really in need', whereas the inter-war period is consigned to oblivion as past/completed 'facts', if not as 'value'. If anything, the period is used as an 'evolutionary' referent.

Unwittingly, therefore, such autobiographies are vulnerable to stylization, to what appears, in a relative perspective, to be excessive quantification. It is a mode which, in its commercial forms (the stories of 'winners' in Benjamin's terms referred to in the introduction), is predicated upon contrast because, invariably, it is torn out of its explicit political and historical contradictions. Ironically, it is the very *detailing*, the insistent and repeated images of deprivation which, in a context of 'welfarism' that has in terms of consistent popular mediation eliminated poverty, makes these treatments of the past seem to emphasize their *pastness*, almost (because so distanced) their 'quaintness' – poverty as landscape. The popularized cultural narrative concedes that there was poverty, appalling housing, and hunger *once upon a time*, but in the post-war period no such conditions remain save in pockets of local difficulty. A general welfare structure is no longer needed and people can assume full responsibility for their own lives without State interference. The figures for homelessness, unemployment, and welfare dependency since the early 1970s which contest these views are successfully ignored by means of a narrative about welfare abuse, 'scroungerphobia', and 'unwillingness to work' and an accompanying stress on individualism, thrift, self-discipline, and enterprise.[5] Such re-writing of the last decade incorporates, assimilates, and transforms elements of that earlier history.

The revisionist process involves a conscious, pre-emptive strike against contending versions of British history, so that the primary site chosen for the wresting of 'meanings' away from a potential opposition has been the inter-war period, with its own version of 'Victorian values', and the Depression (with its psychological over-tones) becomes a 'slump', a temporary postural collapse, a mere interlude among chapters of 'progress'. In this way it becomes possible to extrapolate from certain autobio-graphies carefully quantified images of hopelessness (seven in one room, no shoes, twopence to last the week) and yet from within the same text or range of texts, to mobilize a differing set of abstracted, qualitative images repre-senting 'the human spirit' – tireless mums, resourceful kids, community feeling. The dominant image is that of the *survivor* – figures who 'made it' despite demoralizing conditions, and have lived to 'write' the tale. 'Spirit' is privileged as timeless and eternal, and the physical conditions relegated to the background as timed, period-specific, politically localized. The past becomes a sort of archaeological site which throws up relics, icons of depri-vation as of a 'savage' tribe – where otherness, *not nowness*, is what matters. There is a stress on past 'ways', 'structures', and 'forms' of 'how we used to live', 'in those days'. The 'days of hope' are, in the process, made part of a diachronic, moving theme; the 'hard times' are part of a synchronic grasp only. The reclamation is complete.

Differential reception of texts depends very much upon the dominant explanations and mediations of social relations. It is not suggested that reception is an uncompli-cated, unilateral process. We know that people assimilate, reconstruct, resist and negotiate cultural mediations in a variety of ways. Ideology and 'social' education, however influential, have quite definite limits. However, a mode of writing (or re-writing?) which is structured around indi-vidual experience, excludes the rhetoric and arguments of class, and basing itself on psychological, rather than social or historical, explanations has already built into it a potential for a commonsensical/consensual appropriation, because it is a mode which derives its authenticating forms (e.g. the 'I' narrative) from particular notions of personality, speech, and social relations. Its commercial forms have tended to produce a narrowing, channelling mode. In the absence of substantial research on the readership, or reception, of these autobiographies, any assumptions about their cultural use is bound to be speculative. Broadcast radio and television versions, large paperback sales, and extensive library borrowing indicate, at a very crude level admittedly, a considerable popularity. Most of the texts I have selected for later close analysis are, by no means, passive or uncritical reflections of 'how it was', or mere nostalgic excursions. Each has carved out considerable space for alternative and oppositional readings of the 'past', yet each is also subject to the effects of their positioning within the market economies of commercial publishing. Writing is always inscribed in a network of relays and differential traces which can never be simply 'expressed' by the author, or unproblematically decoded by individual readers. The processes of encoding (every text is traversed by numerous contradictory features) and the social relations of reception both guarantee that no mode of writing can ever be recuperated 'once and for all time' to any single position.

Working-class autobiographies can be appropriated for both consensual and oppositional purposes, but for the latter to be successful these have to be part of a wider political struggle; they cannot simply be celebrated as individual instances – 'gems'. The more effective appropriation is likely to be the one which is keyed in with prevailing codes, frames, and explanations of the events described. In the situation I am discussing, this 'keying in' depends upon the muting of continuity and upon ways of decoding the items of discourse as 'museum exhibits'. In this process, priority is given to those cues which relate to the dominant cultural *schemata* – the structures of commonsensical knowledge.[6] This 'knowledge' functions like a cultural/ideological script, an integrated package of information brought to bear on the interpretation of a situation, or event. For example, it is possible to think of a 'hard times' or a 'world we have lost' script (these may, in fact, co-exist contradictorily in the same 'script'). If such scripts are thought of as a complex mix of memory, anecdote, and mental map, then the circulation of texts which consistently exclude the political and anything beyond the immediate and the local will key in most closely with 'popular inference systems'.

Evidence of such co-option can be drawn from the introductions to a number of examples of the genre. In the foreword to Winifred Foley's *No Pipe Dreams for Father* (1978), Humphrey Phelps writes:

> *A Child in the Forest* brought fame and success to Winifred Foley, but she is still shy and modest; in essence, she is still a child of the Forest. In these tales about the Forest she writes with a touching simplicity and a childlike honesty that is altogether charming.
>
> All of these tales are apparently slight, but they have the power to move the reader to an occasional chuckle and, more often, to the verge of tears. Older readers will remember that dread phrase which occurs in one story – ''im 'ave got it.' *It is a mark of real progress* that younger readers are not familiar with it. If this book does nothing else it should at least make us pause and count our blessings. But it also exemplifies – and Winifred herself is a good example – that even hardships and grinding poverty could not quench the human spirit; kindliness, comradeship, hope and joy still come bubbling out. (my italics)[7]

The text is being used for exemplificatory purposes – it is being recuperated for an ideology of 'the human spirit'. In fact, Winifred Foley's writings are radical, irreverent, 'coarse', memorably written, and full of what Gramsci called, 'that feeling-passion [which] becomes understanding', but the discursive terms and tones of the foreword – dated and platitudinous – have the effect of 'infantilizing' the writing, sanitizing it, and securing it for the rhetoric of progress. The familiar, and recurring, words 'even' and 'count our blessings' are part of this technique of abstraction. The tone diminishes the text, tames, deflects, and domesticates its radical elements, and pulls them inside the framework, or script, of a 'period' genre. It is the verbal equivalent of the sepia photograph. Not that the 'hope and joy' are not in the text, but the syntactic ordering of the foreword ensures that the hardships and poverty are *displaced* by the rhetorical emphasis given to the metonyms of 'the human spirit'. Some continuities are highlighted, others toned down. There is, in other words, a selective, or preferred, continuity. The hardship, poverty, and 'it' are all associated as signifiers of the period being recalled, they are set back in that time, fixed and discontinuous. I am not claiming, obviously, that the foreword 'closes' the reading of the text, but that, by offering a carefully ordered frame, it helps to de-contextualize it – it sets the agenda. Of course, the style of the foreword reveals more about its writer than the text being introduced, but as the first item in the discourse it has a significant placing. A form of 'brokerage' is being exercised. Titles, introductions, blurbs ('these tender scenes' is used for *No Pipe Dreams*) all seem to have a recruiting function. *The ways in which memories are made cannot simply be separated from the ways in which, over the past decade, they have been marketed.* The informing structures of the autobiographies are determined by present concerns. Arguably, those which have been marketed for wide publics are those which, however contradictory in some ways, are promoted because they present 'history brushed with the grain' (Benjamin). Removed either spatially, or economically, from their impoverished origins, 'survivor' autobiographies inevitably have a teleological structure. When things are going 'against the grain' then cultural popularization actively recruits the story of society's 'winners' as they choose it should be remembered.

In another chapter an analysis is offered of the 'Delderfield syndrome' in relation to the re-cycling of his writings in paperback and broadcast television form over the past decade. That he had a wider role in the 'myth industry' while alive is suggested by an introduction he wrote for an autobiography published in 1971, *Tapioca for Tea* by Sarah Shears.[8]

In this introduction Delderfield uses 'truth' like a refrain throughout his text – the authentic, 'unvarnished record'. His rhetoric is filled with a number of other populist terms, like 'what makes real people tick', 'old-fashioned virtues', 'decency-plus-guts' (a very 'English' compound). The task of writing is likened to a domestic craft – 'spun into fiction'; the scale of values restrained – 'modest and sometimes self-educated person': the locality humble – 'an unfashionable suburb'. These terms are not used specifically about the particular book, but about the phenomenon of this genre of writing characterized as 'rare' and 'occasional'. He, implicitly, establishes a 'populist' antagonism between this kind of homiletic 'genius' and élite forms. The book is said to be about 'what really constitutes character'. The profile which emerges is, apart from bearing a close resemblance to a Delderfield novel, the product of a technique which has succeeded in generalizing and popularizing a set of values and assumptions recognizably those of the petty bourgeoisie here represented in a classless form. There is no attempt to obscure the conditions of the 'poor and the underprivileged', but these are placed back in an 'era', in a 'whole complex of society in one tiny corner of a land [again, the localizing] where Welfare *as we know it now* did not exist, and would almost certainly have been dismissed in blueprint as "molly coddling", or an affront to the dignity of the working class' (my italics). No explicit comment is made, but 'molly coddling', 'affront', 'dignity' and the 'working class' are set together in a negative/positive syntactic formation which has its own inference script built into it.

Delderfield concludes, 'it is a world as far removed from a majority today as the world of Agincourt and the Luddites but, for all its cruelties and gross injustices, it had a quality. It is Miss Shears' triumph that she makes you aware of this quality and – dare one say it? – the smallest bit nostalgic for its absence fifty years later.'

The reference 'as far removed from a majority' has, like similar phrasings in Phelps, an age/time factor contained within it as that which follows indicates that, in terms of 1970 experience, the conditions of the autobiography are removed from *everybody*. The comparison with Agincourt and the Luddites (two very different kinds of historical memory) helps effectively to seal off the time of the childhood remembered from the present. No attempt to paint out the poverty is made; instead, a whole era is *periodized*, turned into a 'painting'. History as costume drama can, generically, enclose Agincourt, the Luddites, the Edwardian era, and the inter-war period, within an undifferentiated sense of period. A process of selective eradication and demobilization simultaneously co-opts and edits out. This ideological separation of the processes of working-class exploitation from its systemic formations has enabled these processes, in Raymond Williams' phrase, 'to be dissolved into a landscape.'[9] The introductions discussed so far have a guide book feel about them – the 'past' is regarded as another country, the reader a time traveller.

In concluding this section, two further examples of introduction will be briefly examined. A comparison between H. J. Massingham's original (1944) introduction to *Lark Rise to Candleford*[10] (reprinted in the Penguin version) and the one by Sir Hugh Casson to the Folio Society's separate edition of *Lark Rise*[11] is instructive. Although Massingham's is from a *gemeinschaft* perspective, and therefore limited in some ways, he does bring to bear on the text a sharp sociological and historical analysis of the dislocation and frustration within it. He is discussing a social document and not a pressed flower, even if he does call for a restoration of the peasantry! He sees a working landscape, at least, and not only its 'painterly' dimensions. Its handling of the rural retrospect may well have been appropriated for a vision of 'Englishness' in the Second World War, but its rural romanticism is more complex than more recent stylings of Flora Thompson's work. One particular section is especially interesting:

This is the reverse of a photographic method like that of the fashionable 'mass-observation' because it looks inward to human character and outward to changes in environment affecting the whole structure of society and modifying, even distorting, the way people think and act. Her art is in fact universalized by its very particularity, its very confinement to small places and the people Laura knew. It all seems a placid water-colour of the English school, delicately and reticently painted in and charmed by the character of Laura herself. But it is not. What Flora Thompson depicts is the utter ruin of a closely knit organic society. . . . [12]

Casson does quote a part of this (the last part) but his introduction places emphasis on Flora Thompson's 'miniaturist' scale – 'without ever raising her voice', 'obliquely and tenderly', 'not of large themes but of ordinary lives', 'homely precepts', 'traditional values'. Like many of the other introductions discussed, this one claims for its subject 'the voice of truth', and selects out from the material 'self-reliance and endurance – the capacity to endure without flinching, pain or hardship'. His final paragraph, arguably, is an attempt to restore the placid water-colour removed by Massingham:

She avoided large themes and wide horizons, assembling instead a thousand small details each diamond sharp, to form a total picture and which as a chronicle of a vanished way of life and the values by which this way of life was guided, and as a self-portrait is as modest, firmly rooted and determined as a young blade of grass . . . and no less miraculous.[13]

In reclaiming Flora Thompson from any possible use as part of an 'oppositional' version of the past, re-historicized and continuous, this edition of the text (boxed, embossed, and designed for visual shelf display, not reading) virtually embalms the writing in its own 'organic' imagery. The use of Sir Hugh Casson, a venerated cultural 'trustee', helps in this process because his tone throughout has a patronizing air, even if it is submerged. In writing about L. S. Lowry, John Berger pinpoints this style very accurately:

This tendency to patronize is a form of self-defence:
defence not so much against the artist as against the
subject-matter of his work. It is hard to reconcile a life
devoted to aesthetic expositions with the streets and houses
and front doors of those who live in Bury, Rochdale,
Burnley or Salford.[14]

The popular cultural formations referred to have a function in the networking and relaying of particular ideological orientations, in the construction and reconstruction
of a populist hegemony, which is, basically, very defensive
(it is capitalist social relations which are being defended)
although it affects a *style* of confident patronage. Popular
writings do not initiate, or define, this patronage, but
they are used in orchestrating and interpreting it through
commercial outlets.

Turning time back

Chelsea Child, by Rose Gamble (1979), *A Child in the
Forest* by Winifred Foley (1974) *A Kind of Magic*, by
Mollie Harris (1969) and Helen Forrester's three volumes
(1974, 1979, 1981) are autobiographies which end at a
fairly distant point in time, when the writer left home,
started work, or got married.[15] The main concern is not
only with the specifics of the individual life, but with the
remembered time – pre World War Two, the 1920s and
1930s for the most part. It is their anamnesic qualities
which have influenced their publication. What is focused
upon is a generalized and generational childhood – traces
of the past remembered for their values, attitudes, and
emotions. A relatively low level of 'historical' reference
and context means that as 'value memories' they are incon-
testable and cannot be located simply as being of a
particular time, but as belonging to all time – 'eternal'
values. The emphasis is on recovering *continuity*, a
reaching back to a moment prior to profound and trau-
matic change, a moment which through a network of
relationships connects with the 'certainties' of the Victorian world and before. The 'childhood memory' project is

part of a refabrication of tradition, invented in the face of what might seem to be irreversible change: 'The flood of words from informants presenting "today and yesterday" seems almost like an effort to block the path of change: and if they cannot turn time back, at least to smooth an abrupt break into no more than a gradual evolution.' There is 'a need for the redefinition or at least preservation of the former sense of self-identity of individuals, families, villages, and cultural regions, whose whole consciousness now seems to be in danger'.[16] The process is essentially conservative, but it is not necessarily backward-looking or an activity confined to the Right. A historicized 'nostalgia' (if such is possible) could be a resource for the future.

Each of the works which I shall analyse is based upon the conventional metaphor 'life is a story'.[17] The principal assumption is that each person's life is structured like a narrative, and the dominant forms of narrative achieve their meanings through *coherence*. Given the primacy of coherence (or, rather, a dominant ideological version of coherence) each 'story' draws upon a set of conventions and 'experiential gestalts' which select, foreground and highlight certain aspects while omitting and remaining silent on others. Memory therefore constructs, patterns and plans what is recalled. It is organized around participants, parts, stages, linear sequence, causation and purpose. In other words, the story is based upon a set of ideologically positivist assumptions about time, causality, and truth. The work, because retrospective, will impose a teleological framework upon the 'remembered'. The structure outlined is not, of course, definitive. Other conventions – vignettes, sub-narratives, time shifts – are also deployed, but it does underline the fact that memory is a process of reconstruction, and that the 'truth' of the recall depends as much upon the formal conventions used as the specific content. Direct access to past attitudes and feelings experienced is not possible; what is constructed is a series of *present* inferences from traces (letters, memorabilia, family discussion) of the past which are recoverable. The writer's present view of previous experiences and past emotions forms the referential context of these 'memoirs', what Cynthia Hay calls the 'patterned forms of distortion or schematization'.[18] The accounts are retrospectively 'edited' to fit a particular frame of values – in most cases, 'traditionalist'.

The constant rehearsal of the 1920s and 1930s in particular commercial forms of 'autobiography' arguably has led to the reconstitution of a network of inaccurate, and 'sanitized', resources for that period based upon indeterminate (uncheckable) reminiscence. Experiential accounts of the period not only construct narratives through which the moment can be 'remembered', but they also form the basis of other narratives, so that what comes to be 'known' is not only what is recalled, but what is constructed in already existing 'life stories'. The 'coherence' of the interwar period, the dominant memory of it, is something which is predicated upon a particular ideological formulation in which some aspects are foregrounded, others marginalized. The autobiographical convention – based upon the 'life is a story' metaphor – depends upon what McArthur has called 'the category of the individual [as a] central structuring category'.[19] In formal terms, then, the category of the 'personal' becomes hegemonic and it is this which determines that certain events and circumstances – domestic, familial, and local – are given priority, while broader social and political considerations are minimized. It is almost as if poverty and childhood are doubly articulated as signifiers of a past which has now been outgrown. An evolutionary, developmental model is applied to both person and history.

Lakoff and Johnson say, at one point, 'As the circumstances of our lives change, we constantly revise our life stories, seeking new coherence'[20] and, by analogy, the experiential accounts of interwar childhood form part of the larger ideological project by which 'history' is revised in order to produce a new coherence based upon traditionalist assumptions, a retrospective idealization of lost 'values' inscribed in that period.

As Jerry White comments in *History Workshop Journal*, 15 (1983):

'There has possibly never been a time when the study of our past has meant so much to us. This is no mere product of a sentimental new bourgeoisie. Look at the people's history groups . . . the family history societies, the commercial autobiographies, the lovingly-gathered reminiscences of television and radio and in the press.'[21]

One of the problems with the 'commercial autobiographies' which is the focus of this chapter's analysis, is that, however well-written and graphic they are, they tend to work within what Berger has called a 'terminus' version of memory – the moments recalled are locked firmly in the past. The effects of the poverty, overcrowding, and deprivation described are *dispersed* by the ways in which these are framed, enclosed, and detached from the present. They exist by themselves, part of another time, discontinuous with all other moments. The effect of the retrospective mode is to blunt and make habitual a set of images and perceptions of the period which need to be examined rather than endorsed. The mode itself sanctions certain forms of recall, excizes others. It is a process which is analogous to Susan Sontag's analysis of photographs:

Through photographs, the world becomes a series of unrelated, free-standing particles; and history, past and present, a set of anecdotes and *faits divers*. The camera makes reality atomic, manageable, and opaque. It is a view of the world which denies interconnectedness, continuity. . . . [22]

The past, in the retrospective genre, becomes a set of anecdotes and diverse episodes linked by the structures of coherence produced by the 'life is a story' metaphor and by the category of the authenticating individual – the 'I' witness. Interconnectedness and continuity are conferred by the *genre* of commercial autobiography itself, a series of 'magical' narratives. They displace memory by fixing the period and removing it from meaning: it is no longer explained *in time* but through appearances and images. The commercial autobiography is not, contrary to expectations, an instrument of memory but 'an invention of it or a replacement,'[23] marketed for a particular use as spectacle which relieves us of 'the burden of memory' by circulating a national past based on images, a *semblance* of memory.[24] In Sontag's analysis, 'Social change is replaced by a change in images'. Commercial autobiographies rooted in the interwar period are part of a wider metaphorical process in which a 'hegemonic memory' is being *invented* to replace and discount possible alternative memories. Metaphor is standing in for history and politics as part of the language of power.

The commercial autobiographies to be examined were, with one exception, written by women who 'made something of themselves' and took up opportunities which led to *individualist* forms of mobility, distancing them from their class and locality. They were (with the exception of Winifred Foley) mobilized out of their class, not *for* it. In the case of Helen Forrester she emerged from a complex and contradictory class location, which will be explored later. Escaping from their childhood, the writers return to it almost as anthropologists visiting another country – simplifying and sentimentalizing, or generalizing and classifying. They are published for their *representativeness*, or rather, for the way in which they are constructed within a particular ideology of a representative experience – enterprising, talented, self-educating, resourceful individuals carved out of, and in relief from, their experiential context and not made continuous with it in any way either temporally or spatially – rather like Lena Kennedy's 'heroines'.

Rose Gamble's *Chelsea Child* was published in 1979 and is based on the period 1922 to 1939. From 1922 to 1929 the family of seven lived in one room in Manor Street, Chelsea. In 1929, the street was demolished as part of slum clearance and the family moved into Guinness Buildings, World's End. At the time of publication, the writer was living in an isolated Sussex cottage, having been an art teacher for some years and a buyer in a major bookselling organization in West Africa. *Chelsea Child* was written as a consequence of a series of five-minute broadcasts about her childhood given on *Woman's Hour*. The book itself was also later abridged and serialized on the same programme.

The book opens with a description of the dark, confined, overcrowded space in which they all lived, and with an account of Rose's childhood fears. These are recounted through the use of the exemplifying mode, common to this kind of writing: 'One night I went down with Luli . . .'[25] The bulk of her life was spent in the street. There wasn't much food, and most of what there was went to her father. Her childhood experiences led her to two wishes – one to be grown up, the other to be a man, as, in relative terms, her drunken, alcoholic father seemed to her 'privileged'. Often absent, the father is signified as different from others in the neighbourhood in some ways because of his elegant copperplate writing and casual clerical work. Rose is introduced to the 'magic' of reading by her sister, Dodie, who won a lot of school prizes. The emphasis on reading is a common experience, repeated in all the writings.

Given the appalling sleeping conditions, the lack of privacy, and the unvaried diet, each day is structured very much like any other, and the opening chapter – 'Ethel's ceiling' – synoptically presents their physical and emotional conditions, graphically representing a shared deprivation. The overcrowding is not simply described, it is registered in every detail of the family's experience. Part of the effectiveness of the writing is the way in which the account enables the reader to experience the conditions through the personalized, close-up technique. The second chapter – 'Our Street' – ranges beyond the house to the immediate neighbourhood in which 'poverty and elegance were separated by nothing more than a couple of kerb-stones' (p.18). This is one of several perceptions which widen the angle of observation from the personal and admit present understanding into the frame of remembering. However, given the conventions in which the writing is operating, the observation remains simply as an observation and is not amplified beyond this kind of occasional insight into a political analysis. The book is part of a genre based on memory and anecdote, 'discrete products of self-contained historical reconstruction'.[26] It works within well-defined boundaries of self, period, location and 'reality'. It is a richly detailed miniature, 'marketed' into representativeness by a form of cultural imperialism which makes public extreme instances of working-class cultural experience and deprivation.

The 'Street' is characterized in general terms of its shared habits and customs – gossip, communal games, funerals, the pawnshop, identical housing. The description takes the street out of time, places it in a photograph or a picture, except for the shadow of the war which, again, is an experience registered in all these writings. The main effect is of a gallery of images of a past age, what the cover blurb described as 'a charming and evocative portrayal of a kind of life that disappeared with the Second World War'. It is this insistence on a significant *break* and discontinuity which marks so much of this 'genre', particularly in the way in which it is marketed and popularized. As Ken Worpole says: 'The continuity of experience is not an ideology widely promulgated within the capitalist mode of cultural production.'[27] This stress on discontinuity is linked, on the cover, with another ideological feature of the retrospective mode: 'An immensely readable book, as rich in humanity as its subjects were poor in wordly assets'. A particular ideology of 'humanity' dominates the account – a set of values continuous and 'eternal'. The stylized cover illustrations by Pamela Goodchild reinforce the idea of a kind of life that has disappeared – the time is remembered iconographically: fag-cards, marbles, smocks, scooters, ice-cream carts. These comments reflect upon the *presentation* of the book and not its specific figurations. There are, for example, sharp political insights at times which contradict the simple 'nostalgic mode'.

Another feature of the book, quite common in this form of writing, is the figure of Rose's mother. She had fourteen pregnancies – five children survived – and worked as a cleaner as well as looking after the family. 'Our devotion to her created an indestructible family unity' (p.32). The chapter 'On the Parish' traces the backgrounds and relationship of her mother and father. The mother was a household drudge at the age of nine, having being farmed out as a child, and entered service at thirteen. The father was a shadowy figure, Victorian in attitudes with a 'distant air of superiority about him, despite his shabby appearance'. It is 'Mum', as so often in these narratives, who saw to it that they lived from day to day, as the father 'hated poverty and despised everything about the way we lived, but he was hopelessly enmeshed in both and it made him angry, all the time' (p.35). It is the mother who guarantees the economic basis of family life, she has the central role in the household, both in a material sense and in terms of effective relationships.

The chapter, 'God Bless the Prince of Wales', is structured around the early experiences of schooling, and the writer observes how the headmistress occasionally smiled 'at a pretty or nicely-dressed little girl, but her obsession was with royalty'. An education based upon the three 'Rs' and a rural and Royal version of England emerges from the account. It is also difficult to escape the feeling that although some things are distanced through negative signifiers, others are positively coded to contrast with today, especially 'the strict training in the care of school equipment as a matter of course', and 'discipline was an inherited atmosphere. Our elderly teachers needed little more than their firm voices and experienced eye to maintain the formal routine. Every moment of time in the classrooms was filled with work' (p.57). This resembles the now commonplace memory of 'standards' frequently repeated in criticisms of 1960s methodology with its informality and child-centred processes.

The direct physical, material experience is signified negatively – lack of clothing, poor food, cold, irregular wages – while structures of feeling, or disposition, are positively coded – particularly the mother's resourcefulness and enterprise: 'You will never get something for nothing in this life. . . . One way or the other, you always have to pay' (p.22). The book highlights the main stages of childhood experience – school, play, illness, holidays, 'treats' to the zoo and the pantomime – articulates various temporal and causal connections between the different episodes, and charts interaction at the family, street, and school level. By organizing the retrospect in terms of stages, a typical 'experiential gestalt' is produced which gives coherence to the 'memory' by shaping it as a narrative. The highlighted figures and experiences are invested with retrospective significance, while others are obscured or omitted entirely. The structure of the narrative – the formal conventions of the 'life is a story' metaphor – determines the shape of the account. Trauma, confusion, despair, catastrophe are all structured within particular frames, they are 'staged'. In the narrative form used, the patterned, staged experiences become part of a format in which they represent a phase in an evolutionary, progressive sequence to the implied present state of the writer. As reader we are only in the world of the narrative and not of the narrative's world. There is a conclusiveness about the whole of the retrospective mode – a conclusiveness about that which *was*. The autobiographical mode is in the ascendancy, arguably, because its conventional form lends itself to a particular ideological purpose – the reconstruction of the past without 'history' but in terms of supposedly representative individuals.

One of the strengths of *Chelsea Child* is the way in which it often lays claim to being a general autobiography, especially with reference to shared school, community, and 'life' experiences like 'growing up': 'It was abrupt and final, and your life changed overnight' (p.122). The experience of Rose's parents, sisters and brothers, friends and neighbours extends the net of evidence and generalizes the generational 'memory'. At the same time, it is still organized around certain ideological assumptions: 'It never occurred to us that if anyone was responsible for providing us with a roof it was Dad himself' (p.129). The text tends to construct its perceptions in a social and political vacuum and cuts across a range of complex phenomena by locating responsibility solely in the individual.

The chapter, 'No Miracles for Me', simulates a child-like narrative form – hurried, elliptical, caricaturing, full of energy, wonder, and anxiety. It is based mainly on junior school experiences, with the child's view of the adult firmly remembered, and on the 'coke run' by which the children earned a few pennies. A Sunday School prize marks the first sign of distinctiveness, followed by 'the chance to sit for a special place at a private school, where they had an arrangement to receive a few scholarship girls' (p.165). In retrospect, the 'exceptional' person recalls the moment of signification and difference, the boundary marker. It is not recalled uncritically, as she was a 'special placer' 'well aware of my station', the only one of two in a class of thirty-six. She experiences a kind of 'diglossia' – the need to use two languages – one for school and one for home. In fact, the form itself is 'diglossic', with a standard English linguistic code being used to codify experiences outside of its class-specificity, interspersed with idiolect and dialect transcriptions. Each autobiography is a form of double articulation – experiential and linguistic, as well as temporal – now/then. Her two sisters find work in an art gallery and 'their speech and assurance developed with everyday use' (p.176). This section, in fact, is marked by a dramatic change of register where the 'present' perceptions take over in contrast with some of the former simulations and 'mimicry' of earlier ways of seeing: 'Unconsciously we all began to absorb the values of the shop. . . . We began to relax and speak unself-consciously to posh people, and learned how to handle a saucer at tea time.'

So, although *Chelsea Child* is 'the best picture I know of life in one room'[28] it is also a remarkable document of *hegemonization* whereby class-specific values structured around celebrity and status signifiers are fully absorbed. Rose inhabits the world of art and music and school, and school becomes a refuge from home and neighbourhood

– 'We had lost touch with each other and no longer had anything to say.' The last two chapters rapidly sketch a process of 'embourgeoisement', of *individual* upward mobility. The inclusive street gives way to the 'exclusive group' at school.

By the end of the book (late 1930s) mention is made of the war in Spain, of Jewish refugees, and the outbreak of war. The war separated the family – 'each in turn to survive alone, for which we had been well prepared' (p.192). The last page has a synoptic quality – sketching the fortunes of the different members of the family in the war. The author herself served in the Land Army. The final paragraph combines two salient features of this kind of writing – the enterprising survivor and the disappearance of the pre-war world: 'Nothing was ever the same again. The war swept away life as we had known it and it disappeared for ever' (p.192).

This is the conclusiveness mentioned earlier – the discontinuity which guarantees that 'real poverty' has 'vanished into the footnotes'. Comparable poverty, if on a different scale, is experienced by the one million or more homeless families in Britain today. Additionally, there are substantial arguments by Calder, Harrison, and Pelling (to be considered in Chapter 4) that 'the effect of the war was not to sweep society on to a new course, but to hasten its progress along the old grooves'.[29] Golding and Middleton in *Images of Welfare* demonstrate how deeply the myth that 'it disappeared for ever' has registered, and each one of the commercial autobiographies in different ways adds their own subscription to this.[30] Each one testifies to people 'taking responsibility for their own lives' and 'not going cap in hand' for welfare hand-outs, but surviving inequality and deprivation through resourcefulness, talent, and enterprise, with the act of writing as the final confirmation. In spite of having a struggle, each writer is able to construct a coherent, unified, and meaningful life story: 'She would battle on through, it would take more than a war to defeat Mum. After all, she had been fighting one all her life – single-handed' (p.192). This is the last sentence of the book with the phrase 'single-handed' stressing the individualist trajectory of the autobiographical mode, the key to its 'grammar'. There is little analysis to suggest why her life-experience was so structured, so deprived, other than in terms of the family's immediate situation. No insight is offered into a social structure which, firstly, generates such extremes of poverty and, secondly, makes women relate to the world exclusively in terms of their relationship to the family. A contrast may be found in the memories transcribed in *Dutiful Daughters* of mothers oppressed by their own existence.[31] This book, however, arose out of a very different set of criteria – 'to discover together what is social and shared in our experience' (p.9), whereas *Chelsea Child* seems designed to separate the personal from the political, the individual from the social.

Helen Forrester's three volume autobiography, *Twopence to Cross the Mersey* (1974, paperback 1981), *Liverpool Miss* (1979, 1982), and *By the Waters of Liverpool* (1981, 1983) concentrates upon the 1930s and while many of her experiences are materially comparable with those in *Chelsea Child*, the circumstances of the family were very different.[32] Until the age of twelve, she had been a middle-class girl living in the south west of England, attending a private school and having servants at home. In 1931, after her father's bankruptcy and subsequent quarrel with his mother and sisters, the family moved to Liverpool where the father hoped to find work as an accountant in a shipping company. Unlike other works in this genre, these books do not operate within a familial ideology, as the family, for the most part, is simply a physical entity, with a limited sense of relationship. If anything, the books trace the emergence of the writer from the burdens and irritations of family. The 'fall' is meteoric, and the 'rise' is charted very gradually.

As an account of a middle-class family forced through the Depression to live the lives of the lumpenproletariat in Liverpool, the books are preoccupied with 'background', status, accent, and appearance. Phrases like 'a public school man' and 'an Oxford accent' recur throughout, contrasted frequently with the 'nasal' Liverpool speech. As with all writings of the retrospective mode, the text 'knows its future', so particular emphases, selections, and omissions are made with hindsight. The writer now living in Canada with 'my dear professor and our son' is able to testify to her survival of extreme conditions of deprivation. The sharp close-up on *then* severs it firmly from *now:* there is a double distance of time and life style. Her perseverance at night school and her undoubted courage in facing an emotionally and materially deprived childhood have brought her success in spite of her circumstances.

For much of the time, the writing is largely sealed off from more general or abstract perceptions of society, although the author's work as an unqualified social worker did bring her into contact with many of the most extreme cases in the Depression. In her own case, there are frequent references to the fact that her parents were bad managers and reckless, and there is a distinct impression that she sees their poverty as individually caused (seven children, permanently in debt). In a strange way, this is a middle-class perception of working-class poverty, confined to individual behaviour and motivation and designed to confirm the existing system of structured inequality. Her father's poor wages are seen as inappropriate for 'a public school man', but the larger issue of their inappropriateness is not addressed. As a 'class traveller', although she does acknowledge that many working-class families 'manage' better than her own, there is little insight into, what Winifred Foley calls, the 'capitalist structure of our society'. If anything, a 'non-political' stance is often reiterated. The whole structure of the books is based upon a trajectory of return to her class origins, it is an upwardly mobile path.

Chapter 13 of the third volume is quite explicit about her perceptions of poverty and welfare:

> Sometimes the theories and the interpretations of statistics made me laugh, and I thought of the shrewd exploiters

of social assistance amongst whom I lived. Some of our neighbours know every trick and used extremely agile brains to obtain what they needed from the many agencies in the city; it was almost like a business to them. They were all poor, but it was often not the most needy who received the most help. Now, three generations later, this swindling has become an art, and some people live very comfortably with it. They would probably do equally well if they turned their astuteness towards earning a living. Crying poverty, however, can be a good excuse for shrugging off the weight of responsibility for one's life'.[33]

The books are an impressive record of hardship and also of the way in which a young girl was confined, neglected, and impoverished to a point where she became a passive, silent, deferential, household drudge – self-effacing and subordinated. As a document of sex discrimination and gender limitations they are also a powerful testimony, but the overall project bears witness to the ideological perceptions quoted above – standing on your own two feet, making something of yourself, taking responsibility for one's own life. The books articulate a commonsensical notion of self-help.

As an image of welfare, the quoted paragraph fits well within the framework of the recent backlash, dating from the middle 1970s. In the face of economic crisis, a sustained attack has been mounted upon a mythicized construction of the poor, and many of the ideas and rhetoric used in that 'campaign' are echoed in Helen Forrester's writings – almost as though her evidence is that of a class 'spy' or 'infiltrator'. In Golding and Middleton's introduction to *Images of Welfare* they speak of 'how the crisis in the British economy has become the occasion for a social division of the poor so punitive in its impact as to threaten the very props of the modern welfare state.'[34] The language and arguments of class used in the few instances of analysis by Helen Forrester are those of the hegemonic middle class and its ideology of neo-liberal individualism. The only *continuity* proposed throughout the texts, with the exception of the very first and last chapters, is the one structured around welfare 'scrounging', and a commonsensical disdain for social theories. Her discourse is drawn explicitly from the standard idiom and anti-welfare ideology. The 'undeserving poor' have in recent demonology, become the majority. An individualist morality is constructed around the enterprising person who triumphs over conditions which could lead the indolent and thriftless to moral and spiritual failure. Helen Forrester's retrospective 'Helen' of the 1930s becomes the paradigmatic figure in the case against the 'burden model of welfare'.[35] The key term is *independence*, the characteristic model at the centre of the biofictions examined in Chapter 2.

In *Images of Welfare*, Golding and Middleton convincingly argue that three key ideas form the basis upon which public understanding of poverty and welfare rests: efficiency, morality (of the work ethic and self-sufficiency) and pathology (of individual inadequacy as the cause of poverty). They suggest that these ideas have deep roots in popular consciousness and locate two key periods in which they have been 'fixed' into the prevailing discourse: 1880–1920, and the interwar period when 'ruling images became "naturalized", and the now genuinely mass circulation popular press, bound by its economics to an uncritical acceptance of the social order, provided an authoritative voice for an emasculated reformism more concerned with social control than with the redress of injustice or inequality'.[36]

The 'morality play' aspects of the commercial autobiographies, marketed within economic practices bound also to an uncritical acceptance of the social order, work from well within the vocabulary and rhetoric of the lower middle class and its moral economy – self-sufficient, individualistic, socially isolated, hard working, and perceiving individual inadequacy (Rose Gamble's father, Helen Forrester's parents) as the cause of poverty. A third 'fixing' period of these ideas into prevailing discourse has been the past decade with its 'scroungerphobia' and retreat from 'welfarism' characteristic of the 'new Right'. The biofictions, the commercial autobiographies, and the popular press have all played a significant role in 'revisiting' the interwar period in order to re-naturalize certain dominant images authenticated and authoritatively endorsed by first-hand 'memories' of the time – shaped by present perceptions which, in many ways, derive from the discursive 'commonsense' of *that* period. These 'popularizations' (actively contested by oral histories and worker writings) are a major resource of the production and mediation of the values, concepts and images with which people decode the politics of the welfare state.

The writings discussed in this chapter can be seen as refurbishing and refurnishing a set of ideas, images, and beliefs constituted within the interwar period and made ideologically continuous with the present, while the material conditions 'disappeared for ever with the war'. The process is *palimpsestic* – a historically rooted popular mythology built around the self-advanced individual is laid over a specific personal memory. Ideologically functional images (as Golding and Middleton call them) are dramatized into narrative coherence. Certainly the sub-text of Helen Forrester's writings is 'that we should live within our means' and, by extension perhaps, apply, in Thatcherite terms, the simple standard of good housekeeping to the national accounts. Poverty is the 'hollow-eyed parents and hollow-bellied kids of Charles Dickens' world' by definition, and it is this context, reinforced by the distanced, almost Dickensian, imagery of interwar memories, against which any contemporary claims to poverty are dismissed. Questions of relative deprivation are obscured by 'absolute' discursive forms – visual and verbal. By implying that extremes were, in fact, typical or common, no other levels of poverty are given visibility. The inter-war period is now styled as the 'Golden Age' of real poverty!

Although Helen Forrester's circumstances were exceptional given the family's class situation, there are nevertheless in the writings two dominant generalizations – that the family did not manage its household budget well, incurred unwise hire-purchase commitments and were thriftless, and that the success of the writer showed the social structure to be openly mobile, relatively egalitarian. The former generalization fits in with the responses to questions asked by Golding and Middleton about reasons for poverty.[37] The largest category of answers, they found, referred to the financial ineptitude of the poor. The latter generalization seems to derive from a particular interpretative framework and ideology encoded by the media about mobility and meritocracy. Each autobiography reconstructs a moment of extreme deprivation, freezes it and stresses its exceptional character. They are offered as evidence of the route out of oppression, but, as Benjamin says in *Illuminations:* 'The tradition of the oppressed teaches us that the "state of emergency" in which we live is not the exception but the rule.'[38]

Although I have stressed particular structural and ideological aspects of the Helen Forrester autobiographies, it should be said that they also contain a convincing account of pain, humiliation, hunger, and frustration, and evidence of long hours of tedious work with poor pay. They are also important documents of a number of attitudes about class, sexuality, and gender framed in reticent, euphemistic terms. Helen Forrester's work, particularly, is concerned obsessively with status differentials. At one point when she has her first period and is in terrible pain her sister brings her a cup of tea: 'a coarse china cup on a saucer which did not match'. With the exception of Winifred Foley's, most of the autobiographies share a characteristic dread of the explicit.

Helen Forrester's *Twopence to Cross the Mersey* is mobilized by the piecing together of literally hundreds of linguistic formulations ('our new abode', 'heartily agreed', 'promising faithfully', 'gleaned', 'exhumed'), which produce a distanced mode of observation and a fascinating exchange between the evasive and formulary ideolect of a fallen middle-class family and the actual experience of utter deprivation. The writing is full of clichés and redundancies, possibly because this 'memory' of the early period is based upon experiences she could not have known directly, and the use of an inflated language is part of an attempt to reconstruct 'gaps' in experience dramatically. Both characters and dialogue are caricatured; a mock-dialect is used, and women are always 'stout, untidy, and blonde', the men have 'surly voices' and the toddlers have 'runny noses'. The language used is, perhaps, also characteristic of the self-educated and, in this particular case, is perhaps an attempt to reinvent 'English' English after living for twenty-three years in Canada. This may account for its obtrusive formality of diction. The family's 'elaborated code' of speech is seen, even in retrospect, as what redeemed them from the 'abyss'. However personal the recall, however 'true', it is conditioned by severely restricted codes of perception and observation. This is less true of the writing of the other two volumes, partly because the first one is synoptic, generalized and constructed within a 'timeless time', whereas the others are less impressionistic, more detailed, and have a clearer narrative direction structured around the 'exemplary' individual, not unrelated to Cinderella – 'not all fairy godmothers carry wands' (*BWL:52*). The contrast between her present, slum life and her previous existence is articulated almost as though these are facts of nature, not social structure:

> Almost nothing that I had been taught as a child by Edith or Grandma seemed to have any relevance in slums where fighting and drunkenness were everyday occurrences, where women stood in dark corners with men, fumbling with each other in a manner I was sure was wrong, though I had no inkling of what they were actually doing; a place where theft was considered smart and children openly showed the goods they had shoplifted; where hunchbacks and cripples of every kind got along as best they could with very little medical care; where language was so full of obscenity that for a long time I did not understand the meaning.
>
> Even in my parents' light-hearted group, ideas had been discussed, theories of existence expounded, the war

knowledgeably refought in the light of history. The avail-
ability of music, paintings and fine architecture had been
taken for granted. Dress, deportment, manners, education,
politics, were all taken seriously. (*LM:45*)

No sense is suggested that the two worlds may be interde-
pendent, the condition of one the result of the condition
of the other. As Benjamin says in *Illuminations*, 'There is
no document of civilization which is not at the same time
a document of barbarism.'[39]

The concluding section of Helen Forrester's last volume,
By the Waters of Liverpool, is entitled 'March, 1950'. It
is a 'retrospect within a retrospect', as the narrative proper
had ended in the middle of World War Two. At one point
she writes:

> The grass-covered crater at my feet had been caused by a
> small bomb which had fallen on our first night in our new
> home. Now in March 1950, I proposed to incinerate in it
> the record of all my past life. Before me stretched a brand
> new path, totally unrelated to all that had gone before. I
> was going out to India to marry a gentle Hindu professor
> of Theoretical Physics. . . . (*BWL:278*)

In the opening section of volume one, she describes taking
her 'Canadian-born' son to Liverpool for the first time
and says 'I smiled, seeing it all through his stranger's eyes'
(*TCM:8*).

In a sense, both the opening and concluding sections
suggest the methodology used throughout: the estrange-
ment effect and the abrupt *discontinuity*. The writing is,
at once, a record and an 'incineration' of her past life –
images of the past unrelated to all that has gone on since,
not recognized as being of present concerns. It was simply
once upon a time.

Winifred Foley's *A Child in the Forest* was first broadcast in serial form in the BBC *Woman's Hour* programme
in March 1973, published as a hardback book in 1974,
and as a paperback in 1977. A BBC One Television film
Abide With Me was based on the book. In the introduction, Winifred Foley acknowledges that the book is not

'all my own work' and mentions a range of people who helped shape it. She also mentions her 'sister listeners' to *Woman's Hour* who wrote letters of appreciation to the BBC and to her. The original radio broadcast forms the first part of the published book, the years in service were added as part two. Again, the work of editing and arranging by Sheila Elkin is acknowledged.

I mention all of these factors by way of attempting to distinguish this project from the others – it is a co-operative, 'sisterly', activity. The dedication mentions all the rewards she has garnered as 'daughter, wife, mother, mother-in-law and granny', which is perhaps confined in its gender ascriptions, but the book itself and the writer (as she admits on a Radio Four broadcast in July 1984 with Edna Healey) are full of such ambivalences.

Her work is also distinguishable from the others referred to by the way in which it shows that the poverty in which she lived, the 'state of emergency' in Benjamin's phrase, is not the exception but the rule. Politically active, a lifelong pacifist, her writing does not siphon off now from then, or the political from the personal, but is informed by a knowledge of, in her phrase, 'the capitalist structure of our society'. She has written four bestsellers based on her Forest of Dean experiences and, despite their marketing (cf. my earlier comments) in terms of a 'rural retrospect' – 'the essential Forest of Dean remains very much as it always has been' [introductory note on the writer in *A Child in the Forest*] – the books have a strong sense of identity and of individuality, with firmly drawn characters not generalized caricatures. Rather than a simple enlargement of *then*, bringing that 'moment' into the present, *A Child in the Forest* is an interpretive, as well as a reconstructive, narrative framing the past with hindsight. The language is evocative, direct and non-euphemistic shifting constantly in time, mode of articulation, and register. Sometimes, she stands back and observes, at others there is an impressionistic stream of consciousness effect: 'Carry on, feet, one in front of the other; eyes, don't look to left or right. . . .'[40] Dialect is used frequently and it forms an integral part of the writing, not gestural or caricatured. The writer is aware of her cultural 'diglossia' (she comments on this in the radio broadcast), but the dialect when used seems a heard and spoken transcript, not 'stage' West Country.

A strong sense of values emerges, organically related to the community and family in which she lived – the solidarity and fraternity of miners – and not merely culled from a 'hegemonic' morality. Both mother and father exercized a strong influence on her childhood; her family is described as 'middling' and lying between the 'feckless, filthy and friendly' and the 'prim, prudish and prosperous' who occupied opposite ends of the village. 'Life was wonderful', she says, which fits in with the instant nostalgia imagery now prevalent, *but*, she adds, 'for one constant nagging irritation: hunger'. It is this perspective which organizes the structure of the text cut into themes, 'spots of time' sub-narratives, and critical reflection. Hope for the future is maintained by reading and dreams – a feature common to all these writings. The book has no illusions about the sacrifices made by the 'doubly impoverished' women – economically poor and socially marginal, bearing the brunt of the struggle to keep the family clothed and fed.

The text moves in and out of the frame of time and the immediate family in its cataloguing of tuberculosis, malnutrition, free school meals and strikes. While individualized, the writing does not lose contact with the larger social and economic determinations. Winifred Foley (Poll Mason as a child) is the 'runny-nosed, dirty, raggedy child' of Helen Forrester's caricature. The sense of imprisonment is strong in *A Child*, particularly cultural imprisonment brought about by material deprivation:

> His whole body was covered with taut, angry red skin as though he'd been scalded. His watery, raw-rimmed eyes were nearly blind. He had to wear special shoes for his mis-shapen sore feet, and even in these walking was an uncomfortable process. Inside this grotesque exterior was

a wonderful young man, kind, intelligent, and purposeful.
(p.51)

This is a description of Goggy, who gave her schoolgirl
magazines to read, but although it has some of the characteristics of the set-piece, Dickensian imagery of poverty
mentioned earlier, this is made functional by its close-
up perspective. The set-pieces, the 'stock shots' of the
retrospective mode, attend to the surfaces and exteriors,
the visual clues and cues. The placing of Goggy is made
functional by the paragraph which follows: 'He earned
his living doing a paper round . . . and it took him all
God's hours to walk the umpteen miles on his tender
feet.' This breaks with the 'pressed flower' approach to
deprivation – it re-roots it.

This is extended in the chapter '1926', a moment which
rarely gets a mention in the other autobiographies (it is,
of course, outside Helen Forrester's period):

> The strike was really a desperate cry for the status of
> manhood – to be able to do a full week's work in the pit,
> to be paid enough to fill the bellies of their families. (p.101)

She was evacuated during the strike to a family in Kent:
'Their budget must have been stretched very thin to let
me in, but these warm-hearted people made me feel the
luxury of being welcome', 'They were working-class
people of very modest means' (p.106). This is the only
work in which the deprivation is politicized and there is
a sense of 'class for itself', rather than passively 'in itself'.

The concluding sentence of Part One marks the point,
literally and metaphorically, where many of the autobiographies terminate: 'The little platform became the edge
of the old world, the world I had known, as a child in the
forest' (p.152). The 'old world' is not only seen as a place,
in 'nostalgic' versions, but as a period also – 'in those
days'. Part Two traces the writer's experiences from fourteen to twenty-two in service in London, the Cotswolds,
and Wales – a lost self in a strange new world. The
changed scale of perception is described wittily: 'We didn't
have a policeman in our village but in a place like London

they probably had a couple of dozen' (p.168). It is not only events which are remembered but a particular tonality is adopted to convey varying levels of awareness: 'What harm could possibly have come to me going down a back-alley to help a boy who'd fainted?' (p.170). On her first return to her home everything had shrunk in scale, as had some of her initial naivety: 'I found the words of the Bible illogical and meaningless. "Blessed are the meek for they shall inherit the earth." I wondered when? The snobby lot sitting in the front few rows looked as though they had got a good whack of it, and there was nothing meek about *them*' (p.178). The period in service is not confined to work, but is also the time of the onset of desire and subsequent moral conflicts and misunderstandings.

The final stage of *A Child in the Forest* is based upon the writer's work as a waitress – 'I knew that as long as I was in service I could never be more than a migrant worker at someone else's table' (p.223) – her initial political activity with the young Communists at Mosleyite rallies, and her first sexual experience with the man who became her husband. She spent some time working in a college hall where she received a lesson from a Miss Robson on humility: 'She herself would have to curtsey to Royalty, we all had our place in society, and ducks could never be happy trying to be swans. Far better for me if I knew my place and made the best of it' (p.230). This naturalizing of the social order is 'placed' by the critical nature of the writing. The last chapter 'A Job for Life' opens in a political context, with the writer actively involved in, yet questioning, the anti-Mosleyites in the East End, and closes within an ideological framework based on the domestic and familial – a job for life: 'Now thirty-five years married, we know we found our way. It has been a most rewarding partnership. We started our own family tree, branching steadily' (p.254). The final point, however, embraces the domestic and the political: 'We made our own dreams' – rather than living through the imagery of another class and its fabricated, popularized dreams for the working-class. The book evokes personal, social and political memories of the interwar period, but it does not render them as discrete anecdotes cut off from history, self-contained 'inventions' of 'them days'.

Mollie Harris' *A Kind of Magic* (1969, 1983 paperback) had already appeared in BBC broadcasts and in local newspaper articles when it was first published in 1969, and its reprinting in 1983 was obviously part of the nostalgia industry. The book works entirely within this formulaic mode — a series of sketches of 'yesterday', of 'treasured, unforgettable, irreplaceable happenings', of childhood as 'a time of magic'. The introduction mentions 'magic' 'happy' and 'wonderment' twice, as well as the 'kindness and good humour of neighbours and friends in those *hard-up, happy times*'[41] (my italics). This suggests the 'good old, bad old days' formulation mentioned previously and is also part of 'the rural retrospect': a longing not just for childhood and the past, but for an England pre-industrial and quintessentially rural. The book operates within a 'reminiscence' format: 'the practice of repeatedly recounting or thinking about particular events or incidents in one's life with a strong rehearsal element which can lead to 'refabrication', distortion and schematization.[42] The book's concluding poem provides a definitive record of the 'pressed flower' mode of retrospect, as well as a link with an early [1770] definition of nostalgia: 'The greatest part of them were now pretty far gone with the longing for home which the physicians have gone so far as to esteem a disease under the name of Nostalgia':[43]

> Let Me return
> where the wild rose bloom,
> drowning my empty heart
> in your summer glory,
> cooling my fevered brow
> in the lost fields of home. (p.222)

As well as the 'lost fields of home', the past is also styled as that 'dear Promised Land' and 'heaven'.

With the exceptions and contradictions examined in this

chapter, the *form* of the retrospective mode of commercial autobiography imposes a number of commonsensical assumptions about characterization, interaction, and modes of speech which tend to homogenize what needed to be shown in its complex, ambiguous and contradictory determinations. The 'life is a story' metaphor and the image of the past as end-stopped foreclose the 'truth' in a number of set-piece formulations which, although based undoubtedly on 'experience', operate within a naive realist framework which is not capable of historicizing or articulating that experience in terms other than those structured around subjectivity, omitting, for the most part, the broader economic, social, cultural and political determinants.

The autobiographies examined in this chapter have been based upon a number of conventions of narrative fiction, designed to construct the events of a particular individual's phase of life and to interpret it. At the level of form they can be linked with those novels which will be analysed in the following chapter, works of fiction which derive their narrative form from the conventions of biography and read, in some ways, like third person autobiographies. Both models subjectivize and draw events out of time while seeming to work through time, and confer a synchronic status on their material. A temporal structure is used to perform a spatial function – to produce a repeated and extended emphasis upon one movement bound together by structures of representation which are, for the most part, assumed invisible or unconscious. A particular image of 'history' is constructed which effectively takes the subjects outside of history and into 'story'. It is the way in which individuals are constituted as subjects in *the past as a completed narrative* which forms the substance of the next chapter.

2

A temporary thing

In what has been described as a 'revisionist' history of the inter-war period, John Stevenson and Chris Cook call their opening chapter 'Myth and Reality: Britain in the 1930's' and begin:

> Of all periods in recent British history, the thirties have had the worse press. Although the decade can now only be remembered by the middle-aged and the elderly, it retains the all-pervasive image of the 'wasted years' and the 'low dishonest decade'. Even for those who did not live through them, the 1930's are haunted by the spectres of mass unemployment, hunger marches, appeasement, and the rise of fascism at home and abroad.[1]

A little later on in the same chapter they quote A. J. P. Taylor on the period:

> The nineteen thirties have been called the black years, the devil's decade. Its popular image can be expressed in two phrases: mass unemployment and 'appeasement'. . . . Yet at the same time, most English people were enjoying a richer life than any previously known in the history of the world: longer holidays, shorter hours, higher real wages. They had motor cars, cinemas, radio sets, electrical appliances. The two sides of life did not join up.[2]

The particular fictions I am concerned with in this chapter

symbolically join the two sides of life up. Each one seeks to represent the period in the form of the all-pervasive images described by Stevenson and Cook, *and* the items mentioned by Taylor. Stevenson and Cook (writing in 1977) suggest that Taylor's view has had little influence upon the popular mythology of the 1930s, but, arguably, by now it is this view and an accompanying imagery which has displaced the previously accepted repertoire of the period. The task of re-writing and revising the 1930s has gone well beyond the professional historian, and popular fictions have played a significant role in re-constituting the ways in which we 'remember' the period. Although the fictions I shall be analysing do join up the 'two sides of life', it is a very uneven match in which the 'black years' have become a narrative backdrop against which a whole set of ideological features are developed.

As indicated at the end of the previous chapter, the main concerns of this chapter are with works of fiction which derive their narrative form from the conventions of biography and are structured in ways which suggest an analogy with autobiographical modes of writing, although the historic third person is used. In fact, the use of the historic 'she' is part of a process of authenticating and objectifying what are actually subjectivized narratives. What these fictions share with the autobiographies is an organizational strategy which is close to what Barthes[3] calls the *semic* code, a major device, or set of devices, for thematizing persons, objects or places. This is particularly so of the *period* detail which is thematized repeatedly through a group of signifiers which function like a collective code. Housing, family, childhood, school, diet, work, health, neighbourhood, drink, sex, marriage, clothing, unemployment, hunger, money 'culture heroes' and 'folk devils', class and gender are all 'colonized' by a particular process of signification and take on invariable characteristics. These signifiers, or semes, are used to provide another specified signifier – a named figure, for instance – with its semantic value. In order that the connection is made permanent the attachment process must be repeated.

This is true not only of individual texts but also refers to a larger territory, a 'generic' cluster of texts in which semantic value is given to specific figurations of experience by a repertoire of preconstructed semic codes. One signifier (an image of hunger, for instance) can stand in for all the others. What I have called the iconographic mode of popularized memory operates by this process of continual semic coding and re-coding. This is true at an obtrusive and denotative level of signification, but it also operates *indirectly* whereby semantic value is given to a signifier designed to convey information of an ideological nature, as in those narratives which revise and re-write the interwar period as a temporary, accidental interruption: they extend the discursive range of 'social memory'. The dominant cultural code is formed from within capitalist social relations, and the semic codes organize the narratives according to the implicit 'power-relations' in that code, always being renewed and extended.[4]

I will concentrate on four texts; *Nelly Kelly*, by Lena Kennedy (1981), *Nellie Wildchild*, by Emma Blair (1983), *Opal*, by Elvi Rhodes (1984), and *Polly Pilgrim*, by Marie Joseph (1984).[5] The substantial part of each narrative takes place in the interwar period and has at its centre women who are relatively independent and powerful. Additionally, each text is located within a network of images and symbols designed to codify working-class experience. Except for Elvi Rhodes, each writer has written a number of novels with similar contexts and preoccupations. With the exception of *Polly Pilgrim*, upward social mobility is also a shared theme. Crisis, enigma, trial, and reconciliation all form part of the staple narrative codes of this sub-genre of texts which could be called the 'depression romance'.

Although it will be argued that these novels share many features, it is not intended to subsume them all under a single formula. Limitations of space will not permit more than a brief general discussion of the texts as a whole, so an extended analysis of *Nelly Kelly* is offered as a reading of particular symptoms of structure, style and theme which, to a greater or lesser extent, the other texts share. These popular narratives for women do not only contain anxieties and fantasies commonly found in the feminine romance, but articulate them to a specific personal/political identification located in a moment of deep crisis. My analysis will follow Jameson in arguing that popular culture performs 'a transformational work on [real] social and political anxieties which must then have some effective presence in the mass cultural text in order subsequently to be "managed" or repressed.'[6] In the process of 'management', however, the historical moment is subjectivized and the personal prioritized over the political, to a point where history and politics become simply period markers, or signifiers – the co-ordinates of 'myth'.

The stress throughout will be on the construction of the gendered subject, but reference will also be made to signifiers of class, I am aware of the dangers of an analysis which tends to see gendered subjects standing in for social classes, or for class references to be read as conventionalized gender markers. In these texts, class as a set of social relationships is relatively unmarked, and its characteristic representational form is in terms of generalizations based upon myths of class identity and in the shape of status codings. The point is that it is a central part of the ideological project of the texts that the individualized, exceptional gendered subject stands, not for class, but for *classlessness*, as though 'class' were part of an archive – a periodized 'background', and not a determinate social relationship. The individualist moral culture which shapes each text generates an allegory of mobility, enterprise and the end of ideology and class.

Those versions of the interwar period which stress the 'wasted years' and 'the low dishonest decade' are shown to be an illusion, disguised and defused by the sense of reconciliation and the 'empowerment' of the female. Class incompatibilities fade. The effect of these fictions depends upon the systematic interlocking of two different generic modes of narrative – the feminine romance and the social fiction. It is an eclectic, synthesised mode, but the two forms do not co-exist in any even sense. The one is recruited as a means of renewing the other – of refurbishing the 'unified subject' at a moment when this ideology is seen to be under attack. They are fictions of *transition*, symbolic attempts to come to terms with 'decline', class realities, structured inequality and threats to certain ideological forms and 'eternal values'. The main 'depression' plot is, in a sense, repressed or marginalized and consigned to an iconic context. The mode of romance, arguably, is used to defuse the mode of the social fiction: 'Romance as a form thus expressed a transitional moment, yet one of a very special type; its contemporaries must feel their society torn between past and future in such a way that the alternatives are grasped as hostile but somehow unrelated worlds.'[7] A series of narrative strategies convert/reinvent the political into 'moral essences' with 'character emanation'[8] as the primary causal convention of narratives – hence the titles *Nelly Kelly*, *Polly Pilgrim*, *Nellie Wildchild*, *Opal* – all of which work within an ideology of the centred subject and of *agency;* by converting the secondary male figures into *donors* (in Propp's term), patriarchal relations are suspended or erazed. The interwar period becomes simply a *mediator* which establishes the grounds upon which the final exchange (final, because in three instances, married couples initially are separated) can take place and the compromise formation completed. This formation excizes the 'crisis' (poverty, Depression articulated in broken relationships and in excess and in extremism) not only as a fact of narrative, but of history and of memory. It is displaced from history to myth. In Jameson's terms, the structure of each individual text can be read as a socially symbolic act responding to a historical dilemma, with a double existence as political fact in the interwar period, and a memory which found political form in the post 1945 construction of a welfare society. My argument is that the cultural is being brought in to redress the political – to saturate it ideologically so that, what Bakhtin calls, the heteroglossic or dialogic can be appropriated to a single narrative system.[9]

The whole of the interwar period is seen in the terms of a metaphor of *interruption*. Continuity and the restored pattern are predicated upon a paradigm of the family.

Each text is marked by a series of narrative ruptures differentially coded. In *Opal*[10] the rupture is caused by Opal's initiative and independence in opening a shop, and by her sexual desire which leads to an affair. Her husband Edgar experiences a long period of unemployment to which he responds initially in terms of a political analysis, but gradually comes to see himself, as Opal sees him, as weak and a failure. There is a fairly rapid shift from the economic-political configuration to the psychological explanation of unemployment as a matter of individual pathology. Opal's strength is seen as a further dilution of his power as she moves from house-shop to local 'salon' and, finally, to the ownership of a multi-storey department store which she names after herself. In the process, husband and wife become estranged as Edgar's economic situation undermines his psychic and sexual identity. He eventually finds employment as an insurance salesman and part of his round includes the working-class district in which he and Opal originally lived. She is anxious to sever all contact with this place and memory, and casts it in stock images of the working class seen from a middle-class perspective: 'it could be riddled with germs'. Edgar sees the poverty differently and is aware of the exploitative role of the insurance company, profiting at the expense of the impoverished and powerless.

His attitude is important in carving out a 'sentimental' space to which the ambitious, enterprizing Opal will *eventually* return: 'But what she couldn't understand was, that not everyone was cut out to be successful. She thought that it was simply a matter of putting your mind to it.'

How the narrative restores Opal to the forms of romance is by a process in which she becomes increasingly money-orientated, privatized and isolated as a result of an *excess* of enterprize and an *excess* of desire; she is separated along economic, psychological and sexual lines. She is marked for a period of time as *deviant* because of her 'abnormal', extreme behaviour. The text resolves this crisis of deviance in the form of melodrama. She has a serious car accident and goes into a coma: 'Now it's up to good nursing and nature' (p.190) the doctor says, 'I would like to keep her in this private wing . . . she will need constant supervision for a long time yet.'

She recovers her identity as wife and mother, returns to the store and finds it neglected by staff slackness which has replaced the former 'service' and 'efficiency'. She begins another regenerative process, sacks her former lover, and feels 'the power returning to her'. Her restoration is not completed, however, until a a fire destroys her office at the top of the store, which had previously become her 'world', and she is forced to descend from her isolated tower to share an office with her manager, George Soames, 'a man of medium height, kindly and honest'. He is one of many mediating and moderating forces in the last sections of the narrative.

It is hard to avoid the allegorical pressures of this narrative, particularly the way in which nation-store-private-public-subjectivity are condensed in images and symbolic actions. The language is fairly close to some aspects of Thatcherist rhetoric and the store's recovery is linked with a national economic recovery in the late 1930s. To complete the image Opal returns to her original street and notices the newly laundered net curtains, the freshly painted and varnished houses and doors, and the fact that most of the families are in work. A further image of new housing estates and young couples becoming property owners ties in with A. J. P. Taylor's comment (above, p.61).

The narrative began in the period immediately following World War One, and it ends in the moment immediately preceding World War Two – the inter-war years are seen as an interlude, an aberration; they fall away, slip off to leave the family strengthened and reformed after crisis.

The initial response to Edgar's unemployment was for

Opal to work with Edgar running the house-shop, a way of extending their position by mixing their labour with her pretty productive property, with Opal becoming the wage-labourer in the service sector (she works in a dress shop). This marks a stage where the woman is ceasing to be the sustainer and symbol of virtue in the private sphere which, in a vital contradiction of an ideological attachment to this 'value', accords with the fact that only one in ten households 'conforms to the family ideal of male breadwinner, full-time housewife and dependent children.'[11] It is this Victorian model against which the narrative is working, and through which Edgar articulates his frustration and self-pity.

It is a complex ideological figuration because it dispenses with a particular paradigm (historically located in the 1920s because of the 'failure' of men to sustain their role as 'breadwinners') in the terms of a rhetoric of individualism and the free play of market forces, and yet within an ideology of the family in which 'the self-sacrificing little woman as usual plays the supportive role'.[12] How does the narrative negotiate and reconcile these conflicting strategies? Part of the answer is suggested by Jean Gardiner[13] who argues that, although the government attempts to provide a legitimation for the limits placed on woman by the current recession and the cuts which have accompanied it, at the same time it has to recognize those changes in women's lives and aspirations which are irreversible as a result of experiences since the last war. In other words, a commitment to women's equal rights can co-exist with moral beliefs about the family and traditional values.

In all of these romances motivation, responses, and interaction are seen as a matter of individual temperament and personal psychology. Social and historical co-ordinates are background. Each narrative hinges on unemployment and the 'dole' — the sphere of the disempowered male. The crisis is seen as disturbance and disruption and the narrative takes the form of a quest for an answer to certain enigmas and questions. This is particularly so of

Polly Pilgrim[14] where Harry Pilgrim moves from the north to the south in the search for employment and is forced to leave his family behind. A series of stresses and trials follow both for him and his wife and children. As in the other narratives, desire is again foregrounded but gradually placed by its construction in a context of excess, madness, temptation and, ultimately, the reconciled heterosexual couple. Again and again, a series of metaphors develop the sense that the dominant feature of the period is abnormality, deviance, aberration and excess, variously signified in forms which displace the political – sexuality is the most common symbolic construction. In this narrative there is discord, trauma, anxiety, psychic terror and fantasy, complicated further by generational disruption – Polly and her mother, and Polly, Harry, and their daughter Gatty.

Polly works in a raincoat factory for an exiled Jewish figure, Manny Goldberg and this particular feature of the narrative produces a collocation of unemployment, Jewishness and Nazism which heightens the sense of a specific historical location, an *exceptional* period because of the combination of circumstances – it is marked as a moment of discontinuity which de-mobilizes the larger political analysis.

Polly meets a man called Robert Dennis in the Garden of Remembrance – the metonymic space of war – in which her scarlet coat emblematizes the shed blood of that war and yet, also, she 'made a picture that gladdened the eye'. Reference is also made to the dark, glossy rhododendrons which suggest that the 'scene' is ambiguous – a space of death and desire. Dennis, his hair greying – 'it had started to go that way in the mud of the trenches of Flanders Field' – his arm severed just below the elbow, is a characteristic figure in this genre: the wounded male, damaged either by war or unemployment, or both (as in the case of Edgar in *Opal* and Harry Pilgrim). All the men in these texts are flawed and broken physically and psychically in some way. The whole scenario focuses upon the breakdown of masculinity, or certain codes of masculinity to be more accurate. The woman is seen as therapeutic, the healer/nurse figure in a genre based upon a landscape of remembrance.

This text does acknowledge the 'reality' of the 1930s, tries to deconstruct certain 'myths', admit a 'collective' guilt, and then proceeds to draw a series of reconstitutive lessons from it. It does recognize the need for welfare, but it is, perhaps, the welfare of 'taking care of their own' which is itself part of the dismantling of the welfare state. Elements of an oppositional history are traced through reference to dispossessed weavers, starvation and Luddism, but the collective is condensed into the tragic individual as victim. By foregrounding and distancing this level of struggle (Luddism) like a slide show, or a side-show, the 1930s struggle is, in a way, displaced. The Industrial Revolution simultaneously displaced whole categories of skill and made way for a number of others. The 1930s saw a reversal of that 'progress' – it was another phase of de-skilling and displacement – but this is *indirectly* experienced by Harry in his work as the private gardener of benign owners of production and property. He sees his separation from Polly as a *temporary* thing and the 'whole Depression choking the life out of the North was a temporary thing' (p.72). Again, the individual/class conflation occurs as so often in these narratives. The notion of the Depression as a separation, an interruption, a pause in continuity is linked syntactically through the phrase 'a temporary thing' which is repeated on p.72 of the text.

Robert Dennis, in Harry's absence, stands in as a surrogate husband, but his role is educative, never sexual. His physical 'incompleteness' masks an image of masculinity – 'someone without the air of defeat about them'. As far as he is concerned, Polly is a 'magic' figure: 'All she'd done . . . was walk in through the door to stand in his living-room looking like a *coloured photo* when everything else was in *old-fashioned sepia*' (p.134, my italics). In many ways, this sums up so many things in these narratives. Nellie Wildchild, who comes from the poverty stricken tenements of Govan to become a music-hall star and the Scottish Personality of the Year, is similarly styled: 'She had a magic on stage. As soon as she stepped on the boards she lit up, creating an aura, an electricity about her . . . she shone in the middle of the line like a jewel.'[15] The role of each heroine is to stand out in relief, mobilized, variegated, full of colour, active and dynamic in contrast to the iconic backdrop of 'sepia-tinted' images – the 1930s 'footage'. They are the past, she is the present continuous – the signifier of the future.

Harry 'lapses' by having an affair with Roger Craven's sister, Yvonne Frobisher, but her upper-class position and flippancy almost seems to exonerate him, while Polly, constructed in and through an extensive range of desire imagery, and Robert sustain a celibate relationship which in its final phases marks him as 'fathering' her in her illness. Harry is found work and a home for the family in the south through the agency of the family of an upper middle-class man, Roger Craven, whom he has 'nursed' in his final illness brought about by alcohol and destitution – effecting, in repeated form, the reconciliation and cross-class harmonies characteristic of these texts. All the ruptures and dissonances of desire and the economy are erazed.

This somewhat cryptic summary of a number of texts has perhaps tended to dissolve them into a formulaic model which does not fully represent their complex and, often, contradictory forms which is why I have selected one text in order to explore the precise ways in which environment, class, mobility, individualism, the exceptional and the survivor all figure in complex interaction with the characteristics of feminine romance. Each woman has 'stepped out from amongst the ranks' (to achieve moral or material supremacy, or both), and underneath their vulnerability 'there is tempered steel . . . forged there by herself for survival' (both phrases are from *Nellie Wildchild*). It is noticeable that most of their careers, or successes, are seen as an extension of woman's traditional interests – Opal's career from 'house-shop' to house-department store traces a consumer trajectory built around the female subject and 'furnishing' the domestic – or are 'supplemented' by other indices of femininity, vulnerability for example. Narrative priority is always given to the personal; the 'history' is the site of the individual relationship or profile. There is a simplified moral polarization and schematization.

The fictions referred to in this chapter are, with the exception of *Nellie Wildchild* in some respects, family melodramas in which strong female subjects are constructed as 'modern' women. The texts construct an implicit argument which suggests that 'modernity' and active sexuality arose out of a negative situation – male weakness – and not a positive initiative. It also suggests that this 'reactive' situation generated merely temporary choices and desires, a suspension and masking of the 'real' choices which are to do with family. All of the texts place the issue of female independence and autonomy at the centre of the narrative, but ultimately displace it onto a resolution constructed from familial ideology, with the exception of *Nellie Wildchild*. Here the ending 'celebrates' an impossible love – 'that marriage that would never be', because of the death of the hero in the Second World War. Basically, however, the fictions suggest, as Carolyn Heilbrun points out in another context, 'that women may be "read", their responses deciphered, only if the process reinforces woman's role as consumer, consoler, conquest'.[16]

The simple structure which, supposedly, characterizes 'popular' or 'low status' speech is adopted in order to speak for the whole range of human experience. In this way a particular appropriation of 'human' experience is placed at the centre of the narrative and is made to 'stand in for' *all* experience: everything else is irrelevant or marginal. Repeated use of this form of mediation (popular journalism is a particular instance) has naturalized it to such an extent that it has become recognized as a consensual form of expression, based upon a rhetoric which has rewritten an individualist morality. Linked to this consensus has been the commonsensical idea that 'popular' language is 'authentic' – the speech of honesty, truth and sincerity; the code of the genuine. This is seen as contrary to the 'educated' codes which are distanced from, and stigmatize, the 'popular'. This linguistic populism masks the class-specific nature of differential codes of language and their role in the spread and mainten-ance of power. Ideologies of literacy and limited access to the whole range of lexical and syntactic structures are at the root of this cultural 'diglossia' – the reasons are cultural and political, and not natural. It is a matter of resources, not innate deficiencies or restrictions.

These 'popular memory' romances draw upon a repre-sentational practice which not only simulates the simpli-fied codes of ordinary speech but celebrates it through a range of nostalgic imagery which centres upon women who, historically and politically, were marginalized and fragmented in the period in question. The narratives ulti-mately, but not without contradiction, deliver these women up to an ahistorical myth of domesticity, in the form of the family in particular. Unlike earlier fictions, or documentaries, *in* and *of* the period, the central figure and the narrating voice share the discursive articulation of the text. The authority is *not* that of an outside observer representing the 'working class' to a middle-class read-ership, but these are *insider* discourses – 'I was there'. They are not just eye-witness narratives but part of an 'I experienced' mode. As will be seen later, in specific exam-ples, 'fate', not politics, binds the archive. The visibility of class or gender difference is obscured by the rhetorical figurations of the individualist morality. The heroine is the reference of all and every item in the text. In a not unre-lated manner, Margaret Thatcher wishes to be known, apparently, for having 'shattered the illusion that Govern-ment could somehow substitute for individual perform-ance'. These particular fictions represent popularized forms of the substitution of individual performance for the 'illusions' of Left images of the 1930s.

The centrality of women in these fictions brings them,

in genre terms, close to soap operas, supplemented by 'historical evidence'. Female dependence in terms of the family, the economy, and relationships is carefully charted and a measure of liberation is also described, but this is circumscribed in the ways indicated earlier by the organization of domesticity and sexuality. They are closer to what Janice Winship has called, in another context, 'fantasies of liberation'.[17]

It is not only that women have been restored to the centres of popular fiction (they have always been there in soap and romance) but they have been 're-historicized', taken back to a point of origin – 'hard times' – and, as in an initiative test, have been provided with almost nothing except their own 'guts' and resourcefulness. The fable element is obvious; the fundamental structuring of inequalities in class society has been re-written in the forms of a 'temporary' slump – its moment of 'national' crisis – and the solution to the crisis is emblematized in the figure of a woman who emerges bearing the values and images of a petty bourgeois moral economy, although these are styled as eternal and classless.

The point of the retrospect in these fictions is not to clarify or illuminate a particular historical period, but to re-write it in order to repress the contradictions of contemporary social relations. While structured firmly around a narrative of *change*, they are motivated by a fear of change. They are fictions of continuity and stability (selectively coded) but, above all, of *survival* – supposedly of an individual, but, arguably, of a stratum – economically dependent, but cultural 'standard bearers' of independence and freedom. Currently, the value of equality is now being deeply questioned and counterposed to 'freedom' and 'liberty' and similar abstractions. There are positive arguments now being advanced from the so-called 'New Right' in favour of inequalities, and these fictions, while they cannot simply be subsumed under such a rubric, are symbolic processes which, by constantly stressing the *exceptional* and the *talented*, and stressing *difference*, help to constitute ways of seeing in which socially composed forms of inequality are coded as 'natural'.

Redeemers of the patriarchy?

Lena Kennedy, *Nelly Kelly*[8]
This is one of the fictions of the 'new individualism', with its emphasis on the 'spiritual' mobility of the authenticated working-class subject from interwar poverty and cultural deprivation to becoming a published novelist. Her progress is contrasted with the flat trajectory of her contemporaries, named and unnamed. Nelly is born in the East End of London which is sketched rapidly in a series of economic and environmental negatives. The opening chapter situates Nelly on the point of leaving school – impoverished, bleak, and limiting – and entering a chaotic, depressed world. The Principal – styled as Miss Victoria – instructs the pupils in respectability and obedience. The testimonial from the school is seen as the key to *survival*, a major theme in this novel and the others referred to earlier. By implication also, it is treated as a key theme of the period. Nelly's peers are variously described in terms of their negative physical and mental attributes – 'a large, blousy girl with a grubby face. She already had a child at home – reported to be by her own father', and [about John Hill] 'We must not forget you're unintelligent. Let's say you're good with your hands.' From the outset distinctions are made which go beyond the customary division of mental and manual labour. A set of clichés and stereotypes of working-class life – familiar from widespread and repeated circulation and part of the language of power – indicate the ways in which the text is preconstructed from an 'already known' discourse.[9]

Although the tone of the opening section is critical of the Principal's attitudes, the text nevertheless uses the descriptions of fecklessness, incest, dullness, and slovenliness to suggest – synecdochically – an 'underclass', the characteristics of which are used to set Nelly 'in relief'. It draws upon a pre-cast imagery of the period for its rendering of landscape and 'extras' and reserves its specific articulation for the development of the eponymous survivor. Nelly shares the extremes of poverty of her contemporaries, but is differentiated from them by the fact that she is a 'pretty girl' and has an ambition to write. The two, quite unconnected features, are blended throughout the text into an image of the *exceptional*, another repeated signifier throughout all these texts. On the opening pages it is the stylized Mary – fat-hipped, musty smelling, foul-mouthed: 'Mary sat with her legs wide apart' (which signifies more than her posture) – who is selected as the negative framework for Nelly's *movement*. Mary is physically, sexually, and culturally fixed in a stereotyped class role – one of a series of background profiles blended inextricably with the socio-economic location of poverty. It is an essential part of the narrative method gradually to build up a set of linguistic indicators which establish *physical* or *cultural* differentials which, by elision, become *psychological*. It is, perhaps, this marginalizing of the social and historical co-ordinates of the subject which defines this essentialist mode of individuation. Nelly's life is marked by a whole series of familiar topics – dead sibling, mother dead from pneumonia, a cold, impoverished dwelling – which, given the text's ideological project, have a 'genre' feel about them. Although they are in a sense 'period markers' their specific function is to demonstrate the remarkable features of the heroine.

Part of Nelly's consciousness of her situation is the invention of 'that lovely character who was within her during quiet moments'. Her name was Kitty Daly and she had fair corkscrew curls and always wore a pretty dress. The text 'quotes' from another preconstructed discourse – here specified – produced from within the language of power. The details of the daydream are predicated upon a class 'myth' of boarding school, dormitories, uniform, and holidays abroad. Styled from a schoolgirl romance of an upper middle-class existence, she is Nelly's first creation, a form of compensation – later placed critically. The schoolgirl romance contrasts sharply with her own

familial role as 'mother', housewife, and sweat shop
worker. The polarization is, at this stage, total – she empa-
thizes even with the motherless rats in the sweat shop.
What is being argued here is that her extreme poverty is
somehow paradigmatic: she is the 'ash-girl' of folk tale, a
Cinderella to the girls of the school romance. While Nelly
is loved for her prettiness and dress sense at work, her
sister, Noni, is styled as yet another 'context negative' –
'but she was placid and plump and never cared how untidy
either she or the home was'. This adds further to the
psychological evidence of Nelly's exceptionality, it 'famili-
alizes' her difference to supplement the school/work
signifiers.

So, within a short space of time Nelly is marked off
from a series of negative female signifiers at school, at
home and at work. Nelly becomes the boss's assistant and
is styled as the kind of person who always 'falls on her
feet'. At one point the boss says to her 'My life, Nelly . . .
it's a pity they don't have women prime ministers,' he
joked, 'you would certainly fill the part' (p.69). Not
surprisingly, perhaps, many of the prominent women
figures in these fictions bear a striking resemblance to
Margaret Thatcher, herself a redeemer of patriarchal social
relations in the form of the 'patriarchal feminine' or
'honorary male' scripted from a series of cues provided by
the inter-war period in *its* re-writing of 'Victorian values'.

The conditions of the interwar period are treated *iconically*, through the use of a series of well-known period
signifiers – unemployment, fascist activity, the jubilee, and
communist party meetings – rather than through a close
historical rendering. It is as if a backdrop is constructed
out of the 'known' linguistic and visual indicators of the
period and then spaces are cut out for the heads of the
foregrounded characters. The style claims an insider's
view, but much of the detail seems recorded from the
outside, archivally. In effect, this reproduces the experience of Nelly herself as her environment is encountered in
the form of markers, *exempla* almost, which serve as a
reminder/warning of what she could become if she fails.

The text is composed narratively and stylistically of
'tangled lines'. Her background is progressively aban-
doned. The items in this background landscape have an
allegorical function as evidence in the streets, dwellings,
and impedimenta of the East End of a cultural and psychological fate. All this evidence is designed to set off Nelly's
difference.

When Nelly is involved politically (with the Communist
Party at sixteen) it is again very much to illustrate her own
distinctiveness. The CP activist, Kunner, is always gracious
to Nelly but rarely converses with the other workers, and
Nelly's passivity in the political sense is stressed – the CP
soon 'set about *using* her', to 'educate her *little disciple*',
'*surreptitiously* gave her communist pamphlets to read',
'*even though she didn't understand* much of the talk', she
had *absorbed* the socialist *doctrine*', 'continued to *feed*
her with communist literature', 'a great worker and a great
comrade'. The words italicized (by me) are drawn from a
familiar register of phrases associated, commonsensically,
with political alternatives and suggesting manipulation,
ulterior motivation, and victimizing of the naive. The
naivety of the language used to describe Nelly's 'political
consciousness' is not just character-specific but, by implication, suggests the naivety and over-simplification of the
beliefs themselves. The whole episode – the chapter is
entitled 'A Political Problem' – is recuperated by stressing
two things: Nelly's popularity, and her liking for the *social*
life of the Party. She is elected to go on a student exchange
holiday in Russia, but her father smashes up their home
when he finds out and threatens to 'get' Kunner. Nelly
rushes to the parish priest who proves 'understanding and
kind'. He suggests that she should keep herself occupied
by going to church meetings. The point of the whole
chapter is to indicate Nelly's popularity, her ability to
stand her ground against her father, and, more particularly, to show that she is 'her own person' and belongs
to neither party nor church, ultimately. She resolves the
dilemma by giving up her job as 'this was indeed a home
without a mother.' As well as indicating the features

suggested above, the chapter is also part of a process whereby Nelly 'visits' and 'inhabits' certain characteristic landmarks of the period as part of her authentication. What is registered and narratively 'remembered' is not the landmark but Nelly's response to it, as she is both 'pilgrim' and 'guide' to the period. Her centrality validates her judgements and *places* the experiences. She rapidly sheds her 'need' for a collective solution to the phenomenon of inequality as it becomes *naturalized* as a matter of talent, enterprise, and innate qualities of which she is an embodiment and testimony.

Nelly shifts from adolescent politics to the role of housewife and this stage marks the first of several apparent breaks with particular ideological constellations based on the construction of femininity. Up to this point Nelly's difference has been constructed around 'distances' from her peers and her class environment expressed in physical and behavioural characteristics. Nelly is soon fed up with being at home all day — she is not fulfilled by one of the traditionally ascribed 'feminine' roles. She finds employment in an 'old tyme coffee shop' which feeds her romantic fantasies of class and history [it is run by a Mr King]. Her illusions are gradually punctured — 'the coffee shop's aura of history had faded for her' — and finally her Cinderella daydream — 'poor serving wenches would often meet rich men and end up being duchesses' is shattered when a bowler-hatted, pin-striped 'beautiful guest [at a coffee shop function]' tries to rape her. The incident is related humorously but her 'deb romance' ends when 'she jumped on a tram to take her back to the slum district'. The behaviour of a particular class fraction identified as that which works with money, is generalized and critically placed as part of the dismantling of Nelly's illusions about 'class' and as part of her journey to the world of 'real value' encoded within a framework of lower middle-class ideology.

The text is punctuated with frequent references to Nelly's reading habits and there are several instances, like the one just cited, where the formula romance is revealed in its ideological shallowness. Items of the romance lexicon are systematically discarded as possible 'models' for Nelly, as if she has to develop by challenging a complex set of determinations – genetic, environmental, familial, economic, and cultural-fictional – in order to arrive at a point in the last chapter where she achieves an identity based on a set of what are constructed as freely made *choices*. The analogue of this is the fiction which she herself creates as a mark of cultural independence – the shedding of all her previous fictional 'selves' – in the production of an authentic subject unified, coherent and symbolically reproduced in her novel and her child. The theme of the text, and of the others referred to previously, is the making of the *personal* (an ideology of the personal) out of, and apart from, the political legacy of the interwar period – to accommodate, and incorporate, its memory of poverty and unemployment within a neo-liberal perspective of individualism.

The narrative trajectory, therefore, has an *educational* function as Nelly ends up as the 'truly liberated' woman free from the nets of class, background, history and cultural constructions but enclosed within a *natural* domestic framework. In order to arrive at this stage Nelly has to undergo a series of gender and, arguably, generational tests around questions of sexuality and codes of femininity which are formulated from within the novel's intrinsic contradiction.

The crucial task of analysis is to discover how this challenge is met, defused, and negated by the text – recuperated, in short, for the dominant codes of femininity. Nelly's initial sexual experience is limited, in comparison with her peers, and confined by certain 'Victorian' attitudes. One of the main aspects is female competitiveness which she experiences with her friend Bebe, another of the novel's 'big formed', 'lurid coloured scarf'-wearing figures, designed to emphasize Nelly's 'look', 'taste' and 'difference' and 'uniqueness' – all of which help to signify her final choices as both individuated and representative, in the exemplary not commonplace sense.

'Shotgun weddings', ugliness, obesity, bad skin, consumption are all seen as regular features of her environment but are rarely attributed beyond the individual instances. Having 'outgrown' the political dimensions of this problem of poverty, Nelly's focus is personalized and she begins 'to scribble compulsively in a large notebook'. This is part of her mechanism of escape and will later come to underwrite and consolidate it: 'She wrote of the under-privileged – those who had nothing – and others who had it all, of social injustice and evils.' The notebook is a form of escape and relief from tensions. The problem is diagnosed and the solution is posed in inward terms: a turning away from the collective, a commitment to the liberal humanist model – individual and introspective – with writing as compensation. Linked with this is another individualist model of freedom – escape for the self through mobility and improvement of conditions – 'bettering oneself', 'getting on'. The rhetoric and models of the text come close at times to the ideology of inequality and incentives formulated by Quintin Hogg many years ago but, once more, distinctly familiar in the political rhetoric of our own time:

> . . . rich and poor are united in a common brother-hood, humanity. . . . The incentive of inequality, if inequality corresponds to skill and energy, is one of the main means whereby new wealth can be created. . . . So far from being the cause of poverty Conservatives believe it demonstrable historically that the most decisive steps which have been taken in the past towards a higher standard of living for the mass of people have been taken as the result of this incentive operating on the minds of the few.[20]

Obviously, *Nelly Kelly* cannot be reduced to some kind of simple inflection of Conservative philosophy of the 1940s, refurbished for modern purposes, but the notions of 'incentive', 'skill and energy', 'inequality' and 'the few' all constitute part of the novel's ideological foundations, its naturalizing techniques.

The theme of difference is extended to Nelly's first 'real'

love – Bill – who is a mirror of herself and her values.
He, like her, stands out in relief from his background and
fulfils all the criteria of difference – 'To please Bill, Nelly
had changed her way of living in every respect.' His existence marks out a possible phase of escape – she got some
inkling of middle-class attitudes: 'They seemed to include
a desire for something that had nothing to do with being
posh, for Bill was also really working class.' The ideology
located here is linked with 'respectability' – a code appropriated and sustained by lower middle-class attitudes. Bill
had been stopped once for speeding and 'He was ashamed
at having to go to court and being fined ten bob, and
terrified in case his mother found out about it.' Nelly, who
had lived all her life in what is described as a 'criminal
fraternity' could not understand what all the fuss was
about. An important ideological differential is reproduced
here between the 'respectable' and 'criminal' working
classes. Moving towards Bill does not complete Nelly's
trajectory, although she remains married to him
throughout the text, but is the first significant step out of
her class position: the step we have been narratively
prepared for by all the preceding indices of 'difference'.

The chapter in which Nelly and Bill meet is entitled 'A
Hard Life', as if to explain, and justify, her 'desire' – social,
not sexual at this point. Bill becomes like the notebook, a
way out, a means of helping her assuage her guilt. Nelly
re-casts herself in Bill's image 'he always managed to
choose the middle ground and appease everyone', in the
chapter called 'Settling Down'. At this stage in the narrative (the time is 1935–6) all the signs point towards a a
gradual enclosure of Nelly in marriage, dependence and
subordination, domesticity, housework, and maternity.
She is moving into the codes and value system occupied
by Bill's class fraction: 'They dressed nicely and did not
swear', 'he liked her to look neat and tidy', even if, as the
text acknowledges, the work she does is as exploitative
and demanding as that in the sweat shops. In fact, the
style of 'Settling Down' is over-insistent, edged with the
parodic, although Nelly's upward move is charted

'straight': 'We don't want to get married yet', said Nelly, 'Not till we've saved up enough to buy our own house' [a concern with petty property which is characteristic of her 'new' values]. The style is over-insistent and over-symmetrial in order to offset the 'conclusive' sense of 'settling down'. This styling prefigures later contradictions when Nelly's life-style challenges, through experience, the ideological codes of her encirclement, the dominant gender meanings ascribed to her and willingly (at first) colluded with. In the last section of this chapter she and Bill organize her whole family's move out of Hoxton, and on the bus they see her father and his pal, drunk on a cart.

> Dad spotted Nelly and Bill on the bus and waved his hat, cowboy style, in greeting. . . . Nelly closed her eyes hoping that no one recognized them. She was leaving all that behind her, she hoped. (p.100)

This is a neat articulation of the consciousness mentioned earlier, which distinguishes Nelly. It is a self-consciousness derived from other frames of value, distancing forms, which the ideological project of the narrative will transform into a different kind of *self* consciousness. Her background, peers and her family, even, are seen 'generically' while she alone is individuated through her mobility. The following chapter 'A New Home' supplements the settling down and adds 'gentility', thrift, deferred gratification, bridal virginity, the dual role of worker and housewife, a mortgage, and suburbia, to the developing imagery of change and progress. Nelly's progress is expanded territorially and in terms of her femininity – 'her greatest dreams had come true – she was pregnant'.

Up to this point, Nelly's trajectory is the familiar one traced out in countless fictional experiences – the novel is reproducing an ideological programme for the dominant cultural construction of femininity. The major narrative contradiction comes in the form of the chapter entitled 'Blitz' which takes on a number of symbolic connotations. If the previous ten chapters had all led up to, and prefigured, 'A New Home' (the flight from Hoxton), the Blitz chapter is the detonating structure. The first ten chapters have constructed a discourse of 'normality'. What follows is a contestation of this discourse – a deconstruction.

In the initial stages of the blitz Nelly is nervous and anxious, waiting 'for her man to arrive safely'. The first 'role-break' comes with the loss of her child who is still-born. The death of the baby is the first check to her gender 'fulfilment'. The next comes with the removal of 'her man' when he is called up. The cooking and housework are experienced as a heavy burden and she begins to go to the pub every evening with her Dad and would 'sit and drink herself stupid'. What is happening is a *dismantling* of all the structures developed in the first ten chapters. The drinking is followed by the onset of 'slovenly habits'; she feels hung over each day, doesn't bother to dress and spends the day in her dressing gown. At this point the breakdown is personal and domestic (reverting to 'class' type is perhaps implied): her drinking and slovenliness are just two negations of the codes of femininity which are also class codes and recall the generic conditions of her first East End peers, although she is physically removed from that time and environment.

Her 'recovery' begins with her breaking out of the domestic frame and taking a job again, in a tobacconist shop where she 'becomes the centre of admiration for many a middle-aged and well-dressed businessman', but she refuses all invitations to go out, asserts her married status and determination to 'wait for her Bill'. On his return she feels deeply jealous of his camp life and resents his apparent happiness and comradeship. Her consciousness of the public, shared life of the male sharpens her sense of isolation and rejection. In fact, the war has only magnified and thrown into relief the commonplace social constructions of masculinity and femininity – the one public *and* private, the other confined to the private. His 'independence' cuts across her need for someone to 'need' her. The dependence-independence problem is part of the 'blitz' on the dominant frameworks of meaning.

Nelly is resentful that Bill liked being in the army so much. His first leave proves to be a catalyst for a number of questions about her own separation in gender terms. It increases her restlessness and dissatisfaction, and renews her search for something which she cannot name. Dismissed from her job, she returns to factory work and begins to take some pleasure in the company of other women, and is also stimulated by the open discussion of sexual experiences, but not without contradiction:

> She was actually a little disgusted. She had grown up in a low class district . . . but she had never heard such outspoken comments on sexual behaviour. She was puzzled by the casual attitudes of the well-spoken girls, in particular, who smoked incessantly and dressed sloppily in men's shirts and trousers, their hair pulled back in untidy pony tails. The East End girls seemed to care much more about their appearance and much effort was put into having a nice hair-do and a good dress. (p.123)

Apart from the recurring signifiers – low class, well-spoken – this passage is also interesting because it introduces Nelly to a contradictory image of middle-class values and corresponds quite closely with the popular image of women becoming more emancipated during the war, and the later sections of the novel recall 'feminist suspicions of a drive to reverse this emancipation and get women back ino the home when hostilities ended; by closing the nurseries, by dismissing them from their jobs.'[21] The actual process of reconciliation of gender contradictions and the reconstruction of woman's place was complex and the novel cannot simply be read as a fictionalization of this. On the other hand, the redirection of work back into the domestic and the familial was not a 'one-off' process. It could be argued that recent reactions to feminism, while they cannot simply advocate that 'a woman's place is in the home' have become part of a complex and contradictory articulation. The reconstruction of an ideology of gender distinctiveness has sought to reconstitute women in terms of codes of femininity which do acknowledge work as part of a woman's expectation. At the same time, however, these codes also renew emphasis on traditional roles implicitly, by cuts in welfare provision which, in the name of freedom and community, have brought about a re-adjustment in forms of caring which re-locates it in the family and, by implication, in the female: the private sector of the emotional, the personal: 'If the good Lord had intended us all having equal rights to go out to work and to behave equally, you know he really wouldn't have created men and women.'[22]

The recall of the period 1918–50 is not merely an act of generational nostalgia but, by its *iconic* reiteration of images of community and the family it is re-inscribing the 'Mum' (i.e. unpaid female labour) in the centres of ideological discourse. By-passing the 1960s it constantly returns to the war, especially the blitz, as that moment of 'abnormality' which *explains* the recent phase of feminism. The extract quoted from the novel on the previous page has built into it distinctions which are significant for this – the 'well-spoken girls' exhibit a disdain for the 'look' of femininity, as objects of the male gaze, which has to be restored by the East End girls. Ideologically, the years since 1979, and perhaps earlier, have witnessed an attempt to rewrite the inter-war period and the post-war reconstruction in Conservative terms by some of those previously silenced 'voices of the forties'. One strategy has been to dismantle those characteristics associated with socialism, especially the welfare state, women's liberation, and Britain's 'decline' as a nation. The fictions under discussion do not reflect this ideological process in any direct way, but help to constitute ways in which the cultural process may be seen as part of the construction and complex negotiation of meanings in our time.

Nelly's restlessness is added to by Bill's next leave. She longs to become pregnant again, possibly as a way of resolving the pressure of the contradictions within which she exists. Her notebook becomes another form of escape added to hard work, nights in the pub, and Saturday outings. The chapter 'Blind Date' contains several references to sexual affairs, brought nearer to us by being linked with named figures close to Nelly, including her sister Noni, always contrasted with her as 'fat and sloppy in appearance', 'casual, careless and humorous'.

Noni's husband is killed and Bill goes missing. Nelly goes to an Air Force squadron 'hop' and meets her first *Lover* and *Hero* (as the chapter is entitled) – a young pilot officer. He is contrasted in his strength and good looks with the 'crocks' – the scarred and wounded from all ranks. She becomes 'uncomfortably self-conscious about all the eyes that looked at her so lewdly as the lads discussed her figure and her see-through frock'. She is trapped by, and within, the contradictions of a situation in which she colludes. Barry, the pilot, appropriates her ('Lay off . . . I found her') as an object of desire, and he is marked off from the others by his *difference* – 'obviously very well bred. Every word he spoke was crisply and clearly pronounced.' He is the archetypal masculine hero – a 'top pilot in the Battle of Britain' with whom sex is an exciting experience in contrast with her husband 'for whom sex had been something you just did not get excited about'. Though drunk, not knowing whether her husband is alive or dead, and feeling that 'she had acted like a whore', Nelly completes the breaking of the circle of femininity by acknowledging her pleasure and her desire. She continues to seek justification – 'the only reason she allowed herself to be unfaithful was that Bill did not give enough of himself to her when he did see her'. Within the genre of traditional romance this is an unusual recognition of desire, and it is qualified, in some ways legitimized, by the fact that Barry 'had been so lovely, so refined and well-spoken. He was obviously a gentleman.' The 'cultured voice of the BBC newsreader' announced his death shortly afterwards.

In some ways, female sexuality and desire are displaced onto the fetishised object of desire, who is almost 'seigneurial' in the way linguistic deference invests him with dignity. Despite this, when Nelly returns home, 'she climbed into her bath and scrubbed herself hard; she felt physically and mentally dirty'. (Barry had paid a woman for the use of a room which makes her 'a whore by proxy' she feels.)

Nelly discovers that Barry is from a wealthy manufacturing family, and he is buried with full honours in Westminister cathedral. Perhaps his being a Catholic helps to 'sanctify' their 'mortal' sin. Nelly is impressed 'by the large number of well-dressed men and women who arrived in big shiny cars'. Mortified by guilt, but with the memory of desire, she prays at the memorial service to 'be a good wife, a good daughter, and a good anything that she was likely to become'. She prays, in other words, to be re-admitted to 'the circle of femininity'. This is supplemented by several 'Hail Marys', prayers to the archetypal representative of pure womanhood: 'She felt almost purged, happy, and certainly more at peace with the world.'

This is a baroque chapter, but the contradictions are not simply resolved, nor are the cultural and class 'myths' merely decorative, but remain as part of a seminal schism in 'female consciousness' rooted in desire and its masks and disguises. The class and national position of the 'desired one' almost de-personalizes him, makes him 'god-like' (Christ-like, perhaps), and Nelly's desire is elevated morally, is compensated for by a link with the Magdalene figure of Catholic iconography. She relives her sexual experience by 'writing it up' in her notebook – both a record and a displacement.

Nelly next meets a GI sergeant at a dance, a newspaper man, who is very different from Barry – he is older and ugly and 'has stripes and bars on his arm.' Nelly's relationship with Harry Cross is sustained throughout the book although it takes different forms. He invites her to spend the week with him in Scotland. She is simultaneously drawn and repelled, and while considering whether or not to go formulates another seminal contradiction: 'This is the chance of a lifetime she thought. She longed for Bill to return home [from POW camp], but she knew that once he was back she would no longer be able to have

the fun she could have at present', and 'again she had
betrayed him and again she had enjoyed herself'. Together
with the previous chapter on 'desire', it is this further
code-breaking recognition which the rest of the novel has
to negotiate and recuperate. The visit to Scotland is
accompanied by guilt, anxiety and surprise at Harry's
different form of appropriation: 'but be my baby, let me
look after you. I want to very much'; 'She was so juvenile
in her way, but perhaps that was part of her charm.' Harry
is the 'lovely stranger' as 'father', after the 'aristocratic'
boy-hero, Barry. It is almost as if she goes through a
series of *rites de passage*, psycho-cultural, in which she
encounters a range of male 'incarnations' on her journey
back to the 'monogamous couple relationship' with her
husband. In other words, 'desire' is not something in itself,
part of female sexuality, but is detached and transformed
into a maturation process, where a series of 'stand-in'
husbands prepare the female ritually for her re-introduc-
tion into her male-constructed gender-specific roles of
mother, wife, and daughter.

Nelly confides in Harry her dream of freedom:

> When I was a kid I read all the travel books I could get
> my hands on, and I thought I would like to write books.
> I never really wanted to get married. I used to dream
> I owned a gipsy caravan with an old grey horse to pull
> it and rambled along through green cool lanes. . . .
> (p.164)

This rural romance which names the 'other' of desire —
the outsider gipsy — and the freedom from which she is
cordoned off by her traditional roles and her 'biological
destiny', is interrupted by Harry's 'I remember all the
bloody battles and the pals I saw slaughtered . . .' (his first
published novel is called *Blood on the Earth*). The ritually
shed male blood is heroic, that of the female associated
with shame. Harry, the father-figure, becomes the bearer,
the agent of masculine consciousness who remembers and
tells of the male 'fate' contrasted with the 'female' dream
of Nelly. The week in Scotland is a kind of 'genesis' for

her. Harry articulates the ultimate masculine destiny –
bloody battles and pals slaughtered – as if to remind Nelly
of the larger public role of the male (intercourse as death,
not mere desire of a sexual nature), always close to death
– a role magnified and crystallized by war. It is perhaps
part of a ritual to educate her in the recognition of male
subjectivity and her need to respond to it by displacing
her own subjectivity (in writing – bearing in mind that it
is Harry later who gets her published).

Immediately after the week in Scotland, Bill's return is
signalled and Nelly starts a period of adjustment, prepared
by Harry who, at one point, describes her as looking 'like
a born mother'. Before Bill returns, Nelly meets up with
an old friend Bebe, who has a six-year-old daughter
Melissa, who later becomes a 'Nelly figure' and is
described in similar, exceptional terms: ' a pretty little
thing', 'a beautiful blonde', 'her skin was the colour of
pale gold and her eyes were large and black'. She is also
exceptional in a negative sense as she was born with a
'tubercular arm'. Nelly attaches herself to her as the incar-
nation of the child she 'needs', perhaps to displace her
desire and contain her wish for freedom. Bebe is pictured
as one of the heroic figures of the war – the housewife
and worker keeping the Home Front going, another 'role'
aid to Nelly's development.

On Bill's return, Nelly is still a long way from 'settling'.
She hated housework and had become extremely lazy
about it. She tries to 'return' also with Bill by cleaning up
and having a baby, but Bill wants to wait until after the
war. He uses a 'preventative' and the 'passionate hot
nature in Nelly was never satisfied, though she never said
anything to Bill'. So her desire is repressed and she is
corralled into domesticity – 'tied to the gas stove at
weekends'.

The death of Bebe makes Melissa over into 'the centre
of her life'. Throughout the text, Nelly's problem is one of
de-centredness, an absent subjectivity, and she also makes
efforts to deconstruct, yet also conform to, the 'subject'
proposed for her culturally and socially: 'I must be two

people, one that's good and one that's trying to be good. Bloody funny, the bad one always wins.' This is her way of resolving the problem of a renewed invitation from Harry, and the onset of guilt. She enjoys the passionate love, but 'I intend to be here when the war is over and start again from the beginning with Bill.' Harry is styled at this stage 'as a good pal'.

This 'starting again' is signalled by the chapter 'Demobbed', and it seems to apply to Nelly also – the 'demobilization' of desire. The theme of 'settling down' is re-introduced. Unsuccessful in a final attempt to visit Harry, she decides:

> She was haunted by him, she heard his happy laughter and saw his ugly kind face before her. She could not bear it. It was not easy to forget him. She sought comfort in her journal which was still scribbled in at night. He was a good man, Harry Cross, and she would remember him in her writing. (p.186)

Given the god-like characteristics of Barry, Harry's surname – Cross – seems also to have shades of the religious associated with it. He is certainly linked inextricably both with her journal and her desire – the journal being the form in which her desire is sublimated and recuperated. Meanwhile, Bill's love-making has become more passionate and varied, and Nelly is suspicious that his style has been learned from someone else. When the war ends Nelly is discharged from her work and by Bill: 'We must take separate paths.' He is living with a woman who is expecting his baby. Nelly visits and it is like travelling back through time to her own roots – the woman is described as slovenly, grubby, wearing an old faded dress, lank and greasy, and the house untidy and squalid, 'the product of soul-destroying poverty'. A whole lexicon of details has an anamnesic effect on Nelly. The woman is described as sluttish (linking the economic with the moral and eliding them in a model of personal culpability) and she is straight out of the generic framework of the novel's background – briefly named, mobilized into the plot, and foregrounded. Is the young woman a trapped, 'unescaped' Nelly? Is Bill's desire for her a kind of nostalgia, a way of breaking with his own clean, polite, and 'decent' forms of behaviour: 'he looked dusty and ill-kempt', 'shabby and down and out'? It is almost as if, momentarily, he has slipped into the 'generic' casting of the fiction, has forfeited the right to share the 'exceptional' foreground with Nelly. Bill tells Nelly that 'in some way no one will ever replace you but we have outgrown each other.' He articulates the very experience (with Barry and Harry – the rhyme is intended, I feel, as part of their symbolic role! The more symbolic, the less 'immoral' Nelly's behaviour is seen to be) which she is seeking to eraze by reconciliation with him. It is almost as if, unwittingly, he is punishing her for her transgressions. Certainly what follows is a protracted 'wilderness' experience for her.

Her journal comes to occupy an increasingly large part in her life. Melissa shows signs of growing away from Nelly, and she fears she will look down on her in time. This fear prefigures another, deeper division around their sexuality. Nelly moves to Yarmouth to be nearer to Melissa and meets Leonard, a twenty year old man with lank, sandy hair and thick 'specs' who spoke 'with a good public school accent' – the recurring index of 'quality' in the text. She also turns to the Mass in her search for 'peace of mind' and relief for her 'sin'. After one mass she meets Peter, a Polish refugee, the third 'stranger' in her journey back to Bill. He is 'moody, sentimental, jealous and very possessive', unlike Barry, Harry, or Bill. Each 'stranger' is, perhaps, confronted as the 'other' of one's subjectivity in this existential sense. Peter behaves like an old-fashioned husband, his Catholic conservatism patriarchal and oppressive. She has her desire fulfilled, but realizes that *his* desire lies in her appropriation. It is as if he is the extreme instance of her 'other' lovers – the last stage, the imprisoner, the unattached one also (Barry dead, Harry married). He is, it is perhaps implied, the example which would justify the feminist argument, and so has to be displaced in order to undermine their case. His love is unstable: 'I will strangle you with my own hands if you let me down' – the passion of melodrama. They are both 'refugees' in a sense. Peter returns to Poland:

> Nelly crept up to her chilly attic and lay on the bed weeping. For what she did not know. Because Peter had gone? Or was it happiness at the thought of being free again? She was too confused to care. (p.208)

This confusion, which recurs in different forms throughout, is seminal to one of the central questions addressed by the ideological project of the text – the nature of female freedom. The 'answer' is a coded reply to modern feminism, as well as *or* in the form of, the restoration of the private, the familial, and the monogamous – all seen as aspects of female 'interpellation'. After Peter leaves, Nelly decides that she is finished with men and that she would never again allow herself to be used. She would make a home for herself and Melissa. This echoes the kind of separatism and choice being made increasingly now by many women as a response to patriarchy and the ideologies of femininity inscribed in contemporary codes and practices.[23] Her resolve is checked by Leonard's offer of a 'rural romance' – the nostalgia of his grandparents' cottage. 'Girls my age terrify me' he tells Nelly, and so, in succession to the previous lover-hero, lover-father, lover-husband figures, he becomes the lover as son seeking a mother figure – 'My mother went off with a Yank' (which offers also another possible image of Nelly had she gone with Harry). She moves in with him 'as a business arrangement', another step back towards Bill.

Nelly makes love with Leonard but it is not satisfying, although 'now I have a man of my own and a house to go with it'. This marks a symbolic return to the moment of her marriage, but it is not completed 'ritually' because Leonard is dependent and inadequate in bed. It is at this point of partial return that:

> Feeling an overwhelming passion to recapture her thoughts, she ran upstairs and began to write more about her childhood, and those desperate fights for survival after

her mother had died. Her memory was vivid and clear and her energy seemed endless as she scribbled on and on for most of the day until finally, tired and cramped, she closed her book and came downstairs to cook the dinner. She felt wonderful, released of pent-up feelings after laying the ghosts of her past. (p.222)

The novel we are reading becomes the novel being written by the heroine – Nelly Kelly is Kitty Daly – and the process of writing itself becomes the means of resolving the intrinsic contradiction of the text – desire is sublimated in the creative urge to write. It is interesting that the word 'passion' is used in the extract above in connection with her writing. The 'ghosts of the past' are not only hers, but have a wider collective reference to those of the nation as a whole. In fact, the issue of 'nationhood' is not a casual aspect of the text if Nelly's relationships are considered metaphorically. Her marriage to Bill coincides, in time, with a 'national recovery' after the depression and the abdication, but this is destabilised by the war. During the war she has an affair with one of the heroes of the Battle of Britain, the quintessential test of 'nationhood' encoded then, *and* in memory, as 'heroic' – the emblem of British-ness. She then forges an 'alliance' with an American who remains her 'guide' throughout the text and into the 1950s (shades of Marshall Aid and Nato) – he is the agent who enables her to 'become herself'. Her next relationship is with another ally, a man from the country whose invasion was the pretext for Britain's entry into the war. His totali-tarian personality proves oppressive and, not surprisingly, he returns to communist Poland – a fitting space for his aggressive, old-fashioned, and unstable temperament! Finally, she enters into a relationship with Leonard in the latter half of the 1940s. His youth, dependence, weakness and inadequacy in bed are all linked, implicitly, with the austere reconstruction period of the first majority Labour government. Leonard's callowness and inadequacy, his fear of girls of his own age, and his sexual 'exploitation' of Melissa are all 'period-specific'. What Leonard has to offer is too sectional and parochial to constitute the 'making of a nation', to bring about recovery.

The final reconciliation, on 'equal terms', with Bill, the publication of her novel, and the birth of her son ('and Bill's son was born') all take place in the years after 1951 which marked the return of a Conservative government. It is not entirely fanciful to interpret this text as an attempt to construct something analogous to a folk-memory in which a symbolic liberation from the past is achieved (the past, that is, of what might be called 'Left' memory – the Depression and 1945), by using the popularly dominant symbols of the past drawn especially from the interwar period. By returning to the sites of the Left's imagery it has recaptured them for the 'counter-revolution' of contemporary neo-liberalism which evacuates 'class politics' by, in a sense, placing them back in their 'legitimate' time. This puts into perspective the hard, often bitter decades, but it is a perspective which turns them into a *genre* in which they become part of a graphic economy. The genre is prescriptive and pre-emptive, it represents what John Berger has called(in *About Looking*) a terminus version of memory in narratives which use that 'crisis' as a palimpsest of the contemporary one and posit an end for it in similar ideological terms. The re-writing of the past is part of the re-writing of the present, a means of reclaiming both from oppositional versions in the formation of a series of 'national allegories'.

Prior to returning finally to Bill, Nelly has to retrace the 'oedipal trajectory' in the chapter 'Home to Dad'; she has to resume her role as daughter before assuming her status as wife again. Nelly joins a creative writing group and 'for the first time ever, she felt truly fulfilled'. She publishes her first story and receives her first cheque: 'She had never before been so enjoyably involved in anything that was quite so devoid of sex.' The process of displacement and sublimation of female desire is carefully shaped and rewarded (the cheque). In a climactic scene in the cottage, Melissa and Nelly engage in a generational struggle and Nelly's co-habitation with Leonard and her obsessive fulfilment in Melissa is shattered – 'He fucked me, if you want it in plain English.' This chapter is called 'Something to Live For', which refers to the writing of the novel *Grass Widows*: 'Nelly, old gal', she said to herself, 'I do believe you have found something that makes life worthwhile.' She begins to see writing as a means of getting money and becoming independent of everybody: 'It would be her salvation.'

She meets up with Harry Cross again, now *disabled* and married for the second time. Harry is transformed from active lover to wounded male. His only role now is to help her to get her manuscript published, a kind of symbolic transference to accompany her own sublimation of desire. At first she says: 'No, I can't part with it, it's my baby.' 'She felt sorry for poor Harry. None of his fame would give him back his virility, and only Nelly knew about that.' (A neat ideological reversal of the real relations in the Anglo-American alliance.)

Is there a sense that because of what the war (and in the other fictions, unemployment) has done to men, women must acknowledge the need to resume the nurturant role – would any refusal of this damage the nation's virility? Harry's writing is a compensation for his wound, his amputated leg. The symbol of amputation recurs in these fictions (is it linked with possible sexual emasculation?). This is seen as something the 'modern' woman has got to reconcile herself with, understand, and therefore not become threatening herself. Nelly's writing is, thus, sublimation of her active sexuality (and possible threat), and a cultural recognition of the need to 'contain' female desire in the light of the male's trauma and possible emasculation. It is a peaceful 'settlement' which restores lost territory (in the war with its sexual excesses by women?) – freedom, public status, 'urges' – to the male.

In Yarmouth, Nelly listens to a crowd of Irish boys singing patriotic songs. She identifies with the rebel songs sung in a defiant tone, especially 'Kevin Barry' – 'Do not hang me like a dog. What I did, I did for Ireland.' This helps to restore her to a sense of her own origins and of her own defiant rebellion. This is only a temporary, and sentimental, identification, because, alone and depressed, she tries to kill herself. She recovers, returns home and finds her husband there: 'His whole presence suggested dependability and strength. Suddenly, she wanted him to hold her tight in his arms, then she would really feel secure.' She dismisses the last few years as a nightmare:

> Nelly stopped and took his hand. 'It looks like we have both discovered what life's all about,' she said sadly. The power of his body almost overwhelmed her. He was her man, she knew that now after all those others in between. Even if it had taken both of them all these years to realize that they were meant to be together, it did not matter. They were together now and she was content. (p.256)

All the others 'in between' have to be eliminated, in some way or other, in order to make the finally arrived at options seem like real *choices*. This chapter is called 'An Ultimate Decision'; it is a return to chapter ten, 'Settling Down', with the word 'ultimate' charged with a lot of ideological work. Nelly resumes her broken continuity by stepping back inside the circle produced by the gender construction of femininity first as daughter, next as wife, then in the next chapter – 'Just One Thing Missing' – as mother, and finally, in the last chapter – 'A New career' – as wife, mother, daughter, 'foster' mother, and writer. The final section is a kind of supplement of all the possibilities of 'valid' gender roles for the female. Until the baby, however, she did the 'much-hated housework' and found her 'life dull, but bearable'. She writes romance 'tales' to compensate for not having a child. She returns to the church to pray for a child and for God, 'to make her a good wife, a good daughter and most of all a mother'.

(It is noticeable in the last chapters how there is a 'downturn' in periodization. Apart from the references to the groundnut scheme in Uganda, the building of council houses on a large scale, and black immigration there is little attempt to place the events iconically or historically. Stripped of history, the woman returns to the private, but retains access to the public not through her presence but through her writing. Internal evidence suggests the novel ends in 1953, the moment of the 'new Elizabethans' after the age of austerity.)

The final chapter is structured around a synthesis of 'maturity':

> Nelly soon settled down with her baby son and was so happy. All thoughts and dreams took a back seat. . . . [N]ever had she been so conscious of great attachment to her family. It matured her. . . . She found herself smiling her way through her life as she had done in her teens. (p.268)

The clock is turned back, the years are rolled back, and the intervening period – the one marked by desire and excess, *and* unemployment and poverty – is metaphorically cancelled:

> The neighbours always stopped to chat with her and admire the baby. At last Nelly felt close to them and enjoyed the social gossip.

> 'How nice to see you settled down, Nelly' they would say, 'and to have such a beautiful baby at your age, too.' Nelly took the sweet with the bitter, knowing that they referred to her past misdemeanours. (p.269)

Fully penitent, Nelly is forgiven and redeemed by motherhood and neighbourliness. To complete the picture, Melissa and Leonard are killed in a car crash (the death of the false promise of a raw, inexperienced alliance – spoilt, irresponsible and sexually precocious; teenagers trying to behave like adults – the political analogy/metaphor is not too far-fetched). There is a 'moral' element in the deaths as well. Melissa as the 'Nelly double' has an active sexuality which prefigures the kind of excesses from which Nelly has had to be 'saved'. Nelly takes over their daughter, Clare, to bring up as her own. The family album is now completed with 'the pigeon pair', the boy older and their 'real' child. The process completes the restoration of the centrality of the male in the socio-cultural formation. Bill's only fear was that the baby Clare may be 'abnormal' (because of Melissa's handicap, at least at the literal level, but maybe there is a metaphorical hint also) but she is 'fair as a lily, sweet as a rose' – a real girl, in other words!:

> Poor little Melissa, wherever you are, help your baby to find its place in life. It's our fault that you didn't have a stable background, mine and Bill's. (p.272)

While Nelly is busy with her babies (remembering the spate of post-war publications on child care and 'the growth of love') 'Bill worked long hours and money was scarce but they were all happy. The house had a warm atmosphere of loving and giving and Nelly felt that at last she had reached a safe harbour.'

Bill and Nelly emblematize the faults, excesses, and failures of a generation but have *survived* to guarantee that the next generation will be free of the data of the past, but also will be the heirs of those values recovered from that past and redeemed by the 'sacrifices' of their fathers and mothers.

Harry sends Nelly a letter, mentioning that he is now a divorcee once more, and also that a publisher is interested in her work, *Grass Widows*. She is confused, but 'She could not possibly afford to destroy her happy home now.' The publisher describes her book as a fascinating and original piece of writing . . . with considerable commercial appeal. The book is regarded as 'new', 'fresh' and 'authentic':

> She smiled as she remembered that last day at school when, as a scrawny waif of a girl, she had announced that she wanted to write. She had come so far since then, *despite the hardships – or perhaps because of them.* (my italics)

> She felt a wave of happiness rush through her. Kitty Daly, the grass widow, she thought was like another child she had given birth to years before when her life had been so tough. At last, they were all together now. She did love Bill, she was sure of that and she always had, but she also had her babies to enrich her life more than ever before. She knew then that she would go on writing *as well as*

*being a good wife and a loving mother. And a daughter
too*, she thought, as she watched Dad through the window,
shuffling about in the front garden. Everything was
happening at once, but her life was all working out. She
was fulfilled at last. (my italics) [p. 277]

These are the last paragraphs of the novel. The parts
italicized represent the main preoccupations of the text's
ideological project – its double role as 'history' and
'romance' with its twin themes of rehabilitation and
recuperation. The history 'explains' the significance of the
period 1918–1953 in which the representative, generational individual survived intact *because of* the hardships
endured. These were character-forming it is implied,
unlike the experiences of the 'welfarist' generations which
dominated the 1960s and 1970s. The romance retraces
the sites of 'feminism' and recognizes its 'period' validity,
but it delivers the female back to her *natural* roles, and,
as the final section indicates, re-inscribes the male son,
husband/breadwinner, father to their positions of
centrality vis-à-vis the female (this is done structurally –
she 'felt', she 'thought', she 'smiled', she 'watched') who
is 'margined' and restored to the passive tense.

The novel is a working out of the stages by which
recuperation is brought about. The term 'recuperation' is
being used in the sense employed by Michele Barrett in
Women's Oppression Today:[24] 'The ideological effort that
goes into negating and defusing challenges to the historically dominant meaning of gender in particular periods.'
She talks specifically of the ways in which women's liberation has been accommodated by the various media, and
Nelly Kelly is, as I have demonstrated, certainly an
instance of this. I would wish to extend the range of
this recuperation, however, as indicated previously, to the
ways in which fictions also have a role to play in negating
and defusing other challenges – political, 'Left' imagery,
for example – to the historically dominant meaning of
politics in particular periods. At several levels in the past
decade, attempts have been made by the 'Right' to recap-
ture lost ground and to contest those discourses which

offer a 'Left' explanation of the contradictions of the
1930s. The whole process is part of a wider campaign to
re-colonize and dominate areas of meaning which have
been partially liberated from the structures of power.
Cultural fictions have done as much to constitute the 'field'
of this selective revision of the past as have other scenarios
of 'preferred memories' of the *real* reconstruction, which
is claimed as long-term as opposed to the short-term,
welfarist reconstruction of the 1940s in response to the
'abnormalities' of the 1930s and the war. The 'voices of
the forties' have returned to re-record *their* versions of the
past in a series of public discourses on the family, marriage
and mothering.

Memories are made into fictions out of a variable range
of themes and formulas. The 'pieces' which constitute
these memories are, in a sense, all there, preconstructed,
before the particular text is fashioned. The overall structure and 'signature' of each text is specific – the active
foregrounding of the survivor figure – but the socio-
cultural spaces and period benchmarks have an archival
feel about them. The texts are developed from a particular
'grammar' of narrative which is exteriorized, crafted
around utterance – there is always the strong presence of
an authenticating voice, even if the narrative is third
person – and based upon the deployment of a repertoire
of stock images and topics, standardized formulas and
themes. This rhetoric and narrative system depends upon
repetitions, garrulousness, fluency and amplification. It
sounds like an oral composition – it has its roots in popularized forms of expression: personalized, anecdotal, and
'commonsensical'. It lacks the formality, abstractness, and
class-specific redundancies of the so-called 'elaborated'
code, but, like any other form of expression, it has its own
redundancies.

In fact, the notion of redundancy could be used more
widely in analysing the discourses as a whole because there
is a sense in which, what I have called the 'archival' matter
of the text is progressively shed as the plot develops and by
a form of symbolic transfer the *witness* aspect of 'spiritual

mobility' is stressed. In some instances there is social and material mobility also, but it is secondary to the metaphysical, quasi-magical element. Any transformation and re-structuring takes place outside the history and politics, and is reposed in the unity of the individual female subject. It is almost as though the narrative discards the inessential features of the initial 'situating' material – the overt markers of deprivation. Within the text, and popular-memory narratives generally, *that* past has become another place, designated as the 'other', a unified period of bleakness. The principal narrative stress is placed on discontinuity and redundancy – the past is locked in the past, signified by the proliferation of 'stills' of the period, iconic markers.

The texts operate by inviting the reader to participate by *image*, or icon, in past events, and by *ideology* (that of an individualist rhetoric) in contemporary perspectives on that imagery. The narrative mode is analogical, as each icon and structured episode is designed to provoke recognition of the codes which commonly express the period and to identify them in terms of the central figure. All glimpses of the time start with, and from, her. We do not necessarily remember the period, nor do we need to, the codes of narrative and iconography remember it for us. These codes propose a unitary discourse of memory, and 'interfere' with history, resist it, by closing down the period discursively – it is allowed no 'reality' beyond that constituted by the text itself. Our movement back through time is illusory; it is not a discovery but an erasure. The past becomes the Past; the thirties, the Thirties; the depression, the Depression. A reification process is involved. The originality, the particularity, is reserved for the central figure alone. The setting (what I have called the archive) is seen to be recurrent, common, patterned – anthological – a matter of organizing the already known, already existing selected passages. The contrast is between what Barthes calls 'the voice of banality' and 'the voice of singularity'.[25]

To develop another point of Barthes, I would argue

that the period 'history' is analogous to the *pose* in the photograph – the 'look', style, objects, clothing all gathered for their photogenic, or anamnesic, qualities. It is this which can help to determine and contain the period for those who have no memory, or even for those who have. For those who have, the process is complicated, as the offered 'stills' are variously resisted, or assimilated and used to supplement the currency of remembering. Although the narratives depend upon a *continuing* series of images and actions, I would argue that there is a fundamental contradiction between the 'synchronic grasp' of the period detail and the continuity of the individual trajectory. The latter develops within the paradigm of a *fictional role*, the former draws upon data which have the rhetorical status of fact – it is the 'this-has-been' (Barthes) of the documentary realist method. It corresponds with our 'newsreel set' of the inter-war period; its effectiveness depends upon our knowing that it has an 'actual' referent which is being quoted from. The fictional role, on the other hand, depends upon *constructing* (rather than quoting from) its own ideological referent. We 'know' the 'fate' of the period – its outcome; interest is transferred to, and transfixed by, the fate of the singular figure, who acts as mediator of the extended moment, colours it.

The constant return to the pre-war period is not just a matter of nostalgia, but an attempt to revisit the conditions of a generational past, and to locate *singular* women who take on a representative role by, simultaneously, *guaranteeing* the future and exorcizing the past: the symbolic transfer from history to myth, politics to 'person', male to female. The fictions are constituted within a rhetoric appropriated from the 'lexicon' of feminism, but *rewritten* in the terms of an individualist ethic and a culture which gives primacy to a particular form of the family and woman's place within it. The fictions are partly works of cultural reclamation, partly works of resistance to contemporary feminism. They are essentially *revaluations* – a revisiting of the 'archaeological' site where the need for 'welfarism' was discovered – logging it in the stock

images of our time and 'unearthing' other finds: self-determination, enterprize, strong and independent women,
living their own lives and making their own decisions in
ways which made the men seem clumsy, emasculated, and
inept.

In most instances, the men's situation is given a circum-
stantial explanation – the First World War and unemployment. Their 'incompetence' is located historically. The
women move from the periphery by default, so to speak,
which suggests a *temporariness*, a matter of time. It is
enough to establish credibility by celebrating their deva-
lued, and undervalued, skills but it also suggests that
women can *displace* men (for the time being while men
recover 'generationally'). It is also another way of
suggesting that strength in the sphere of emotions and
feelings is a female prerogative – men are preoccupied,
and weakened by the public and social.

The repeated negative signification of men and women
(especially) who break with the moral economy described
above indicates how these fictions are concerned with the
collapse of a particular order – signified as 'moral' but,
ultimately, economic. This is why the classic moment of
crisis of that order is so frequently the context for fictional
explorations at a time when the order is, once more,
perceived to be in crisis, but the values are being widely
circulated. It is over-simplified to suggest this, but is hard
to resist seeing this crisis in its familiar symbolic form of
the weakened male – given the patriarchal relations of
capitalism – in need of the sustenance of the traditionally
dependent, but momentarily independent, female. If the
weakened male 'stands in' for the imperilled capitalist
order, the independent female 'stands in' for the 'moral
economy' of the petty bourgeois stratum. The fictions do
not reflect, but actively re-constitute and reconstruct an
'idealized economic and moral order'[26] based on the
survival of a refurbished and 're-imaged' moral economy.
They are fictions of restoration and symbolic power,
designed to 'roll back the welfare state', renew self-direc-
tion and 'limited sovereignty': control.

In the concluding chapter of their book on the petite-bourgeoisie, Bechhofer and Elliott explore a number of facets of its moral economy with particular reference to retrospects:

> Retrospects occur or are resuscitated at points of important social change . . . their purpose is not to explain, to render intelligible the shifting patterns of social relations, rather it is to give comfort and hope to those who long for a return to the imagined joys of an earlier era. . . . The 'retrospect' sketches the shape of a prior order but offers no historical comprehension of the real framework of structural relations which supported it.[27]

> In surviving, the petite bourgeoisie demonstrates the viability of small-scale capitalism and in its periodic mobilisations it calls for the defence of a previous and apparently desirable social order. In this way it plays a significant role in the ideological servicing of contemporary capitalism, in the successive efforts to recapture the sense of capitalism as a historically progressive force.[28]

It is a way of attempting to 'remoralize' capitalism, to construct a set of images through which the 'joys of a simpler, freer, more competitive economy are sung'.[29]

Another very significant cultural *displacement* is taking place in which 'history' (1918–45) is invoked as an explanation of, as well as accessory and witness to, the separation of the female from the male. The dominant signifiers of this separation are war, unemployment, and poverty. It is as if the female is forced to find a mode of representation which *sublimates* the desire for independence/liberation in the form of a historical deviation, a slump – almost as if the woman is apologizing for, yet also justifying her behaviour as a form of prescribed, 'involuntary' rebellion from the nineteenth century certainty that the worker could keep his wife at home as a sign of virility, almost:

> Thus the protection of the family and the securing of the woman's place within it was regarded as integral to the fight against the employers and the brutalizing effects of working conditions. And gradually the ability of the

worker to keep his wife at home became a sign of working
class strenth, of prosperity, of better days to come.[30]

It is difficult to establish how general this practice was,
but it is a deep ideological presence in most of the texts.
Economic strength/weakness is conflated with individual
virility/emasculation. These fictions structure the female
subject within an explanatory history in which the male
is finally restored. They offer a metaphorical representation of the inter-war experience through works of restoration designed to offset male insecurity and fears of
female separateness and independence – economic, sexual,
and cultural. They are, ultimately, romances of heterosexual reconciliation. Separation is seen not as ultimate
but as a temporary diversion occasioned by recession and
war.

The fictions are produced simultaneously within an
acknowledgement of changes in the position of women –
indeed they narratively represent these – and a denial and
recuperation of these changes by their narrative framing.
'Traditional' feminine values are expressed, and contained,
within a partial 'feminism', or, more precisely perhaps,
within a rhetoric partly appropriated from it. These
fictions are metaphorical explanations of the ambiguities
and contradictions inherent in women's position in society
at this moment. They succeed in superimposing a very
powerful image of the individual upon the memory of the
collective – the 'left' imagery of inter-war marches, for
example, which are seen, ultimately, as ineffective.

Another 'collective' potential is 'sisterhood', but this is
negated by the active competition between women, and
the series of linguistic indicators which structure negative
and positive codes of femininity and morality. The collective, group, crowd, branch, whatever, threatens to bring
the disappearance of the individual. An attempt is made to
historicize and 'psychologise' the explanation of individual
actions through a number of supposed metaphors of the
female psyche in which women are seen to become
conscious 'authors' of social processes. They are enabling

fictions built around images of female empowerment in particular ideological forms. This is part of a process whereby successive ideological efforts are made to negate and defuse the 'challenges to the historically dominant meaning of gender in particular periods'.[31] Although, as indicated above, the fictions 'return' the female to the patriarchal fold, it is not a simple adjustment, as a number of ideological positions have to be re-defined and re-negotiated. Each fiction is marked, at some time or other, by a *breakdown* and it is this which signifies the moment of recovery, the onset of renewed relationships. Nothing can be simply regarded as a 'given', but each position has to be fought for, navigated, and achieved. The family is a primary example, and each fiction enacts a kind of rebonding, a re-securing of dispersed and fragmented codes. The unified subject, marriage, femininity, maternity, the family, the household, and filiation are all subject to challenge, in varying degrees, in the ficitons and each has to be relearned as part of a resumption of interrupted continuities. The interwar period is styled as a disjunction, an interruption, a rupture not only at the economic level, but at the ideological level as well – it provides the narrative logic of what might be described as *fictions of parenthesis*.

This represents a crucial ideological intervention in current debates about the period, because as Andrew Gamble and Paul Walton point out:

> In many ways the 1930s marked a watershed. Far from being some accidental interruption to the smooth path of capitalist development, the depression exposed the tendencies inherent in capitalist accumulation. It clearly revealed the changing structure of capitalist markets and the need for the state to play a much greater role in the capitalist economy.[32]

In the scenarios I have outlined, the watershed is seen in terms of role crises, and the resolutions foreground the strong and enterprizing individual, standing in for and masking the increased intervention of the state. The fictions are constructed around the notion of an *accidental*, not symptomatic, interruption. The division between an increasingly dominant corporate capitalism and a declining sector of small capital is ideologically reversed by the making prominent of the moral economy of this sector, and by disguising the changed nature of the economy through a narrative rhythm based upon downswing and recovery, effected by individual settlements around the conventional, deeply structured, wisdoms of monogamy, the family, and femininity. The 'natural' is brought in to redress the vagaries of the social.

The fictions are a kind of re-scripting, a making positive of a period we are accustomed to scripting negatively, an attempt, perhaps, to restore a broken link in the chain of signification of the representation of women. On the one hand, it recognizes a particular situation as being historically specific, and yet in so doing it re-eternalizes codes which it has abstracted from the historically specific. This is a vital contradiction in which an unstable economic and political period is linked analogously to another level of instability: psychic, familial, sexual. The plots of these narratives use this conflated instability as their reference points and their structuring bases. The one stands in for the other and suggests a mutuality of resolution in terms of harmony after rupture, displacement and fragmentation – destabilization. Contradictions are thus personalized and controlled. Categories of gender are replenished after a phase of disturbance. By superficially linking the private/public worlds they are, in fact, disconnected and made separable for ideological purposes. The fictions reinvest in privatized relationships and depoliticize the interwar experience, while appearing to 'cover' the period. The strong women, the eponymous subjects of the text, are 'reconstructed into redeemers of the patriarchy'.[33]

3
People like us

The previous chapter discussed the ways in which certain fictions established a periodized environment in which the specific biographical situation was used to position individuals in the common-sense world based upon, what Schutz[1] called, the 'stock of knowledge at hand' created from particular typifications. These stocks of knowledge form an ideological configuration, a framework of understanding, in which people make sense of 'everyday life'. 'Everyday life' as it is constructed in fictions depends upon the deployment of pre-constructed, taken-for-granted discourses based upon what is represented as 'natural', 'intuitive', 'instinctive', and 'obvious'.

> In the everyday, the activity and way of life are *transformed* into an instinctive, subconscious, unconscious and unreflected mechanism of acting and living: things, people, movements, tasks, environment, the world – they are not perceived in their originality and authenticity, they are not tested and discovered but they *simply are there*, and are accepted as inventory, as components of a known world . . . [it] is a world of confidence, familiarity, and routine actions.[2]

In R.F. Delderfield's fictions, the subject of this chapter, such an 'inventory' is actually constructed by a process which, using the biographical situation, constitutes society in terms of a specific subjectivity condensing in itself characteristics of a national allegory. The primary emphasis in the fictions is on the local (the school, the suburb), the ethical, and the voluntary in ways which suggest these as the roots of a national consciousness. The social bond is emphasized throughout but this can only exist through the agency of 'consenting' subjects. The main focus in this chapter is on the means whereby Delderfield generates narratives based on a lower middle-class 'memory' of the past, selective and particularized yet naturalized and generalized, which forms the basis of the narrative form. A group, or stratum, which is socially peripheral becomes symbolically central.

Delderfield's fictions are based on a concept of individuals whose roots are in classic liberalism, and themes of historic continuity and national identity related to ideas of a mystical and transcendent bond between citizen and state predicated upon *community*. The social imagery of the texts is constructed from the 'fracturing of liberalism into its conservative and radical tendencies',[3] with its contradictory blend of 'authority' with 'freedom'. The narrative model is *developmental*. People are held to be capable of developing individual talents and powers in a society whose purpose it is to make possible a life-long educative process. The narrative model is closely linked to Delderfield's image of social change – gradual and evolutionary – and its subjectivity structure – self-realization and moral growth. The *educative* process at the centre of his fictions explains why To Serve Them All My Days, set in a school, is the fullest exploration of the themes of liberal democracy, 'ethicalization' and paternal authority. The school is the paradigmatic form of change, self-development and community:

> Liberals . . . naturally gravitate towards the middle ground
> in politics from which they seek to mediate between the
> competing claims of capital and labour. . . . [They]
> proclaim the merits of private enterprize yet renounce class
> privilege . . . seek to extend material security and cultural

opportunities to the poor but refuse to identify themselves fully with any particular section of society.[4]

The 'middle ground' is the point of intersection for the conflicting tendencies in *People Like Us* (1964) and mediation is the key role played by Algy Herries and later David Powlett-Jones in *To Serve Them All My Days* (1972). Each text confronts the potential destabilization threatened by social tranformation (located specifically in the interwar period) with a narrative synthesis of compromise and conciliation constructed in a 'national space' with community (school or neighbourhood) as the local, organizing instance of the nation. Potential antagonisms around class are defused by this ideological synthesis of community.

It would be erroneous to give the impression that the inter-war period has simply been recovered as 'archaeological' evidence of a neo-liberal individualist ethic. The emergence in 1981 of the Social Democratic party, the subsequent 'battle' over Tawney's legacy, and the 'populist' appropriation of inter-war references (cf. Owen's *Facing the Future* (1981) with 'Let Us Face the Future', and Shirley Williams's *Politics is for People* (1981)) were accompanied by a number of cultural revivals centring around figures like Priestley, Vera Brittain, and Delderfield. Throughout the last fifteen years or so, television drama has sustained a 'memory' of the inter-war period through adaptations, on an epic scale, of a series of bestselling 'middlebrow' classics of the period, such as *Fame is the Spur* (1982), *The Citadel* (1983), *The Stars Look Down* (1975), *My Son, My Son* (1978), *The Good Companions* (1980–1), and *South Riding* (1973). With the exception of *Days of Hope* (1975), there have been few original drama productions based on the period. It is difficult to analyse the reasons for this fairly consistent *fictional* attention to the inter-war years, except to indicate that the production values which characterized these versions had the effect of distancing, closing-off, and encasing the 'memory' by a preoccupation with periodization, details of style and image, and a ritual process of narrative reference. The basic values of each 'classic' were derived from a moral liberalism concerned with social injustice. The same kind of ethical centre, although emerging from a different class fraction, informed Vera Brittain's *Testament of Youth* (television production 1979).

The ways in which these television versions of inter-war 'classics' have been used to construct memories needs to be considered in terms of a sentimentalizing effect achieved by 'costuming' the period. At their moment of original publication many of these fictions were welcomed as radical cultural interventions in a political struggle over poverty, injustice and unemployment. They were hailed for their 'realism'. The problem is that the 'realism' of that period, in the costume drama of television adaptation, becomes the 'romanticism' of ours.

It is always difficult to gauge the effectivity of any particular ideological intervention, but it would be true to say that, *at the level of rhetoric and symbol,* there is a convergence between the moderate imagery of Social Democracy and the ethical liberalism of the inter-war 'classics'. The latter helped, at the cultural level, to constitute the foundations of a liberal consensus which the former have, in some ways, sought to salvage by the kind of 'alliance' reminiscent of the 'integrationist' rhetoric of Priestley and Morrison in the late 1930s and war period based on a commitment to liberal democracy: 'the reasonable citizen's response to crisis.' Its focus is on 'nation' and not 'class'[5] and its policies replete with contradictions.[6]

There have been several Delderfield television adaptations in recent years – *People Like Us* (1978), *To Serve Them All My Days* (1980), and *Diana* (1985). With the exception of London Weekend Television's *People Like Us*, the format of each one has followed the realist paradigm of the epic social romance, individual struggles framed within a serial, hindsight version of 'popular history' structured around the already mediated newsreel evidence of the period in question. The specific emphasis of the dominant narrative articulation is on the individual trajectory, sustained by the 'always already there' commonsense of the preconstructed 'history'. The technical resources deployed in these productions are drawn from the 'stock' conditions of television 'realism': the 'landscape-costume-look' authentications. The time of these chronicles is 'a march-past of purely typed, anonymous and interchangeable beings'[7] (apart from the specific figurations of the named individuals). It is what Althusser, in another context,[8] describes as 'empty time'. The diachronic mode, with its semblance of life, change and movement, in which 'history' is passed through the filters of ideology, is used to construct a synchronic codification of values as stationary, natural, universal and timeless. The primary identification of these fictions is with the 'myths of bourgeois morality' – within the codes of a moral-liberal conscience. In this way, through this *treatment*, the 'memory' of the inter-war period [signified in certain period markers – strikes, poverty, unemployment] can be accommodated because it is predicated upon a resolution at the level of the ethical, not the political: 'In this sense, melodrama is a foreign consciousness as a veneer on a real condition.'[9] To pick up Althusser's phrase 'foreign consciousness' and apply it to populist writing like Delderfield's is a useful analogy of the methods (and those used in the TV adaptations), by which he disguises problems and conditions by a process in which 'people' overcome conflict and contradiction by adopting modes of perception 'borrowed' from the bourgeoisie, the bourgeoisie who construct 'the people' in its classless, mythicized sense: 'the people that one forces the people to be'.[10]

'The people' as specific interpellation is being used here in the sense developed by Ernesto Laclau in *Politics and Ideology in Marxist Theory*,[11] where he talks of 'different types of interpellations (political, religious, familial, etc.) which coexist whilst being articulated within an ideological discourse in a relative unity'. It is the coexistence of different types of interpellations, the constitution of individuals as subjects through ideology, and the relative unity produced by narrative *coherence* which characterizes Delderfield's fictions in the form of a condensation of a range of otherwise contradictory positions. Delderfield creates an exhaustive, epic scale of narrative in which one central interpellation – the moral community constituted from within the private and domestic sphere – operates as a symbol of a range of others, stands in for them, as well as neutralizing them by a mode of displacement.

Both *People Like Us* and *To Serve Them All My Days* begin with a moment of historical and narrative violence – the First World War – which registers as a profound disturbance and interruption of the nation. In the television versions both texts end with the Second World War, another 'interruption' but, this time, narratively marked by 'the recovery of homogeneity according to a movement of reconvergence – reinvestment which, precisely, realigns, contains the violence anew'.[12] Violence, asymmetry, contradiction and heterogeneity are narratively constructed and displaced by the closure of the resolution. In both texts, the First War is not only a physical/material violation but moral and ethical as well – it precipitates an extended *crisis* (the inter-war period) which it is the purpose of the narrative to rehearse and resolve. The Second War is similarly marked as a physical/material violation but *not* a moral – ethical one, because the narrative process has developed a series of identifications which depends on 'the inscription of the subject as the place of intelligibility.'[13]

In Laclau's analysis, which refers to processes which have analogies with Delderfield's practice, the 'agents' are interpellated as 'the people' not in the terms of a popular-democratic struggle, but in the terms of an antagonism towards a series of negatively constructed signifiers, partly constituted from within the dominant bloc (e.g. bureaucracy, the interventionist state) but also, and more importantly, signified in corporatist (i.e. trade union practices) and 'deviant' interpellations such as, in Delderfield's terms, active female sexuality, 'extremism', and an excessive preoccuption with money. It is an interpellation of 'the people' which emphasizes its *active* identification through its ideological content while concealing its essentially passive construction, its abstractness.[14] This is particularly true of the social sector at the centre of Delderfield's fictions – the lower middle class – which is separated from the dominant relations of production, with a diffuse set of 'objective' interests. Delderfield re-presents the sector as the 'place of intelligibility' in his narratives, ideologically centring the economically 'marginal', and harmonizing/homogenizing a diffuse and contradictory set of interests.[15]

Popular democratic interpellations are, in themselves, not necessarily articulated to any specific class position, but the narrative effectivity of Delderfield depends upon its articulation of 'the people' with some of the central symbols and values of the lower middle class. It is not simply that the lower middle class is identified as 'the people', but that a lower middle-class ideology of 'the people' (it includes, in *To Serve Them All My Days*, Algy Herries; the retired Indian judge – 'trained to keep an open mind' – who chairs the Governors, and Brigadier Cooper) is articulated throughout the texts. It is those who are constituted within a particular ethical-moral interpellation which fulfils the role of condensation by symbolizing all other forms of interpellation – political, religious, national. It is 'classless', consensual and predicated upon an image of Britishness, its 'national character'. The family, neighbourhood (suburb) and the school are the principal interpellative sites in *People Like Us* and *To Serve Them All My Days* which condense all others. It is an inadequate and erroneous articulation from the point of view of the dominated class, because it fuses democratic interpellations with the ideology of the dominant class. Laclau analyses this as a characteristic of Social Democracy. Separated as it is from the dominant relations of production in society, the lower middle class's identity as 'the people' is far more significant than any class perspective – its popular-democratic ideology (clearly delineated in Delderfield) exists within the ideological discourses of the bourgeoisie *and* of the working class, but in these particular narratives 'working-class' identity (e.g. Jim Carver and David Powlett-Jones) is condensed and articulated to a lower middle-class affiliation which is, itself, dependent upon the ideological discourses of the dominant class. These 'intermediate sectors' have almost exclusively an identity as 'the people'.

Drawing together

Delderfield tries to produce texts in which the ideological position of the hero is meaningful for the whole community and, by extension, the society/nation – one unitary and singular belief system, a general code in which every specific message elsewhere is transmitted. The narratives present what is offered as a 'national community', and the ethical symbolism that constructs it, not just as a collection of individuals or a physical territory but a cultural space in which 'belonging' is an active moral process. This is seen most sharply in *To Serve Them All My Days* which I will come to. But firstly the ways in which a 'historical memory' is constructed in *People Like Us* to 'think' the community's specific crises will establish a valuable context for examining the more extensive 'national parable' in the former novel, based as it is upon a distinctive mode of expropriating *implicit*, taken-for-granted symbols of identity, value, nation, people and social order.

People Like Us was first published in 1964 as two separate novels: *The Dreaming Suburb* and *The Avenue Goes to War*. The former was broadcast on radio in 1958, and the television serial, *People Like Us*, combining both novels was first shown on London Weekend Television in 1977–8. In the introduction to the paperback edition (1971) of *The Dreaming Suburb* Delderfield makes plain his intention of using the suburb symbolically: 'They might be any people, of any South London suburb, indeed their lives throughout the period 1919–40 might be the lives of any suburban dwellers, on the outskirts of any large city in Britain.'[16] The repetition of 'any' indicates the level of generalization at which the narratives operate. 'These people are, for the most part, unsung, and that even though they represent the greater part of Britain's population . . . it is time somebody spoke of the suburbs, for therein, I have sometimes felt, lies the history of our race.'

What Delderfield is chronicling is the 'history' of 'the silent majority'. The use of the term 'race' evokes images of the 'island race' and of a distinctive, 'imagined community'.[17] In fact, the importance of Delderfield lies not in the pseudo-historical constructions of the inter-war period but in the production of a series of narratives which interpellate subjects within an ideological discourse based upon an imagined nation-community – 'people like us', as argued earlier.

The suburb is seen as part rural, part urban – 'rus in urbe' – ecologically dependent upon the city, but with its roots in a rural image of Englishness – *Manor Park Avenue*.[18] The important thing to notice at the level of narrative formation is that the writing has the ideological effect of a *record* of the period, whereas it is a re-recording of contemporary mediations of the period: history as 'collage', registered through a subjective filter and as a 'bird's eye view'. The text draws upon a composite repertoire of preconstructed fictional, journalistic, and historical representations inscribed in 'popular memory' by constant re-iteration in 'memorable' (i.e. already known, familiarized) narrative structures: history as story. The fiction simultaneously offers itself as recorded memory, definition *and* way of seeing the past.

By its intensive focus on 'characters', the text is able to determine what is seen of the public and the 'historical' and, more significantly, *how it is seen*. By concentrating the 'gaze' on the personal, generalized through a number of period icons, it is able to *disperse* the 'look' at history.[19] In effect, history becomes 'background', something analogous to, what in television terms is known as, the *stock shot*. History becomes a subscript to the biographical.

Metaphorically, in writings like this, the author goes out
and 'rents' historical footage from the stock of generic
representations – e.g. the General Strike or the Blitz –
previously compiled in, and by, generational memories.
To extend the analogy, the narrative formulation consists
of 'live' action in the foreground by characters established
within the text and internally validated as *belonging* only
in the text (although conceived within a realist paradigm)
combined with a 'filmed' scene in the background. It is
the narrative *form* which produces this 'process shot' in
which, by a complex ideological switch the credibility of
the subjects in the text validates the history as *rear projection*, which is a form of reversal of the actual historical
process under capitalism, a liberal 'distortion of interest'
– which seeks to foreclose subjective experience: 'Nor
is there space for the social function of subjectivity. All
subjectivity is treated as private, and the only (false) form
of it which is socially allowed is that of the individual
consumer's dream.'[20]

Such fiction produces a complex and contradictory
positioning. It gives priority and space to what is coded
as personal experience, and also sees this experience as
more than an individual problem (through its image of
neighbouring) but its representations, in part at least,
provide a 'false' space for experience by the suppression
of history. The image of 'the people' in *People Like Us* is
a product of a lower middle-class ethic and set of values,
and *not* of the empirical evidence of the experience rend-
ered in the fictional suburb. The latter derives from the
former; in its ideology of 'the people' the reverse is postu-
lated. The 'people' are constituted as subjects of fictional
discourse according to a specific cultural and social
formulation.

An effect is created, ultimately, of a homogeneous,
small-scale, inward-looking society based upon and bound
up with a particular locality. Each figure is bound, in
some way or another (even negatively) by reference to the
Avenue. The pattern which emerges is what sociologists
call the 'folk-rural' society. This is the effect of the *fictional*

transformation and mediation of the raw data of the initially established suburb in its ecological terms – size, location, and demography. The 'folk-rural' effect is produced by the narrative technique of intersecting episodes, networking of characters, familiarization through repeated signifiers, and an illusion of change and movement brought about by, what I would call, a 'rhetoric of history' – newsreeled, headlined, and synoptically reported. Everything is authenticated at the level of *local* experience; the suburb becomes both record and filter. The 'history' becomes a medium of distillation; it is appropriated as *witness* and *evidence* simultaneously.

Thus, out of an image of *intensive group life* Delderfield moves towards a social ethic which has been defined as 'that contemporary body of thought which makes morally legitimate the pressures of society against the individual'.[21] Delderfield reconciles this social ethic with the ideology of individualism by producing an image of society which sees it as the sum total of its *exemplary* representatives, not as systemic. It could be suggested that Delderfield is attempting to render a collective image of liberal individualism. There is a crucial society/people elision, a masking of the structured and stratified. Society is simply 'people like us'. This can be regarded as being constituted within the main movement of individual states and interests necessarily *modified* by the newer demands of a changing social order. It is, ultimately, a 'progressive' view of history as an unfolding narrative, a view which marginalizes all other contending views; struggle is held to be solely an individual matter.

However, some values, dominant in surburban life, are not represented unproblematically – witness the forms of familism, consumership, and career. Many of these are represented negatively, in the form of separation, divorce, and still-born children. The family and marriage are shown under pressure, and, in fact, the family is by no means seen as the ideal unit. There is, in volume two particularly, an emphasis on *reconstruction*, on the formation of new affiliations and alliances – the notion of neighbourliness/comradeship, perhaps, which cuts across inter-war social aspirations and values. The narrative re-constitutes the 'memory' of the 1940s in terms of extended family, the wider community, and the idea of the need for a *welfare* society. We also need to keep in mind the context of the texts' production and reception. They context changing political identifications (based on consumerism) by the production of a 'political' reminder, a collective memory, an alternative resource. A set of popular ideas exist about what constitutes the suburban way of life. These are mostly negative. Delderfield deliberately explores the suburb as a positive resource of a socio-cultural identity; he stylizes and advances the 'suburban' as the modern equivalent of the 'yeoman' – the essence of Englishness. A crucial aspect of the hegemonic process is to construct 'acceptable' narratives based on the shared stock of common sense of those groups on the boundaries of the dominant class. Delderfield deploys a particular rhetoric and develops a system of narration which 'substi-tutes for the idea of classes the idea of different peoples [this 'island race'], and this idea applies to the struggles of enemy and rival class the *vocabulary* of the history of invasions and conquests.'[22]

In some ways, Delderfield's mode of writing with its liberal pluralist codes and its symbolic constructions of the middle stratum suggests that 'each of the classes in the society is the vehicle of its narrative system',[23] a conden-sation of desire in the 'dreams' focused in a series of repeated 'narrative propositions'. In this respect the revival of Delderfield in the form of television serials in recent years has contributed a number of *retrospective* 'ideo-logical narratives' which have installed a 'generational' common-sense version of the past in a dominant position. Delderfield's ideological narratives represent an attempt to 'conceptually equate the elements of what in fact remains a hierarchical structure',[24] part of a larger project of re-inscribing liberalism at a time of perceived crisis. His narrative 'syntax', as described earlier, is itself based on constructing a *symmetry* conforming to existing social arrangements, a cultural *form* which corresponds to the prevailing forms of social relations under capitalism. This kind of narrativity is one of the 'mechanisms of bourgeois hegemony . . . which allows the capitalist class to partly control the symbols and values which play a role in the identities and aspirations of the members of the subordinate class'.[25] This suggests the limits of the liberal democratic 'thesis' underpinning Delderfield's narrative ideology, which consists of 'long chains of representation' related to the individualistic mode of liberal democracy's characteristic form (the vote) – a 'natural', 'neutral' form like the 'realist' mode itself. These narrative forms are, effectively, forms for registering the preferences of particular class interests through 'preferred' cognitive styles. This mode of *representation* (monological and 'conciliatory' – *convergent*) is firmly dissociated from struggle as an element of the social process. Its ideological resolutions correspond to a model of 'conflict-free interest accommodation'.[26] 'Popularization' is itself a process of 'narrative imperialism' in which a certain representational form becomes preferred as *the* representational form.

The subject who occupies the 'place of intelligibility' in *To Serve Them All My Days* is David Powlett-Jones, the scholarship-winning son of a Welsh miner, invalided in the First World War and awarded the military cross. The book was first published in 1972, came out in paperback in 1973 in two volumes ('Late spring' and 'The Headmaster') and was first televised in April 1980. The cover of the 1980 paperback describes Powlett-Jones as a schoolmaster of rare talent. This links with a crucial aspect of petty-bourgeois individualism bound up with what Poulantzas calls the 'myth of social promotion'[27] which underpins the whole project. The upwardly mobile miner's son becomes the headmaster of a minor public school, becomes a part of the bourgeoisie 'by way of the individual transfer of the "best" and "most capable" '.[28]

The History Man

> This time he looked back across the centuries for his sign,
> ranging eras as far back as those of Alfred, Hereward the
> Wake and the bloody chaos of Stephen's reign. Things
> must have seemed pretty hopeless then for those holding
> the short end of the stick, for the poor and landless. . . .
> But something gainful had emerged from it. Magna Carta;
> Simon de Montfort's so-called Parliament; centralized
> government; and a rule of law under Edward I and later
> Henry VII. Nothing much, perhaps, or until Cromwell and
> his successors won a constitution from their overlords, and
> city merchants held backsliding kings to ransom. It was
> always a long, pitiless haul, with any number of backward
> lurches, but, finally, inch by inch, democracy had been
> dragged onward and upward, and he wondered, fitfully,
> who did most of the heaving when it came down to
> bedrock. It wasn't the privileged and the wealthy, and it
> wasn't the masses, thrusting upward from below, for
> almost all their efforts had been swiftly neutralized by
> reaction. If he was asked to name a class to which most
> of the credit was due it would be that section of the
> community he had once affected to despise, the petty bour-
> geoisie, and who were the petty bourgeoisie when you
> thought about it . . .? They were the kind of Englishmen,
> Scotsmen and Welshmen who were neither rich nor poor,
> intellectual nor illiterate, well-endowed or down-and-out,
> the section who sent their sons here, to a place like
> Bamfylde, to acquire, through books, example, and above
> all, a mingling of and a sharing of ideas, a creed of
> common sense and tolerance.[29]

The school is set in a rural wilderness and the years spent
at the school are seen as a healing process in which the
rural represents a notion of Britishness, quiet and essentially pre-industrial – a lower middle-class arcadia. The
novel constructs its central figure in a way which renders
his physical and mental invalidity a metaphor for a
broader process which the war is seen as bringing to the
surface. The text enacts an extensive process of rehabilitation and recovery, a reinvestment based upon a number
of new alignments and coalitions to form a coherent

pattern. Those most deeply scarred by the war come from the working class, hence a working-class agent (promoted in the field to the rank of lieutenant) is singled out to negotiate a space within 'middle' England. The narrative becomes a metaphor of convalescence for the class 'survivor', allowed to flourish in a small, tightly knit community through a secular form of magic. The basic narrative proposition is a secular resurrection, with the war imaged as crucifixion.

The narrative is concerned with bringing the past into the present (especially in the television adaptation) not necessarily to interpret it, but to repeat its moment of a re-convergence of an idea of Britishness, which breaks with an 'overdose of jingoism' and discards the heroic, militaristic athlete of muscular christianity, invoking instead an Arnoldian vision of liberal humanism based on an informal, democratic rapport between boys and teachers (witness the nicknames). Both text and teacher are concerned with *modern* history as part of a project (evidenced by the passage quoted at the beginning of this section) designed to put together the component parts of a lower middle-class ideological ensemble as *representative* of national character. In the guise of articulating a tradition, Delderfield is, in fact, *inventing* one.

David is seen as needing to recover in an enclosed community; the school becomes a secular monastery, a place of moral vocation – 'privacy within a community of people'. The lower middle class 'subject' is reconstituted within ideological codes of masculinity different from those celebrated in 1914 jingoism. The school is spartan, threadbare, friendly – 'like an old and shabby rectory' – the constant religious infrastructure of the narrative. The head, the Reverend Algy Herries is an old boy of the school, part of a dynastic legacy, emblem of a heritage broader than that of the school. He became head in 1904 – 'I came in on the radical tide', part, that is, of the Liberal era of 1906–14, wiped out by the war (cf. Dangerfield's *The Strange Death of Liberal England*[30]). The school is voluntary aided, an important point, suggesting a 'mixed economy' identity. Founded by a disciple of Thomas Arnold, the school operates on the basis of a liaison between local people and the county authorities, an early instance of a 'state' initiative, but with the stress on the *voluntaristic* tradition. All the real decisions are made by Lord Hopgood and the Old Boys, an ensemble of aristocrats, tradespeople, local government politics and the church, which shows the lower middle class as a dependent stratum with aristocratic sponsors.

Herries sees himself, god-like, as a 'potter at the wheel', his key images adaptability and survival: 'They learn a little tolerance . . . and how to see a joke against themselves, and how to stand on their own two feet. But, above all, the knack of co-operating. I'm not too insistent on scholarship' (p.28). He sees education as having a well-defined end-product – 'a second chance'. Herries refers back to the Civil War and the 'something very practical' which emerged from it – 'Parliamentary democracy. Two steps up, and one and a half down. That's my view of history. British history, at all events' (p.28).

David comments on the fall in these values since 1914, but Herries assures him that the lesson will be learnt. 'Out there, everyone below the rank of field officer has had a bellyful of patriotism', David replies, but Herries argues that patriotism is the first step on the road to civic maturity and that David had survived for a purpose – 'I still believe in a Divine purpose.' The purpose is to 'help head other survivors in the right direction, maybe', 'to preserve our way of life'. The tone is modest, moderate and decidedly abstract, part of a narrative constructed at the moment of intense debate about Britain's entry into the EEC. It is close to what Priestley, writing in 1934, called 'that inner glowing tradition of the English spirit'; 'It is little England I love.'[31] Both writers share this 'Little Englander' mentality, made fashionable again with the 1981 Nationality Act and fears of 'being swamped by people from other cultures'.[32] Bamfylde is a metaphor of 'little England' – the nation in miniature.

The self-discovery of the individual is linked to that of

the nation – i.e. the values renewed in the inter-war period formed the basis of victory in World War Two and, by analogy, need to be revived again today. The narrative amounts to a rite of passage, as David passes 'over the threshold into an entirely new world'; he is seen by Herries as a bridge over a generation gap: 'your gap, caused by the war, is semi-permanent. It might take twenty years to close' (p.43). In like fashion, the inter-war period in the past decade has been constantly used as a 'bridge', a way of stepping over the period of the post-war 'settlement'. The school is isolated, its building 'seedy, scarred and very shabby' but, in another teacher's terms, 'it is a first-class, second-rater', which is perhaps a way of formulating an identity for post-imperial Britain, providing a 'moral' role for the country.

The relationship between Herries and David is that of father and son, a spiritual-ideological bonding in which the representative of bourgeois values initiates his acolyte in the 'sacred knowledge' of the class, breaking with the 'biological' ties and codes of birth and class origin:

> He had a curious afterthought then, concerned with a squat, bowlegged, round-shouldered man, who had died underground in the summer of 1913, a man who, even then, had had unwavering faith in him. . . . It was as though his father, feeling the darkness pressing in, had called for help on his behalf, and Herries, walking his rounds on this high plateau, had heard him across the width of the Bristol Channel. (p.51)

This is a neat narrative encoding and mystification of what Poulantzas calls 'the myth of social promotion', a meritocratic ritual. The characteristics of working-class experience and ideology in the text merge with, and are invested with the forms of, lower middle-class ideology: 'This presence of working-class ideology in the petty bourgeois ideological sub-ensemble always tends to be dominated both by specifically petit-bourgeois ideological elements and by the bourgeois ideology that is also constitutively present in the petit-bourgeois sub-ensemble.'[33] The father's death in 1913 is not an arbitrary narrative element, but both event and timing become part of a necessary ritual preparation for the construction of the 'middle way' class alliance out of the crisis and violation of 1914–18. Herries, it is said, is 'a past master at reconciling extreme points of view' – and *reconciliation*, its *locus classicus* seen as being in the inter-war period, is the paradigmatic theme *and* form in Delderfield.

This whole process is part of a narrative of what sociologists have called degrees of 'interest-distortion'[34] between the different classes. As most of the dominant conceptions, theories and *forms of representation* are functionally connected with the culture of the capitalist state, then the process dramatized repeatedly by Delderfield is part of the ideological problematic of liberalism – the absence of problems and concepts which have not found narrative forms.[35]

The ascendancy of the autobiographical mode, the construction of the subject as the place of intelligibility of the realist narrative, and the extensive use of the first-person narrator all suggest a functional link with the *private* ownership of the means of production of the capitalist state, and means that all the retrospective narratives which bring the past into the present in order to construct a future, are *monological* in form – teacher to pupil, father to son, and writer to reader. So, although 'Thatcherism' may be rightly or wrongly identified as *the* current 'political' problem by the Left, I would argue that a deeper and continuing problem is the dominant Liberal cultural forms available for 'thinking' the future, or even 'thinking' the present conjuncture. The institutionalization in television serials, and other narrative forms, of liberal forms and modes of representation (monological) mean that 'interest-distortion' can never be simply encountered by 'radical' interventions at the level of content, but must be constructed in 'dialogic' forms of narrative organization. It is not, therefore, the content of Delderfield's fictions alone which account for their extensive use on television, but the individualistic, monological narrative codes – a form of cultural opportunism which characterizes much of commercialized popular narrative. They are monological structures of narrative designed to *mobilize* the individual.

The dominant metaphors in *To Serve Them All My Days* are healing, recovery, sense of renewal, and resurrection. Boys and women (infantilized) become secondary agents of this, the bringers of *reconciliation*. Bamfylde's sheet anchor strength is its *predictability* with any innovations linked with tradition. The nation is seen as flexible, 'bending', capable of balancing opposites and extremes.

The principal figure undergoes a series of ordeals – war, death of his wife and daughter – which are given shape and cohesion by the ethos of Bamfylde. The history he teaches, like Delderfield's narrative, 'fits in with today'. He compares life on the plateau and life in the valleys and links them by tradition and obstinacy – a tenacity. Bamfylde is seen as a unique place – 'up here on its own and with its own way of life'. The environment is invested with a mystical power of rootedness, and is used to show how the individual is a 'shallow-rooted plant' dependent upon 'the strength of a cluster of root fibres that ran just below the surface'. This organic imagery has a social extension when reference is made to the comradeship of the war. The narrative project is designed to effect a compromise between these extremes – to strike a balance of rationality, tolerance, and give and take. Bamfylde/England is 'spiritualized', mystified in the form of a moral/cultural identity which is unique and is the foundation of *character*. One particular interpellation thus becomes a symbol of all the others as part of a consistent ideological discourse – 'steadiness, continuity, and a touch of genuine idealism, but it also has – how the devil can I put it – post-war optimism, and a broadening of outlook that's been achieved in all kinds of ways since people got the war into perspective' (p.221). The description of the 1920s and of the attitudes generated in criticism of them, repeatedly, suggests the debates of the 1960s and 1970s. Schools like Bamfylde lost their direct grant or voluntary aided status in the late 1970s and most have since become independent. Both an educational structure and ethos of a particular relationship is being sustained, a mixed economy of state help and local initiative. 'To see things and ourselves as they and we really are, not as fashionable trends and fashions project them, generation by generation.' This inflects a traditionalist perspective in the face of 'trendy' changes like those in the 1960s. David also speaks in favour of system, organization, chain of command, like the army, church or a well-run business. The system is pre-eminent, although in constant need of adjustment. The narrative is filled with different versions, and images of, this systemic, core paradigm-tradition, order, and authority: the symbols of 'patrician hegemony'. The notion of a team, of people 'pulling together' is ever present and Herries describes the keystones of liberal democracy as patience, tolerance, good fellowship, and the ability to see someone's else's point of view; a *passive* interpellation articulated to the ideological discourses of the bourgeoisie.

In Part Five of the novel, as Herries the traditional 'moral force' recedes, politics enter explicitly in the form of Christine Forster – upper middle class, and university educated. At this stage, David has shed his working-class 'valley communism' and come to 'regard pit politics objectively'. His brother's politics are seen as sectional and class-bound, while David welcomes Christine as somehow 'legitimizing' Labour's position: 'I think it's encouraging, a person like you, with a good degree, coming over to us.' He also thinks the miners have been unfair to the Labour Right – the embryo 1930s SDP – some of whom defected to the National Government. Christine is treated patronizingly, styled, reduced and placed in gender terms, and her initial 'Left' positions conflict with David's increasing 'moderation' – 'It's time you chaps dropped your nineteenth century slogans and started persuading the floating voter that a Socialist isn't a home-grown Bolshie.' By constructing these positions from the perspective of the central figure, Delderfield de-radicalizes Labour and marginalizes the 'Left' either through consigning the miners to the periphery or by encoding Christine in sexist terms – infantilized, decentred like all the females in the text. Her approach is, nevertheless, 'clientelist' and social-democratic, 'to even things out a bit'.

The period 1917–42 is used, palimpsestically and metonymically, by Delderfield to recode the period 1945–70 – the grid of the one is laid over the other. When Christine asks David to speak at her constituency adoption meeting in Somerset he addresses the theme of the 'Monmouth rising' which, as Christine says, was 'a case of the people versus the others, and that's good enough for me'. The whole of this section corresponds exactly with Laclau's analysis of 'the ideological crystallisation of resistance *to oppression in general*, that is to the *very form of the State*'[36] one of the principal bases of 'popular traditions'. David refers to 'the Englishman's struggle to wrest power from the hands of narrow, sectarian interests, and prepare the ground for real democracy', 'an impulse that has brought the Englishman into conflict with local tyrants down to this day, a determination to have a say in how he is taxed and governed', 'entrenched privilege', 'dying for a principle', and 'today we are privileged to hold the torch. Not only with a vote but *under trained leaders*' (my italics). Oppression is styled in the terms only of its aberrations, its excesses and not its persistent structural presence of class exploitation. *Class* struggle is replaced by the abstraction 'Englishman' – the 'individual' interpellation related to an individualist culture seen as going back as far as thirteenth century yeomen. Popular-democratic interpellations are incorporated in a model of parliamentary democracy – 'have a say', 'the vote', 'trained leaders'. The structural trajectory of the passage is based upon the idea of progress, history as a providential unfolding.

Throughout the narrative, the nation-person symbolization is sustained in the terms of a privileged identity. The fundamental imagery ('this island race') is based on what Barnett has called 'Churchillism'.[37] Trench warfare toughens and makes David more resilient; his hunger for social justice has been replaced by Bamfylde as a way of disarticulating him/the people from the *national* political space (he declines to become a parliamentary candidate when invited because of loyalty to the tribe/school). His father's death coincided with Sarajevo, Beth and Joan's with the General Strike, Alcock (the polarizing, stability-threatening figure) dies in 1931, the moment of the *National* government. Alcock – the colonial – commits suicide and his ashes are sent back to Cape Town, in a sense placing him back where his 'un-Englishness' belongs, overcoming his disruptive presence.

David sympathizes with Ramsey MacDonald and the idea of a coalition, to which Christine is utterly opposed. Their relationship 'becomes' the 'coalition', she induces restorative peace and emotional re-awakening, 'the bridge between him and personal fulfilment'. This metonymic encoding reduces the antagonism between 'the people' and the power bloc to a relationship of simple difference – the nation/person transforms it into a unitary/continuous discourse. Sir Rufus's speech to David about what are regarded as his 'radical' politics confirms the notion of the 'neutral' state (in the form of the judiciary) and re-iterates 'it's mostly a matter of milieu and mine happened to be different' – a discursive levelling on the basis of simple difference and evacuating *class* from its form:

> I have few real convictions left, but I can think of one. This country, although it still has a great deal to learn, maintaining a free society. Its party politics, to me, are a charade. They have a part to play in the democratic process but they remain a charade. This is going to be a stormy decade, and will almost certainly end in a drawing together of all shades of political opinion, here in Britain at least. (pp. 383–4)

The abstractions of 'country', 'free society' transcend the 'democratic process' and the charade of 'party politics' – it is a 'patrician' vision of Britishness, invented to displace the visibility of stratification, inequality, and power. David becomes increasingly 'parochial' and 'insular' in preparation for the moment when Britain will 'stand alone' in the opening period of the war. The whole retrospective grid has this teleological structure, as the future of the past is, of course, known – the narrative dramatizes an *already completed historical period* and reconstructs it in the terms of an 'invented tradition' based upon a health metaphor of the 'national body' – emblematized by the 'socially promoted' working-class person of talent, whose merit is rewarded. His political affiliations have shifted to Bamfylde – 'the symbol of old-style Britain', and he puts his faith in 'tradition, ripeness, habit and continuity' but is still antagonistic to 'oppression in general' and excess: 'I'm still Bolshie as regards the fun and games chaps like you play in Threadneedle Street. If we'd guillotined the whole damned crowd of you in Trafalgar Square, maybe I wouldn't be doing this now [leading the School Corps]' (p.447). The person addressed is an Old Boy now a stock-broker, and the imagery draws upon two revolutionary moments, but reduces them to the scale of the school. The language is reminiscent of Priestley's popular, cross-class patriotism in *Out of the People* – it focuses on the abuses of the 'old gang' not the capitalist relations which are its foundation. The whole of this section (Part Seven) is entitled 'Island in a Torrent'.

With the benefit of *hindsight*, the narrative is organized around a series of events with a known, historical provenance, and these are rehearsed in the terms of narrative propositions which make the characters ventriloquial figures articulating positions (on pacifism, Spain, and re-armament) which simplify them and produce what Benjamin called, 'history brushed with the grain'. All the episodes exist to be deciphered like symbols, and as the narrative reaches its final stages the ideologies of British-ness accumulate. Christine, having lost the candidature at Openshawe South, because the Party Chairman was a pacifist, takes over the prep-school known as 'The Cradle', an appropriate space for a Delderfield female! Her summary of the Party Chairman's speech (p.451) sounds like a parody version of unilateralism – passive, 'wishful

thinking' – and reminds us of how often opposition to
CND has been constructed round a selective re-
reading/writing of the issues in the 1930s. Christine has
been a pacifist and an advocate of disarmament, but
'matures' to the 'dominant position'. David's position is
now described in terms of the myth of 'objectivity' –
pragmatic, empiricist, commonsensical, in fact. This is all
part of the double articulation of the discourse – the histo-
ricist reconstruction of the period and the contemporary
perspective. Disarmament, Spain, re-armament, have their
echoes in the Cold War, Vietnam, and the EEC. Spain is
described as 'a local quarrel'.

The last section is entitled *Re-Run*, which underlines
the whole of Delderfield's enterprise. World War Two
mirrors World War One, but the jingoism and false patriotism, the heroics, are evacuated. World War One is
displaced by the 'popular' rhetorics of World War Two –
'total war', 'survival', 'more muddle if we win, a living
death if we don't.' The key word here is 'muddle', one of
those self-deprecating, quintessentially 'English' characteristics. In the war, the roots of 'Britishness' are more clearly
articulated. When Carter's school is evacuated to
Bamfylde, one of the staff is an amateur archaeologist
with extravagant theories about *Middle*moor (Bamfylde's
site) being the real site of Arthur's Camelot. All of the
contributing images of the narrative come to rest in that
symbol – the mystical, romantic origins of Britishness.
Bamfylde is the heart of 'middle' England – 'tolerance,
equality of opportunity, the true essence of democracy,
small 'L' Liberalism, and British standards of equity and
fair play' (p.552).

None of the values described in themselves are class
specific but they, like many other elements of democratic
and popular culture, are irrevocably linked to the class
ideology of the bourgeoisie through monologic liberal-
democratic discourses which dispense with 'all that red
flag flapping [which] never fooled me, and never fooled
anyone else' (p.552). Bamfylde is described as a place
'where they had imbibed a little of the ethos of the island,

and its struggle over twenty centuries to fashion apparatus capable of accommodating free will with justice and human dignity'.

The text carefully distances itself from some of the more crude manifestations of patriotism and articulates a 'vision' of Britishness which is best described as 'mystical common sense', a set of beliefs based on the idea that:

> English institutions, like no other in the Western world, were the result of slow growth from Saxon days; that, like a coral reef, precedent had fallen upon precedent, erecting a bulwark of liberty, creating institutions such as Parliament or constitutional monarchy. Many centuries and much tribulation had been required to bring these to perfection; their antiquity, their slow growth, endowed them with a special virtue, and British history, therefore was a moral as well as political example to mankind.[38]

Delderfield's two principal narrative propositions are based on this evolutionary, little by little, model of growth combined with a belief in the *providential* nature of England's history. The realist narrative form is itself providential in its structurings. It encodes a form of nationalism which underpinned imperialism and, yet, was also effective in dramatizing the struggle against Hitler. Delderfield is the supreme popularizer of this 'Whig interpretation of history', which, Plumb argues in *The Death of the Past* (1969), is/was particularly active among the lower middle class, although it pervaded the dominant class's imagery also for many years, and played a key role in the construction of the Falklands.

Certainly, the concluding pages of *To Serve Them All My Days* are encoded almost entirely in these mythic terms – 'an offshore island holding out under a non-stop bombardment'. The long passage on page 566 [quoted at the opening of this section] is the fullest fictional articulation of the myth in post-war writing. The passage erects a Whig version of history which places the petty bourgeoisie at its centre, the social formation presently vital to the interpellations of 'authoritarian populism', whose moral economy provides the social basis of 'Thatcherism' as well as the power of the small business ideology of economic liberalism derived from the 'Whig' myth. Further, such a history also enacts *syntactically* the democratic popular interpellations of the intermediate sector – 'neither rich nor poor, intellectual nor illiterate, well-endowed or down-and-out' – the signification is placed in the fulcrum words, and the remainder of the passage works within a similar 'middle' rhythm of balance and moderation. The passage reproduces in synoptic form the whole trajectory of the narrative. It emphasizes *continuity*, the handing on of a legacy. David's latest recruit to the staff is a receiver of this legacy as he re-capitulates his own initial situation – invalided out of the war, scholarship boy, son of a mill-worker and a 'mother who keeps a corner shop to help out' – a significant combination. Bamfylde may be 'secondgrade' (like Britain after the war) but 'academically and socially, that is, not in any other way'. After the Battle of Britain, Earnshaw (the new staff member) says:

> 'We're on our own now. It's up to us, all of us, not a gaggle of generals . . . and not cluttered by Allies either. That always affords a better field of fire. . . . I keep making comparisons. The performances we put up against even bigger odds at places like Crecy and Agincourt. . . . Allies slow us down somehow. Politics keep coming into it and we lose unity, sense of purpose and direction. We'll win all right.' (p.570)

'Allies' also interfere with the *providential* nature of British history. This speech is a classic instance of the Churchillian 'stand alone' rhetoric which still has a powerful resonance for the 'island race'.

The sense of continuity referenced by Crecy and Agincourt fits in with the 'Whig' interpretation of the unfolding of British history, and it might well have registered (in 1972) with lower middle-class opponents of the EEC – 'Allies slow us down, somehow. Politics keep coming into it and we lose unity.' Northedge's evidence for the lack of active support for the EEC supports this possibility.[39] The final image of the narrative is of the school (nation) as an enormous family, a recurring 'trope' in ideologies of Britishness (cf. Orwell in *Lion and Unicorn*). If the function of all ideology is to constitute individuals as subjects, Delderfield's narratives position the individual as British subject.

Delderfield's 'history' sees the struggle against, what is variously constructed as, the dominant bloc as being solely conducted in the terms of 'democratic' struggle, separate from any consideration of class. His work is composed from within a number of ideological ambiguities and crucial historical elisions and displacements. It exalts 'yeoman' values as abstractions and constructs a form of patriarchal populism. It chronicles 'resistances' and articulates them to different versions of society in such a way that their potential antagonism is neutralized. His narrative system combines the characters, events, and settings so as to suggest the relative *continuity* of selected popular traditions articulated in readily identifiable emotional symbolism. Delderfield is popular precisely because 'popular traditions' constitute the complex of interpellations which express "the people"/power bloc contradiction as distinct from a class contradiction . . . in so far as ' "popular traditions" represent the ideological crystallisation of resistance to oppression in general, that is, *to the very form of the State* they will be longer lasting than class ideologies and will constitute a structural frame of reference of greater stability'.[40] These ideological symbols are also, as Laclau shows, 'the residue of a unique and irreducible historical experience and, as such, constitute a more solid and durable structure of meanings than the social structure itself'.[41]

As of this moment, the dominant ideological discourses still have connotative power over the fragmented, disarticulated popular interpellations, mainly because they have succeded in 'capturing' elements of these popular interpellations for their own articulation. The organization of the State may be in crisis, the economy may be unstable, but there are few signs that the forms for *popularizing* ideological discourse are showing any significant weaknesses. At the present moment 'Thatcherism' and forms of 'liberalism' have monopolized the articulations of 'the people' (particularly in its re-writing of the past in the terms of 'popular traditions'), even though some forms of populism – as yet not capable of generalization – do have a partial, if still suppressed, existence: the peace movement, 'local socialism', black struggles, feminism, and defences of the health service.

Delderfield works with narrative conventions and familiar themes which 'have sturdy historical roots and are tenaciously entwined in the psychology of specific popular strata',[42] an ideology produced by social forces which have become part of our 'common sense' – a 'natural' way of perceiving and understanding the world; 'natural' because largely uncritical and deeply sedimented. Gramsci also uses the term 'good sense' which approximates to the practical, empirical 'common sense' used in English and by Delderfield. In fact, Delderfield's texts are a composite of common sense – commonly/popularly held sets of assumptions and beliefs – good sense, and the folkloric – 'beliefs, superstitutions, opinions, ways of seeing things and of acting, which are collectively bundled together under the name of "folklore" '.[43] Delderfield's fictions are constituted within a diffuse and relatively unco-ordinated network which is the basis of a generic form of thought common to a particular period and popular tradition. In a sense, he does not simply *reflect* this generic form of thought, he has played a substantial part in formulating it, in making it *generic*. He makes unitary and coherent a fragmentary and contradictory collection of ideas and opinions, gives form to a 'narrative becoming' by developing discourses in which the resolutions seem to originate in the propositions of the narrative itself, and not derive from already existing forms of thought.

Delderfield's fictions document the historical effectiveness of the 'common sense' of liberalism which he constantly re-enacts, dramatizes, and transforms. That 'liberalism' still has such a 'generative' capacity, is capable of being sustained in different narrativities (novel, play, television) in its forms of 'common sense', is part of its power to create 'the folklore of the future, that is as a relatively rigid phase of popular knowledge at a given place and time.'[44] At a time when seemingly endless representations of the future are being cast in the discursive forms of the past, it is not surprising that Delderfield's fictions have become a staple form of 'transcoding' for television. He uses the 'folklore' of the past to create a 'folklore' of the future because it is based upon a durable structure of meanings.

For Gramsci, common sense is seen as aggregated and internally contradictory forms of thought: the incoherent (not systematic) set of generally held assumptions and beliefs common to any given society, the product of concrete social activity by the ruling bloc seen from a historical perspective. Common sense is not ideology, but has been generated by its processes and social transformations. It has the force of obviousness. 'Mass-popular' ways of seeing are not critical and coherent, but disjointed and episodic; a series of fragmentations of what were originally produced, in ideology, as unitary and coherent. Though a popular fictional text offers itself as a resolved and coherent unity, it contains within it many 'references' from the disjointed and episodic features of common sense. The popular text is, like personality in Gramsci's analysis: ' . . . strangely composite: it contains Stone Age elements and principles of a more advanced science, prejudices from all past phases of history at the local level. . . .'[45] Later, in the same analysis, he refers to the ways in which philosophy has left stratified deposits in popular philosophy, and it is this phrase, together with 'an infinity of traces' (which have not left an inventory) which help to identify quite precisely certain features of popular fictional forms in relation to ideology.

In dealing with common sense, Gramsci was concerned with ideology at its lower levels, (which do not simply repeat the dominant, but assimilate, transpose and domesticate it), as the repository of popular beliefs, myths etc. and as a means of dealing with everyday life. It has a confirmatory and consensual effect. 'Naturalization' was seen by Gramsci as a key mechanism of common-sense thought, as it closes knowledge, ends debate, and dissolves contradictions. Similarly, as we read a popular fiction, meanings are composed by blocks or groups of signification, of which we grasp only the smooth surfaces, imperceptibly joined together by the movement of sentences, the flowing discourse of narration, the 'naturalness' of ordinary language.[46] The ways in which common sense 'naturalizes' the social order is analogous to the ways in which the structures of fictional discourse 'naturalize' the order of signification in the text, so that the reader responds to their formal solidity (however 'neophobe' and conservative) and their imperative character in producing commonsensical norms of conduct.[47]

Delderfield's chronicle structures work fundamentally on the basis of a popularized historic compromise; he is constantly re-writing the historic articulation of 'the people' in the terms of the ideological discourses of the bourgeoisie, incorporating democratic-popular interpellations of 'resistances'. The repeated narrative formulations render the relationship *invariable*, its historic specificity displaced by the notion that 'choice is a way of life', that what is being established is 'a state of mind'. The fictions have a 'gatekeeper' function in that they are a dominant cultural form in which the local 'infrastructure' of a lower middle class is linked to the superstructure of the 'national' society, a stabilizing role. The 'fractional' is, therefore, given a national articulation on an individual basis through representative figures. The 'local' is a moral space basically, an order based on harmony, stability and tradition, durable structures (cf. Algy's 300-year-old 'thinking post' in *To Serve Them All My Days*) which will withstand stress, crisis and disruption. Unexpressed, but implicitly threatening this moral space is the 'mass society', and Delderfield echoes the people/masses debates of the 1930s.

Methodologically, Delderfield's narrative constructions depend upon the assumption that the 'data' they use are the sole basis of the generalizations they deduce and the moral lessons they draw. This is what Stedman-Jones calls 'the poverty of empiricism'[48] – the positivist methodology of the realist narrative. The creation of traditional mythologies giving a historical sanctity and priority, an *active* presence, to the self-image of a class fraction normally characterized by its passivity.

One particular narrative code is privileged and becomes naturalized. It is based on an evolutionary paradigm. The *logic* of the narrative – causative, unitary and continuous – validates the larger ideological discourse in which it is articulated. A new 'subjectivity' is proposed by re-organizing the 'memory' of the inter-war period in the terms of 'the people' – a rhetorical and emotional abstraction designed to restore an interrupted *continuity* drawn from a reconstructed 'popular tradition'. The basic form of the writing is 'methodological individualism' – all sociological explanations are reducible to the characteristics of individuals – which is the 'classic' form of popular codes of realism. This is linked with the functionalist argument that social groups, in Delderfield's case the lower middle class, have emergent properties, characteristics which are produced when individuals interact but are not simply reducible to individuals. Delderfield's construction of 'the people' combines aspects of both methodological individualism and functionalism: 'There is a dialectical process in which the meanings given by individuals to their world become institutionalized or turned into social structures, and the structures then become part of the meaning-systems employed by individuals.'[49] This neatly formulates the basis of philosophical liberal humanism which is at the root of Delderfield's narrative images and metaphors.

The re-birth of the past

There is no sense in which Delderfield's fictions can simply be articulated to a coherent set of ideological positions at the moment of their circulation in the form of television drama (1978–85). The ground vacated by consensus politics has been fiercely contested by a number of conflicting, yet often overlapping, forces. The argument of this book is that this ideological struggle at one level found expression, was reproduced in, a diverse, and contradictory, range of popular cultural forms.

It would be tempting, and methodologically convenient, to articulate Delderfield's fictions to one particular position – say that occupied by the emergence of the Social Democratic party. However, it will be demonstrated that, whatever its practices and policies may be, Conservatism has been busily constructing an extensive populist rhetoric and symbolism which draws heavily upon the self-imagery of the petite bourgeoisie – weakening the State, living within your means, standing on your own feet, the liberty of the individual, respect for eternal verities, Englishness. As Bechhofer and Elliott point out:

> In all this the small businessman becomes symbol, representing, it is claimed, the virtues of an old order to which we must return if our economic fortunes are to mend and our society and polity be restored to health.[50]

These 'virtues of an old order' are clearly expressed in the colloquial articulations of Margaret Thatcher:

> I want decent, fair, honest, citizen values, all the principles you were brought up with. You don't live up to the hilt of your income; if someone gets the bills wrong you tell them, you don't keep the extra change; you respect other people's property; you save; you believe in right and wrong; you support the police. . . . We were taught to help people in need ourselves, not stand about saying what the government should do. Personal initiative was pretty strong. You were actually taught to be clean and tidy, that cleanliness was next to Godliness. All these ideas have got saddled as middle class values, but they're eternal.[51]

Invoked here is a myth of a past 'moral economy' marked by certain salient features and 'memorizable' symbols. Delderfield is the virtual 'laureate' of this moral economy, its most effective chronicler in a series of narrative re-iterations from 1958–72. Wilfully 'old-fashioned', the texts speak to, and of, a generation [growing-up and coming to maturity in the inter-war period] in a method which condenses individual, class, time, history, and nation into a symbolic memory of permanence. Again, the 'leap' from Delderfield to Thatcher would be neat and convenient, but this would be to mistake the person for the phenomenon, and to locate so-called 'Thatcherism' too readily in a particular form of Conservative politics. Conversely, the kind of symbolic transfers and rhetorical condensations at which Thatcher is, admittedly, very adept, should be seen as part of a larger process which seeks to re-discover selective versions of the recent past and articulate these with what is thought of as the 'middle ground' of British politics. A 'middle ground', moreover, which all contestants agree has to be constructed with 'radical' equipment.

In this respect two useful conceptual frameworks are: J.H. Plumb's distinction between 'history' and 'a past' in *The Death of the Past*,[52] and Michael Wood's use of 'nostalgia' in 'You can't go home again' originally published in *New Society*.[53] By 'a past' Plumb means collections of half-remembered, often repeated and often embellished tales of a specific past of a specific people, which, through constant repetition, bind that specific group of people together – in Delderfield's terms, 'people like us'. The 'us' both refers to, and constructs, a group identity. The interpellation of 'the people', as in 'our people' (Thatcher) or *Politics is for People* (1981) (Shirley Williams), is an attempt to provide an ideological binding which will hold together an uneven, and contradictory, set of forces.

For a particular generation born before 1934 the 'inter-war' past is a crucial element in its identity. More complex, though, is the way in which a particular class, or class fraction, is constituted within a 'class-memory' of its past – a narrative of values and ways of seeing extrapolated from, and interpellated within, a particular period. If you perceive that the values of your 'class' are under attack, you necessarily cast around for explanations, for symbolic 'scapegoats' – Macmillan's 'stop-go' economic policies, post-war welfarism, the corporate state, trade-union power, the 'permissive' sixties. These 'scapegoats' are all recognizable features of the kind of 'populist' imagery adopted by 'Thatcherism' and partly appropriated by the SDP. This 'moral economy' of the class in question has to be readily located in specific and visible cultural forms, in familiar symbols which relate to the *group* whom it identifies, and reminds its younger members of the group of its 'origins'. Such cultural forms are designed to renew the 'class fraction's' memory. If a 'class' feels alien, or exiled from the *present*, it can superimpose upon the present the familiar and normative 'ideals' of its 'past'. What matters is the memory, not the fact. This common-sense memory binds the class together.

I am not suggesting that recent British politics have simply been a matter of securing the 'lower middle-class' vote, as the SDP's transatlantic and European style, and the Conservative government's obvious commitment to international capitalism and 'market forces', patently disproves this. I am suggesting that a number of ideological 'narratives' adopt a rhetoric and symbolism predicated upon the 'preferred memories' of the lower middle class. A complex process of co-option has taken place in which being 'modern' and 'up-to-date' [i.e. as opposed to nineteenth-century socialism] is linked to a scenario which values the 'past'. Such a 'past' is impervious to history, and gives full play to mythical elements, and not just those based on the Grantham 'corner-shop'. The memory of victory past (e.g. the triumph over the 1930s depression and, above all, in the 'people's war') reinforces the strength of loyalty and identity. As Thompson, and others, have indicated, the almost complete appropriation of the war by the Right has enabled the 'real history' to be *unwritten*. So, in myth, Dunkirk becomes an 'epic', and, in the constant re-telling, this *selective* stock of 'preferred' memories is replenished:

Jim at once saw what he was getting at and approved. It matched his own feelings about the Avenue since Churchill had taken charge of the war. The levelling of the fence would be symbolic of the unity of the British, of the sinking of party differences and social distinctions. . . . [54]

Delderfield's fictions take the inter-war period as *the* definitive ideological narrative in which the 'people-nation' interpellation is complete. The *coalition* of values, attitudes and classes predicated upon a rhetoric of concili-ation is developed through a series of events from 'history' recalled through the perspective of the lower middle class. In this way, the events are co-opted by a particular class appropriation severed from the working class – styled as the 'masses' – and the dominant class – styled as the 'privileged and the wealthy'.

He was sixty seven now and it was time to take stock of his convictions. His own life did not seem to have amounted to much. He had wasted so much time on politics and it was only now that he was coming to realize that *politics were really people*, the kind of people who lived in these Avenues.[55] (my italics)

Britain's *survival*, it is suggested in narrative after narra-tive, came from 'out of the People' in Priestley's definition. This kind of past, as Drucker says, depends upon its *vivacity*, its familiarity. To be meaningful it has got to produce a vast supply of iconic documentation. It also depends upon a certain amount of cultural *simplification*. Fictions like Delderfield's reconstruct the missing codes, the tribal 'gnosis' or arcana, of the special provenance of a lower middle-class past, which is re-presented as the nation's past in the form of a folk-memory. In folk-memory, in myth, 'the events of the past are frozen in memory'.[56] The diachronic is simply a vehicle for the synchronic grasp. Delderfield's 'future' is projected as 'palimpsestic', the original period has been effaced in order to make way for a second writing to take place.

   It is not surprising that in the face of deep social anxiety all political forces should turn to the 'middle ground' [ideologically] and to that class fraction, which given the current economy, has no future beyond that of a 'cultural resource' in the form of 'retrospectives'. In a conjuncture marked by instability and unevenness, the *coherence* of lower middle-class narratives of 'moral economy' are a valuable resource.

When the Masai were moved from their traditional lands in Uganda to Kenya, they handled the cultural trauma and sense of dissonance by giving all the new territories the names of their former land, hills etc.[57] In this way time and change are immobilized by the *re-creation* of memory. This is an active process of cultural intervention, analogous to the cultural productions of the present and future in the terms of the 'inter-war' past. The breakdown of norms governing social interaction is recuperated by the production of 'enabling' frameworks which place speculation, fear and anxiety within permissible limits, which screen off the 'unthinkable' and 'unimaginable'. If a sense of decline and breakdown at several levels in society – political, economic, personal – is condensed and displaced onto a sense of *moral breakdown*, this gives space and time for some kind of ideological 'in-filling' which masks the real contradictions.

Michael Wood's essay on nostalgia offers another useful means for exploring the phenomenon I have been describing. Nostalgia, he says, speaks to a sense of loss and 'all flights into the past . . . are boarded in the present.'[58] This was the point being made earlier; Delderfield's narratives simply deploy the past for a way of talking/thinking about the present. 'Whatever its object or its content, it is a way of behaving *now*.' Wood addresses the problem interestingly in the form of a person/generation image: 'you can't pick up the halves of a divided self before the division has taken place.' For Delderfield, the division took place in 1945, which is why so many memorials are being constructed to it. To see the present ideological conjuncture in the terms of a 'divided self' is a useful metaphor. Wood refers to the movie *Let the Good Times Roll* in which 'time seems both to pass and not to pass.' It is the 'historical' footage which encodes 'time passing' – it is our perception of the 'performers' [in the film] or the 'values' (in the novels) which 'stills' time:

> What nostalgia mainly suggests about the present is not that it is catastrophic or frightening, but that it is undistinguished, unexciting, blank. There is no life in it, no hope, no future (the important thing about the present is what sort of future it has). It is a time going nowhere, a time that leaves nothing for our imaginations to do except plunge into the past.[59]

That was written in 1974, and we would possibly have to add the 'catastrophic' and 'frightening' to Wood's description. The way in which the Falklands War at the level of spectacle, rhetoric, and symbolism represented a tragic 'abandonment to the visions of yesterday' has already been well documented.[60] Interestingly enough (for 1974) Wood links the urge for nostalgia with 'all that talk of the need for moderation in British politics, of the need for a brave new middle party', as our present conjuncture is characterized by yet further bids for the 'middle ground'. We could, he says, 'find ourselves camping out indefinitely in our current landscape' which is why so much energy is invested in creating a future based on a past landscape. The historical time, 1918–45, becomes an *ideological space*.

Wood contrasts two modes/styles of nostalgia – that 'for the great, final, dwindling days of something that has vanished' and 'a nostalgia for the early days of what we have . . . a beginning of the end nostalgia'. The kind of retrospective I have been analysing combines elements of both – it is nostalgic for a particular kind of nostalgia! The 'beginning of the end' nostalgia locates the germs of all our current discontents in a particular moment. This kind of recall pictures us 'poised on the brink of what we were to become'; 'nothing really seems irrevocable'. It is the 'revocability' of the period from 1945 which Delderfield's fictions are motivated by. 1945 is seen as the time *before* things turned out as they did, the time when they might have gone the other way. Certainly in terms of television, nostalgia has developed into a substantial *genre* which indicates not simply a sense of loss and a time in trouble, but a general abdication, an actual desertion from the present.[61] 'Nostalgia' as a genre is a dehistoricizing process, it refuses to dissolve the special provenance of our particular past; if anything, it fetishizes that 'provenance'.

There are important distinctions to be made within particular *styles* of the nostalgia genre. For instance, the 1977–8 LWT production of *People Like Us* was built around elements of charade, and pointed to itself quite self-consciously as 'periodized' – 'costumized' at the level of iconic clothing, song, transport. It directed attention to its 'impedimenta' *as* impedimenta. In Wood's terms, this was made up of 'trips to the past, allusions to it, implications of the past in the present', not a revival of but a 'quotation from' the period. This doesn't invalidate the very strong narrative emphases [marked by the *dominant* realist codes] on the ideological components of lower middle-class 1918–45 (the novel, incidentally, ends in 1948), but it does complexify possible reception, it doesn't 'effect a closure'.

Wood further suggests a distinction between the 'nostalgia provoked by an old photograph, say, and the nostalgia provoked by a movie that looks like an old photograph. In the one case, a piece of the past is experienced as lost; in the other, a general sense of loss makes us look around for a piece of the past that will suit our present feelings. We haven't lost it because we have only just made it up.'[62]

In the LWT (1977–8) production of *People Like Us* an interesting dialectic of styles was developed which was based upon a productive interaction between both categories of nostalgia distinguished by Wood. By 1980, the BBC One production of *To Serve Them All My Days* had stylistically severed itself from the mixed codes of representation used by LWT, and settled for the production values of 'saga realism' and, in some ways, closed off the possibilities of differential reception. The subsequent productions of *A Horseman Riding By* and

Diana (BBC, 1985) used the same format. One must be cautious about generalizing from such instances, especially as budgets and markets are material determinants on production decisions [the LWT series was produced when drama was still very much a priority in LWT's programme planning without the later pressure on budgets], but the difference between the 1977 and the 1980 productions do suggest a shift in emphasis towards a 'look around for a piece of the past that will suit our present feelings'. The BBC versions of Delderfield, with high visibility given to initial class differences – sharper than in the novels – and equally high visibility given to the reconciliation of these differences, suggest that their emphasis isn't on something we have lost 'because we have only just made it up'. In other words, it is 'good television' precisely because the structures used are consonant with folk-memories of 'a past', and are designed to reconstruct a site of conciliation predicated upon a lower middle-class ideological formation. The BBC's Delderfield aimed at the kind of coherence predicated upon the unified petty bourgeois subject, using *the* code (of realism) and suppressing the voices of other, off-stage codes. It is *not* a perspective of textual 'quotations', but the unitary discourse of 'common sense': a paradigm, not of *that* period, but of *our* period. The 'naturalness' of 'common sense' language never points to its 'signifying' characteristics – that which denotes its 'fictionality' but is based upon an illusion of *completeness*.

The battle for the middleground

We need to ask what ideological struggles marked this particular conjuncture? The SDP offered themselves, initially, as a more effective means of tackling poverty, promoting citizen participation in government, and securing accountability of institutions through decentralization. Emphasis was placed on the 'social market' and the withdrawal of the state from the provision of welfare.

> The SDP's survival ultimately depends on splitting off the radical middle class from the organized working class, and

detaching with them in the process a sufficiently large
number of skilled workers.[63]

According to Hilary Wainwright[64] David Owen in his
book, *Face the Future* (1981), is concerned (like Delderfield) with a transformation of attitudes, not power: 'The
central focus [in explaining this decline] must be the failure
of managers and workers to trust each other and to co-
operate effectively together.' Bernard Crick[65] describes the
SDP (or, rather Rodgers in his book, *The Politics of
Change* (1982)) as in danger of creating a 'purely
rhetorical middle ground of fantasy parlour politics'. This
seems to be precisely the ideological effect of Delderfield
– to furnish the images, characters, and symbols of this
rhetorical middle ground, contested by all parties (despite
the radical claims of the Tories to disdain it). Crick
attempts to define 'social democrat' as the position of
those who are not egalitarians but who wish for 'a Fair
Society or for Social Justice' in the sense of some perceiv-
able relationship between merits and rewards.

Again, this is familiar territory and closely resembles
the values and relationships adumbrated in Delderfield –
especially *To Serve Them All My Days*. The ethical
element is more strongly encoded in Delderfield than in
the SDP. In another article, 'The Many Faces of
Socialism'[66] Crick develops further his analysis of 'social
democracy' and says they talk about 'liberty', 'tolerance',
'equality of opportunity', and 'fairness', all recognizable
characteristics of 'Britishness' described by Priestley,
Orwell, and Delderfield – what Crick calls 'procedural'
values which point to how things should be done to make
the present system work, rather than bring about social
change. Owen's own endorsement of the 'social market
economy' has been described by the *Financial Times* as
'Thatcherism with a human face', and Hugo Young[67]
wrote of Owen fashioning 'a new synthesis, part socialist,
part nationalist, emphatically patriotic'.

It is the formulation of a 'new' synthesis from past
materials which seems to be the key to a whole range of

political and popular cultural writings of this conjuncture based on key phrases such as 'change', 'future' and 'people'. Owen's maiden speech (16 May 1966) was astonishingly 'Delderfieldian': 'the radical spirit which has run through Plymouth for generations. This is the city from which the Pilgrim Fathers embarked on their voyage to the New World. This is the city which welcomed the Reform Act with peals of bells. It has a great radical tradition. It is a Cromwellian city.' The speech could have been written and delivered by David Powlett-Jones had he decided, after all, to leave Bamfylde for politics when asked. The reiteration of 'radical' suggests a certain special pleading, designed for rhetorical effect. It is a 'petty bourgeois' radicalism, the kind of 'Britishness' conjured up by the invocation of Cromwell (cf. *To Serve Them All My Days*, p.28). The rhetorical opportunism deployed in the maiden speech is an attempt to meet what Stuart Hall calls 'the hankering for the centre and coalitionism [which] has been a very long part of the scene. It is partly a response to and a product of democracy. It is also one of the responses to class politics that there should be parties and issues that cut across class so as to contain it.'[68] Peter Jenkins saw the SDP, correctly I think, as a symptom, and not the cause, of a political realignment.[69]

Both Conservatives and Social Democrats have attempted to develop a rhetoric which cuts across class, which severs the party/class connection. 'Thatcherism' carries out 'Right' policies while addressing a 'moral centre', 'the virtues of an old order', 'eternal values'; 'Its project is to fracture what exists, to shift the balance of forces. Then some longer term, more moderate political force might come in and produce longer term solutions but on political terrain much more favourable to capital, which has the unions very isolated, the shop stewards' movement undermined, and the unions boxed in by legal restraints.'[70] The evidence of the past few years suggests that there is certainly some kind of 'middle ground' consensus over these issues. Strongly linked with this is Thatcherism's neo-liberalism – choice, freedom, competitive individualism, and self-reliance. These 'values' are not simply confined to the Right, but are components of a 'populism' built into a sustained antagonism to any form of Socialism. In order to occupy any of the ground of this populism, the SDP/Alliance had to make a number of accommodations in order to 'break the terms of the post-war settlement'. I have argued that the ways in which the terms of the post-war settlement have been broken have not simply been political, but also cultural. The 'post-war settlement' has been abandoned/dissolved by re-writing it in the terms of a 'myth' of the inter-war period – a myth predicated upon Britishness, liberalism with a small 'L', the idea of coalition politics as opposed to class-bound party politics, a reinforcement of the centre, and the war.[71] Thatcherism does not, obviously, express, or reflect, these characteristics but it was successful, *at the time* [1975–9], in recognizing the ideological territory staked out by these long-persistent 'hankerings'. It didn't create new forms, new attitudes – it filled a vacuum, 'a centrist' tendency without a credible 'centrist' political form. Until the Falklands War, the 'centre' was rapidly being taken over by the Alliance, who exploited the symptoms of a very real erosion of long, taken-for-granted, political formations – an erosion which, arguably, goes back to the late 1960s/early 1970s, and not entirely unrelated to the EEC, despite both Conservative and SDP/Alliance commitment to Europe.[72]

In his book, *Descent from Power* written in 1974, F.S. Northedge talks about psychological aversions to 'going into Europe', and the class basis of the relief after De Gaulle's second veto in 1967.[73] The Heath government (1970–4), and certainly Wilson (1974–6) advocated a strong European role for Britain, yet despite the 2:1 'Yes' referendum vote, the popularity of such a role among sections of the working-class, and certainly the petty bourgeoisie, was never high. The implications of entry for the 'small businessman' were potentially very negative.[74] Thatcherism has attempted to show that 'Heath's conviction that there was no future for Britain in any attempt to restore its political influence in the world from an economic basis which had been shown time and again to be too small' was erroneous.[75]

The rhetorical terms of Thatcher's speech to a Conservative rally at Cheltenham Race Course on Saturday, 3 July 1982 (in the aftermath of the Falklands War) will indicate what I mean.[76] The speech is bound together by references to 'our country', 'our people', 'this nation', 'the real spirit of Britain', 'the new mood of the nation', 'the spirit of these times' [' . . . the NUR came to understand that its strike on the railways and on the Underground just didn't fit – didn't match the spirit of these times.'], 'Britain's recovery, which all our people long to see', 'the mood of Britain', 'our Task force', 'We have ceased to be a nation in retreat.' It is a contentless, empty discourse.

The speech explicitly addresses itself to tradition:

> When we started out, there were the waverers and the fainthearts. The people who thought that Britain could no longer seize the initiative for herself.
>
> The people who thought we could no longer do the great things which we once did. Those who believed that our decline was irreversible – that *we could never again be what we were.*
>
> There were those who would not admit it – even perhaps some here today – people who would have strenuously denied the suggestion but – in their hearts of hearts – they too had their secret fears that it was true: that Britain was no longer the nation that had built an Empire and ruled a quarter of the world.
>
> Well they were wrong. The lesson of the Falklands is that Britain has not changed and that this nation still has those sterling qualities which shine through our history.
>
> This generation can match their fathers and grandfathers in ability, in courage, and in resolution. We have not changed. When the demands of war and the dangers to our own people call us to arms – then we British are as we have always been – competent, courageous and resolute.[77] [my italics]

Twice reference is made to the fact that Britain/we 'have not changed', the qualities – 'competent, courageous, and

resolute' – are not grandiose or over-stated. The tone, if
anything, is relatively 'modest' but it would have been
likely to register far beyond the 'party faithful' at Cheltenham. It refers to a stock of already known, and agreed
upon, 'values' immediately recognizable as 'British',
evidenced by history and tradition, and re-iterated in
countless popular cultural forms in recent years, including
the adaptations of Delderfield on television. All of these
are cultural evidence which denies 'that we could never
again be what we were'. Apart from a certain jingoism,
the last chapter/episode of both *To Serve Them All My
Days* and *People Like Us* fits within an ideological
continuum encoded by the linguistic presumptions of this
speech. The Falklands were, in a sense, irrelevant – they
were the site for a long-delayed replay of World War
Two, an action recall of 1940–5 with 'Churchillism' as its
paradigmatic form. The fact that Thatcherism is deeply
attached to American capitalism, and that US nuclear
bases cover part of Britain, was less relevant than the fact
that a memory of victory past was being invoked to recall
the strength of group loyalty and identity: 'Those who
have governed Britain in the days of decline entered politics or were in their youth when Britain governed a quarter
of the globe and lorded it over international conferences:
certainly their education in English history has been a
study of the country as a great, perhaps the greatest, Power
in the World.'[79]

Arguably, the responsibility for sustaining that
'education in English history' has partly passed from the
schools to popular cultural forms which have generated a
widely circulated range of productions based on 'retrospective thinking'. It is not incidental that David Powlett-
Jones is a historian, nor that he is intent on teaching
modern history and equally concerned to point any
parallel between previous history and contemporary
events. He is both model of, and metaphor for, Delderfield's whole 'methodological individualism' and a paradigm for the retrospective tendency in some recent popular
cultural forms. Their task, like his, is to displace history

with the psychological and cultural 'realities' of the past
– in Plumb's terms, 'the past becomes the theatre of life'.
Explanations of the past, in cultural forms, are, like rituals,
essential for social stability, and therefore an essential part
of government. 'Myth . . . provides for the worker; the
official past is the property of government.' Plumb also
adds, significantly, that 'the personal ownership of the
past has always been a vital strand in the ideology of all
ruling classes.'[79]

The Falklands Task Force, the Thatcher speech, were
part of the 'theatre of life'; a ruling class – recruiting well
beyond itself – was renewing its claim to the ownership
of the *present* by constructing a 'moral continuity' with
the past – breaking up the post-1945 settlement. As Plumb
also says, 'where the service of the past has been urgently
needed, truth has ever been at a discount'.[80] There is no
question that over the past decade the Conservatives had
reclaimed 'ownership of the past', and its ideological
pressure has found many cultural expressions. The
SDP/Alliance had little access to this 'ownership', although
over the Falklands and VE Day Owen's 'patriotism' was
very evident, but it tried to co-opt, and represent, a
number of values seen as part of that 'past', particularly
'certain terms of the traditional liberal political lexicon'.[81]

The 'conciliation' imagery so prevalent in the popular
cultural forms I have discussed and will be discussing, and
the resolution of contradictions, links with what Raphael
Samuel describes as the way in which politics can correspond to a 'class *unconscious*, and in the case of the SDP,
the fetishisation of the uncontentious seems at least to be
congruent with, even if it cannot be simply explained by,
an unalienated social state'.[82] An argument based on a
'class unconscious' is problematic and it is very doubtful
whether any simple class-party articulation can be made.
However the notions of the 'uncontentious' and the
'unalienated' form a very useful link with the popular
cultural narratives predicated upon the contentious and
the alienated, yet resolved within a framework of conciliation and consensus. Perhaps there is some kind of

correlation between what might be called a 'cultural economy' – i.e. aesthetic judgements and, even, 'narrative preferences' (middlebrow) – and political forms of expression. Certainly, the working class in these fictions is either invisible, unregenerate, or *individually* upwardly mobile. Samuel claims that the SDP wishes not to improve the working classes but to abolish them. Many, if not most of the writings under discussion, begin with characters signified as within, or closely related to, working-class 'culture' [accent, occupation, housing, environment] but none ends without having brought about a transformation in the character/characters, designed to neutralize contradictions and the 'residues of class fear'. The keynote is social cohesion, unification, and the visibility of the moderate middle class represented, frequently, in the form of a 'lower middle class' version of 'the people' – a symbolic composite of a number of 'commonsensical' traces of different class indices. The ultimate effect is one of 'classlessness', which ties in with what Samuel calls the 'SDP dream of a classless society'.

Although the Social Democrats did not explicitly address the inter-war period, they were nevertheless beneficiaries of cultural constructions which sought to 'forget' the actually existing conditions between the wars which, in Shirley Williams's phrase, 'bred the socialist challenge'.[83] She seems to suggest that these conditions have been forgotten almost as a matter of course, rather than as part of a constant process to intervene upon the 'memory' of the period and reconstitute it in 'contemporary terms'. She fails to see that what she terms the 'intellectual vacuum in conservative thought' has not only been filled by monetarism, but also by a 'cultural scenario', reconstituted from the inter-war period, which supplements and justifies monetarism. 'Many of us may feel its [monetarism's] influence arises from the maturing of a new generation of conservatives whose folk memories of the depression have faded or even vanished.'[84] Their memories may have faded or even vanished, but other 'folk memories' have been actively reconstructed in the form of 'personal ownership of the past'. This 'ownership' consists of a systematic evacuation from the 'depression years' of an active working class as a class, replaced by individual denominators of enterprise and aspiration. Shirley Williams, in the same passage, says that 'Nevertheless, conservatism has the wind in its sails. The Liberals, the progressives, the Social Democrats, have exhausted the conventional thinking of the post-war years.'

Like Thatcherism, Williams also seeks to 'break the post-war settlement' [exhausted, conventional thinking], deconstitute the working class as a class, and recruit its members to a construction of 'the people' in which they exist unaccompanied by (unencumbered by?) the repertoire of traditions, memories, and symbols of an exploited class. In the name of 'the people', both Conservatives and Social Democrats have engaged in a struggle for the working-class vote, severed from its class/party connection. In the cultural fictions, representatives of the class are individuated and either de-classed or 're-classed'. The 'hankering' for the centre Stuart Hall described is not only part of a wish to cut *across* class but, in SDP terms, to *cut out* class.

As Raymond Williams reminds us, in *The Country and the City*:

> in every kind of radicalism the moment comes when any critique of the present must choose its bearings between past and future. And if the past is chosen, as now so often and so deeply, we must push the argument through to the roots that are being defended: push attention . . . back to the . . . moral economy from which critical values are drawn.[85]

So, although the SDP's constant reference is to the future, the provenance of social democracy, as claimed by Shirley Williams, places the party quite firmly within the 'moral economy' of a traditional order – gentle, pastoral and humane: a pre-industrial image of rural England. In her conclusion, a further dimension to this 'England' is added by addressing the ideology of the petty bourgeoisie. So, far from being on the edge of extinction, the lower middle class in the past few years has found itself the centre of attention for a number of 'political' sponsors. This has been supplemented by, perhaps constituted by also, its extensive 'cultural sponsorship' in the popular fictions of the paperback market and television drama. If, as Shirley Williams suggests in the same conclusion, 'people in large numbers are difficult to manage', then the scale of operation long practised by the petite bourgeoisie looks like reviving. Both its 'moral economy' and its economic and social practices have been actively co-opted by competing ideologies. 'The battle to decide what the new politics will be like is just beginning. It is possible, just possible, that it will be a 'politics for people'.[86] This is the last sentence of her book, completing the people-nation conjunction which has formed the axis of so many of the popular cultural forms examined in this and previous chapters. The people-nation conjunction is also the characteristic form which many recent and widely available representations of the Second World War have taken and will be examined in the following chapter.[87]

4
Everything British

It has been argued throughout this work that the period 1975–87 has witnessed a consistent attempt to establish continuity with a 'suitable historic past', designated approximately as 1918–45. In this chapter it will be shown how imagery of the Second World War has formed a crucial part of this 'suitable past'. The dominant impression given by these constructions is not simply of continuity but of *resumption*, resumption that is of an interrupted tradition. Using Hobsbawm's concept of 'invented traditions' it will be seen how 'the history which became part of the fund of knowledge or the ideology of nation, state or movement, is not what has actually been preserved in popular memory but what has been selected, written, pictured, popularized and institutionalized by those whose function it is to do so'.[1] A particular set of inflections is given to a specific past in order to generate and shape models, or paradigms, of the present. In terms of World War Two the key stagings and reconstructions of imagery have drawn upon the Blitz, Dunkirk, D-Day and VE Day. Although each of these has been subject to extensive questioning,[2] they have also been part of a huge symbolic re-investment conducted in popularized, ritual terms in the celebration of anniversaries for example, which were made (in 1984 and 1985) 'the focus of everything British', as the commentary on a film based on the Royal Family in the war put it.[3]

The memory of World War Two has been mediated in such a way that it has become part of what we all 'know' about the war as part of a process of selective popularization. In order to be effective, such ideological representations have to make coherent and 'natural' that which is partial, episodic, and, possibly, contradictory. Popularization depends primarily upon the re-casting of the existing iconography of film, writing, television – the media-dependent imagery of known cultural forms. Memory has to have image, tone, landscape, accent even. This process is part of what Raymond Williams calls 'the selective tradition': 'that which, within the terms of an effective dominant culture, is always passed off as "*the* tradition", "*the* significant past". But always the selectivity is the point; the way in which from a whole possible area of past and present, certain meanings and practices are chosen for emphasis, certain other meanings and practices are neglected and excluded.'[4] An important feature of this activity is the way in which these 'certain meanings and practices' are recruited to the 'core ideology'.

The endless 'representations' dealing with the war currently popularized have less to do with the war itself than with a symbolic return to that war in order to reconnect with the 'land that time forgot' or 'the time the land forgot'. It is, in effect, an archaeological site in which, it is claimed, the natural, the national, and the universal images of Britishness have been buried, superimposed upon by the 1945–75 period – the prolonged 'wilderness years'. As Dawson and West carefully point out, in *National Fictions*, Churchill's war position depended upon a compromise with Labour which facilitated the Beveridge Report and post-war reconstruction. But as they have shown, the facts of *this* unity and commitment have been obliterated by the extensive cultural renewal of images of the nation which privilege a Churchillian rhetoric isolated from its complex and specific context.

A selective, and simplified, reconstruction of World War

Two, combined with the invention and repetition of Cold War images, has produced the ideological effectivity of the Right's 'defence' argument. It is vital to stress the combination of the two rhetorics, because neither would be effective on its own. A process of ideological displacement guarantees the re-formation of the 'nation' as a meaningful, symbolic system in the face of multinational and international capitalist realities. Britain's last (and lost?) 'national memory' was constituted in, and by, World War Two, it is implied. Whatever else it signified, the Falklands war was certainly used as a theatrical pageant, a parade of popularized images of British past power — part of a cultural bid to align the present with a carefully edited version of yesterday.

The 'nation' and 'the people' are interpellations which are designed to disguise the differentiation of social classes to such an extent that to appropriate the war metaphor for oppositional uses, as in class war or struggle, is to risk the denomination 'political', and to place the 'sectional' over the 'national'. The colonization of *forms* is almost total, a tribute to what Barthes calls the full effect of 'bourgeois ex-nomination', its *naturalization* of what originated in class-specificity: 'the function of myth is to empty reality' — 'things lose the memory that they once were made'.[5] This chapter is concerned with establishing ways in which 'memory' was made at the time of the Second World War, and how it has been constructed in retrospects since.

In talking of 'deconstructing' or 'liberating' myth, or 'populism', another complex problem is encountered, because, in Hall's analysis, 'it [populism] feeds off the disappointed hopes of the present and the deep and unrequited traces of the past'[6] and 'Any myth with some degree of generality is in fact ambiguous, because it represents the very humanity of those who, having nothing, have borrowed it.'[7] 'Popular consciousness' is *not* 'false consciousness' (as this presupposes the pure existence of its opposite, 'true consciousness') and 'the people' are not simply 'dupes' of the ruling class or the mass media, but make 'coherent' lives out of the existing stock of symbolism and metaphor. Meaning is commissioned from the available symbolic systems – awareness of omissions, absences, is a politicized, lateral mode of perception which can never become *popular* until the rhetoric of power becomes increasingly tautologous, lost for 'signifying' explanations. The 'popularized' is, precisely, power in its cultural form – a de-politicized *mediation*. Analysis needs to take account of political determination as well as cultural *representations*. Simply 'uncovering' the representations yields nothing – in fact, the 'uncovering' metaphor denies the complex processes involved in *re-presentation* – the stress is on the reproductive capability: verbal-visual productions, distribution, consumption and reception under capitalist relations of exchange.

By way of illustration, I shall concentrate upon three books written during or shortly after the war but not published until much later – *Mrs. Milburn's Diaries*, (1979, paperback 1980), and *Nella Last's War* (1981, paperback 1983), and Stanley Rothwell's *Lambeth at War* (1981) – and one written in recent years, *One Child's War* by Victoria Massey (1981), (also broadcast on the radio). The choice is very far from exhaustive, but the range suggests both the 'national myths' already discussed and some memories of 'the people out of step with World War II'. Some consideration will also be made of Andrew Davies's *Where Did the Forties Go?*, published in 1984, because it deals with the way memories of past events can influence the present and the future, and styles itself consciously as a 'popular' history.

Why should publishers choose to issue in 1979 or 1981 diaries written by relatively 'obscure' women in the war? Is the war, or the women, the principal motivation? Were the decisions influenced by the 'ubiquitous presence (on a truly massive scale) of "representations" dealing with the war, which are widely available today across a range of cultural forms'?[8] Or was their publication part of a process which stimulated the production/reproduction of 'representations'? Was it part of an intellectual nostalgia for the recovery of the 'unity' of a 'popular memory' – 'a left ethnology proceeding, through village chronicles and memoirs of the people, to transform a voyeuristic relation to the people into one of inheritance.'?[9] The scale of 'war representations' seems to be part of a 'right' ethnology in which the day-to-day 'scripts' of what is constructed as 'the people' are recruited to the public/national reference system, particularly in its traditionalist inflection around the natural and eternal verities – the nation-family couplet: 'people are shown not what they were, but what they must remember they were'.[10] The re-writing of the past is a site of struggle in which those generalizations which articulate most closely with the constantly revised 'national' ideology are likely to be perceived as 'real memory'. The Right *images* a simple past which, it suggests, has been blocked and repressed by the period 1945–75; its task is to fill in gaps in memory, to re-historicize [in its terms] the present by re-capturing past memory – 'to make out what has been forgotten from the traces it has left behind or, more correctly, to construct it'.[11]

These reconstructions/reprints/reproductions can be seen as constituents of a larger framework for interpreting the present, as well as what Ranciere calls, 'an amnesic culture of commemoration' [bearing in mind that 'forgetting' is a crucial part of remembering]. The dominant modes of representation (this is to say nothing of contradictory 'messages') work within a set of inscriptions 'by which the image of the social consensus is offered to members of a social formation and within which they are asked to identify themselves. It functions as a reserve of images and manipulator of stories for the different modes of configuration (pictorial, novelistic, cinematic).'[12] It is this 'reserve of images' (repertoire) which the configurations *share*, despite their different inflexions. As Ranciere argues, against Foucault, there is no value in claiming to recall *the* popular memory since this might only be an instance of the latest re-inscription. Those 'memories' are selected which help to constitute a *unitary* memory; the potentially *divisive* is either omitted or carefully inscribed as divisive/deviant.

This has not been theorized and in order to provide an analysis, I have used Stephen Heath's essay 'Contexts'[13] which draws upon recent psychoanalytic writings. He quotes Lacan at one point: 'Is this, as it may seem at first, an emphasis on the past? Things are not so simple. The history is not the past. It is the past insofar as it is historicised in the present – historicised in the present because lived in the past. The path of the restitution of the history of the subject takes the form of the restitution of the past.'[14] The contemporary re-writing of history is part of a socially motivated/class-specific ideological process which foregrounds 'the category of the individual'[15] as a *natural* structuring practice. The *testimony* of individual women and men (mainly women in this case) authenticates the presented 'record' and fits in with the notion of the primacy of the individual as a category of cultural discourse. The *form* of the discourse guarantees/validates its meaning. So the past is rewritten with both 'great' individuals [King, Queen, Churchill, Montgomery] and 'lesser' individuals, linked structurally by the organizing principle of the 'representative' individual – leaders and 'people'. An individualist morality has been re-written into popular memory of the war.

Representations of the past are implicated in a process of ordering, and narrating; it is, however structured, a historical discourse. Heath suggests that in classic cinema 'family romance is there as the point of such a discourse' ... 'the constant force of the narrative of history given is familiar and family history: individuals, lives, passions, mothers, brothers, sisters, sons, daughters, the whole panoply of domestic conflicts. History is shut in to that order, provided with the perfection of a story ("a closed discourse with both a finality and an end").'[16] Finally Heath argues, 'History is not an immanence but a production of discourse, the guarantee of which for the historical film is present, political, in the present political relations of the spectator to history and to his or her history in this film.'[17]

The usefulness of the war for the constructions of national memory in its populist inflexion is that it is 'a closed discourse' and 'popularization' can be shut in to that order, given the perfection of a *story* – an effective ideological narrative. In *Nella Last's War, One Child's War, Mrs Milburn's Diaries* – the familiar and the familial (even if shaped around lack, loss, absence, evacuation, incompleteness) are the 'cement' of the discourses, as they are the 'cement' of *popularization*. Whatever their reception, they are marketed as interpellant 'memories', addressed to the 'family romance' we all experience. Britain was a 'family at war', its conflicts 'tidied up' by retrospective 'fictions', fashioning and refashioning popular memory.

Strangely, the two books written during the war offer two challenges to the ideological sketch offered here. *Mrs. Milburn's Diaries* are marked by repeated attempts to *publicize* the private – in the form of notices on the WI board, letters to the local papers, extracts of her POW son's letters sent to the editor of the *Coventry Telegraph* and to the POW magazine. The diary reflections express a ceaseless desire for self-publicizing: governor of the Council Schools, Land Army, WI etc. – to the point that the 'private' is almost evacuated. *Nella Last's War*[18] questions the 'biological imperative', particularly self-sacrifice for her husband which she sees increasingly as a 'deformation' and which forms the 'latent' narrative of her record. The recuperative value of these books lies in their representativeness, their generalization, with the women styled as 'mother' and as 'Englishwoman'. Middle-class English women have always had an 'allotted' public space (voluntaristic). Nella Last's introspections are private and never surface in action, and, moreover, are 'placeable' as a response to the aberrant conditions of war – her 'feminism' can be shut in to that order, end-stopped by 1945.

As contesting social images are shaped from a common

stock of references and concepts, no single appropriation of a particular form of writing can ever be complete or finally closed off. Separation, loss, homelessness, rationing, black market activity, air raid shelters, bombing, saving, conscription, shifting sexual mores were all part of the experience, or at least awareness, of most people in World War Two. How this 'experience' is deployed, its forms of representation, varied considerably but, recently, Conservatism has utilized a rich imagery drawn from the war which has convinced many people that its version of both the war and, by extension, current social reality is 'authentic' and 'natural'.

Nella Last's War is a diary compiled during the war by a conservative, lower middle-class woman living in Barrow for whom the war experience produced an awakening of consciousness about her role as a woman which, in many ways, challenged, and challenges, traditionalist ideologies of 'a woman's place'.[19] Certain aspects of the diary, therefore, do not fit in with the dominant imagery of the 'national memory', because one of the characteristics of the current 'siege-mentality' is a defence of the 'feminine' tradition.

The marketing of the book, however, attempts to recuperate this contradiction, in some ways, by styling the publication 'A Mother's Diary', and by using (in the paperback edition) a photo of the author on the front cover, permed and wearing her fur, foregrounded against a scene of street devastation. The scene is faded and indistinct and dominated by the 'period' marker of the oval photograph. The cover both salvages the past and announces that it is gone for ever. Additionally, the edition uses as an epigraph: 'next to being a mother, I'd have loved to write books', a quotation from the diary. What is being generalized, made publicly 'meaningful' is her 'motherness'. The specific experience – Nella Last's *war* – remains firmly grounded in the private. What is being marketed is a construction of the diary which codes and categorizes it in order to signal a limited range of possible interpretations – personal, domestic, local, narrow. Churchill or Montgomery's 'experiences' are *history*, they are image-makers, national constructs. A personal-public division is being reaffirmed. *War Diary* by Nella Last would have emphasized the *war*, the chosen title marginalizes the war and prioritizes the mother/the person. The production of the *book* builds in a 'preferred reading', although, obviously, it cannot foreclose other possible readings.

There are two other interesting 'production' factors which need attention. The first is that the diary was originally published (in 1981) by Falling Wall Press, edited from over two million words written from 1939 until the 1960s. The decision to publish only the 'war' section suggests that the 'reconstruction genre' determined the production, rather than the diary 'in itself':

> We decided that we would edit the book only if Falling Wall Press were going to publish it. The press's commitment to the experience of 'ordinary' people, and especially women, combined with the certainty that we would have complete editorial control and be able to determine the design and presentation of the book, were crucial factors in our feeling able to undertake the huge editorial job involved.[19]

What is said about the Press is true, it is a small, radical press with a 'progressive' record, and the document *is* unique. The editors have supplied notes to guide the reader through the diary and to set the story in the context of the major events of the war 'from the point of view of the writer'. It is clear that what was intended was a 'representation' which would in some ways challenge the Conservative 'national popular' memory of the war. This it does, but the problem is that in the paperback 'construction' of the diary a particular cultural form is being proposed which defuses its 'radical' challenge.

The second factor of importance is that the diary was, in its original form, a letter diary written for Mass Observation which explains its formal properties and the ways in which it was shaped in response to questions sent by

MO – the material on dreams and relationships are particularly noticeable. So, it is a 'private' memory with an archival structuring, part of a larger project, sociologically and anthropologically conceived, in which the 'personal' was already constructed at a potentially generalized and representative level. If, as the editors say, Nella Last was 'recording . . . the texture of her times', the way in which that texture was registered depended, in some ways, upon a primary ordering beyond the writer. The record was generated, of course, from the already existing pattern of personal and social interactions, the local and domestic referents, which shaped her daily experience, but the mental landscape revealed owes a lot, in structure not detail, to the originating archive. A diary is itself an ordered narrative, it is 'narrowly' retrospective, systematized, partly by the 'memory' of the day and, in this case, also formalized (given *form*) by the MO methodology. These reports from voluntary observers were not designed to be published [so avoiding at least some degree of self-censorship], but they were used as the basis for critical and quite radical reports by MO, the findings based on an 'anecdotal map' of Britain. This context suggests a possible element of 'performance', and self-consciousness about interaction and about language, a disposition to analysis, and the 'transactional' nature of the recorded observations – i.e. did the material fit into the framework, or did the framework determine the selective perceptions? MO's premise was based upon 'the science of ourselves' and *Nella Last's War* is a remarkable instance of extensive self-analysis combined with a stock of set expressions designed to interpret circumstances of abnormal occurrence. The diary as published has three elements – the 'historical' space of the editorial notes, the 'mental' space of the awakening observer, and the 'conventional' space of the middle-aged Barrow mother and wife. It is the complex and contradictory relationship between informant and her testimony which could enable the document to be appropriated by the 'Right' for its 'popular memory' and also for an 'oppositional' construction of 'popular' memory. In the fictions previously studied, similar contradictions are sited and resolved – here the contradictions are unresolved in a form of writing which inhabits the boundary between private and public in its provenance and its forms. Its representational codes admit double and contradictory articulation as part of a conscious and unconscious refashioning of the past.

The diary is constructed around a subjective/objective dialectic, indicated by the differentiated 'spaces' already mentioned. The 'mental space' (the private private) perspectivizes the 'conventional space' and vice-versa. In the 'conventional space' she is aware of, and possibly overcodes, her 'typicality', her 'ordinariness'. This space is a particularized, local reflection of components of a traditionalist ideology – moral, familial, passive, self-reliant.

The 'conventional space' is also defined by the WVS Centre, the shop and the canteen – all of which she invests in very heavily as a form of 'service'. At the same time, she recognizes that this service is part of a sublimation, what she calls 'a kind of "polishing up the dark side".' The feeling of crumbling somewhere inside, the sense of something which started dying, together with her 'nerves' and fixated dreams of shipwrecked sailors compose what I have called the 'mental' or introspective space of the diary. In this space, she speculates and dares to name her mostly sublimated fears and frustrations, she generalizes her situation from woman to women, speculates about her possible representativeness and whether the war will release people from taboos and inhibition: 'After all these peaceful years, I discover I've a militant suffragette streak in me, and I could shout loudly and break windows and do all kinds of things – kick policemen perhaps – *anything* to protest' (p.77) and 'I suppose you would think I was putting a brave face on it if I told you I'd sooner *die* than step into the frame you make for me. Do you know, my dear [to her husband], that I've never known the content . . . that I've known since the war started' (pp.90–1). In some senses, even though there is frequent

reference to having the things which 'make a woman's
life', the diary registers a form of 'breakdown' (euphem-
ized as 'nerves'); or, rather, the diary *is*, rather than registers, the 'breakdown' – it is the *form* which it takes. In
the 'conventional space' of home and centre this breakdown never takes place. The diary is a liberating mode:
'A woman was expected – and brought up – to obey, and
we had not got far from the days of Victorian repression:
men expected to be masters in matters widely to do with
sex' (p.159 – thoughts prompted by a question about the
war's effect on sex in a MO questionnaire, which she
answers indirectly by recounting a story told to her by a
parish nurse). She regards herself as 'in rhythm now,
instead of always fighting against things' and freed from
the 'slavery years of mind and body' when she had to do
what her husband liked. The *rhythm* is both expressed in,
and partly created by, the form of the diary. The central
contradiction is formulated in response to her son,
Arthur's, comment 'You make home too attractive, dearie
– and it's turned into your prison,' when she reflects 'But
when I look at my husband's tired face sometimes, I
wonder what else I could have done.' Yet, she is opposed
to the conscription of women in case they will not settle
later to homes and children, at the same time as she feels
'thoroughly out of time' because she has a 'growing
contempt for man in general' and no longer thinks herself
'odd' or 'uneducated', although she also feels that she
wants to cry 'Mothers UNITE. Let's all be old-fashioned.'
So, 'emergent feminist' ('I can never go back to that
harem existence my husband thinks so desirable' – p.289),
advocate of Beveridge, critic of Vera Lynn's 'nostalgic
whine', and yet also voting for Churchill, 'We got a real
shock when we heard our Conservative member had been
beaten by 12,000 – we simply could not believe it.' This
latter remark re-incorporates her into the conventional,
shared space of a class-fraction and generation which the
diary has repeatedly interrupted, broken up.
In what the diary's editor calls 'the unusual self-
consciousness of language' what we see is not some kind

of 'innate tendency' but an effect produced by the MO framework – an opening up of alternative perspectives prompted by an awareness that there was in London a 'receiving set' for whom there was the need to 'anthropologize' herself and her locality – perhaps, there is even a consciousness of the class/metropolitan difference of the 'receiver'. This awareness is another perspectivizing, generalizing characteristic – it lifts the diary out of the private, problematizes the 'personal', and also sets into motion a profound questioning of the MO assumptions about 'the men in the street', 'ordinary people'. This is the 'performance' element which unfixes the point of view (a *Mother's* diary) and dramatizes it. What the editor calls the 'idiosyncratic frequency with which Nella Last puts words and phrases into inverted commas' (p.318) is precisely the anthropological 'technique', part of an extensive quotation from her linguistic/cultural/generational stock and from her 'tribal dialect'. This is the 'mental space' entering the conventional. The published text has removed almost all of these explanatory 'quotations' and traces – seeing herself from the outside – in the interests of 'readerliness'. What we lose is the 'writerly' text.

At one point (p.296) Nella Last speaks of the 'false sentiment my generation had been reared with, the possessiveness which stood as the hallmark of love, with no regard to differences in temperament, inclination or ideals . . . when a person of limited vision, or just plain fear of life, could crib and confine more restless spirits'. In a broader sense, this 'false sentiment' of a generation is the lived experience of *Mrs. Milburn's Diaries* in which the writer, unproblematically, 'thinks' categories of 'Englishness', the social imagery mobilized by a class in the terms of national 'unity', expressed in symbols constructed around 'moral entrepreneurship' and a 'patrician morality'.[20] It is this structure of 'symbolic' Englishness (the diaries are sub-titled 'An Englishwoman's day-to-day reflections') which is the principal organizing feature of the diaries, predicated upon a total identification with a traditionalist script in which 'one's' position is infinitely generalizable: 'one' is 'everyone'. It is not a simply a matter of content, nor of attitude, but also a question of *discursive form*. Mrs Milburn is a self-styled 'moral entrepreneur'. Her attitudes resemble those described by Mary Lee Settle: 'The people seemed not so much changed by the state of war as shrunk by it; they seemed to be protecting oases of comfort or stability and gave a sense of hiding and hoarding, not material things – the English were too honest for that – but habits, a way of having days, old wornout prejudices that no longer fitted the circumstances. We may look back with a mistaken nostalgia; but that is youth we miss, not the state of war – where we were shrunken, cramped in gesture, acquiring those habits which protected and hid us from some abstract force no one could name but which threatened loss and exposure.'[21] This analysis in *All the Brave Promises*, part of a complex and profound 'memoir' of World War Two by an American who served in the WAAFs, helps to focus on the 'reconstruction genre' itself: it seeks to liberate a nostalgia in which 'repeating the same ritual year after year is a way of *stopping* time, of keeping it fixed at some point in the past' thereby 'mythologizing' the past in the process.[22] This not only locates the 'reconstruction genre' but also helps to place the methodology of *Mrs. Milburn's Diaries* – the euphemistic language is part of a habit developed to 'protect and hide', to 'deprivatize' the emotions by performance, gesture, lexical 'indexings' which constructed a 'deflective', 'transcendent' mode of discourse which *distanced* loss and exposure. This helps to explain how, *discursively*, Mrs Milburn handled her son's five year imprisonment in a POW camp. The 'hiding and hoarding' is linguistic/cultural as well as a traditionalist reflex. This raises the larger question as to whether this public/private discourse, with its 'litotic' structure and highly affirmative images of 'Englishness' is war-specific, or part of the habits of a class or class fraction – a feature of its ideological entrepreneurship in which the 'national' is systematically inflected in its *local* representations. The war is both background and *medium*. The *Diaries* were published, in 1979, as part of a broader cultural mediation, a popularization, not of the war itself but of the war as a re-discovered symbolic space, selectively appropriated to mobilize images of 'Englishness' deployed in a contemporary power struggle over meanings, attempts to negotiate and produce hegemonized 'memories'.

Unlike *Nella Last's War* these diaries were not prompted by MO, or any other agency, but they were not simply 'private'. The structure, the language, and the references suggest a certain 'public' aspect, an awareness of an audience. From time to time an entry refers to comments made by friends who had been sent copies of the diary, and also to family readings of the previous year's record. This indicates a target circle of readers/listeners who could be assumed to share the attitudes and values. Certain habits of phrasing, almost a class fraction 'argot' at times, strengthen this sense. A similar awareness of a 'public' characterizes the way in which she sends her son's POW letters to the local evening newspaper and to the POW magazine. This stems from a particular kind of rural middle-class ideology, the need to be confirmed repeatedly at a public level of existence – opening fetes, WI secretary, Church, friend of the Cathedral, Council School's governor, British Legion, Land Army administration, and Mother's Union. This ritual behaviour is a particular mode of interpellation – a form of empowerment, a way of sedimenting the 'patrician hegemony' in, and through, local forms. What the diaries reveal most sharply is the continued existence of marked class divisions – the family's gardeners are simply referred to by their surnames – Wilks, Robbins etc. The two cars, the good clothes, the relatively easy access to 'black market' goods, contrast sharply with Michael Foot's 'restrospective' on the war: 'It was a democratic society with a common aim in which many of the class barriers were being broken down.'[23] Mrs Milburn does talk of 'mateyness' and of getting to know her neighbours through various house-to-house collections (not otherwise) but her 'world' is nevertheless one in which everyone is firmly 'placed'. As Laurence Harris has said: 'the private ownership of capital meant that the economic basis of the old class structure was unchanged . . . wartime Britain's social divisions were class divisions . . . the essential character of the capitalist economy was reproduced during the war.'[24]

The diaries articulate a number of positions from deep within the ideological character of the capitalist economy – its symbolic/cultural forms of 'Englishness' with cultural dependence upon 'significant others'. There is the personalized/familiarized identification with the monarchy, with the King seen as 'Head of our great Family', as keen attention is paid to making sure the Union Jack (bought for her husband's birthday) is hung correctly. She sees herself, her family, her values as emblematic, representative – standard bearer of the dominant ideology: 'We had invited our friends James and Edie to a chat and sherry at 11.30 a.m. because the black-out makes afternoons difficult.' The editor stresses this 'representative' quality: 'Of course many millions of women throughout the world had shared that experience of war, and in many ways Clara Milburn was not very different from them.' In addition to this, the editorial suggests a sexist categorizing: 'Being a woman, she also wrote of her clothes and her garden. Being an Englishwoman, she wrote a good deal about the weather.' Her 'old-fashioned' qualities of womanliness and Englishness are offered in 1979 as a counterweight to 'feminism' and a lack of patriotism. Her testimony is clearly separated, by the editors, from those of 'generals, politicians and pundits' in rather condescending fashion. Though published prior to the Falklands War, many of the sentiments expressed come close to the 'gotcha/rejoice/our boys' newspaper rhetoric with *its* echoes of 1940. In fact, the Falklands War was the supreme instance of the 'retro mode'.

The diaries combine personal 'notation' with reiteration of the public events of the war culled from radio and newspaper. It is hard to avoid the sense that the war is being experienced vicariously as an adventure. The appropriation of 'news' reproduced with specific inflections

('The Finns are wonderful . . . and manage to hold out against fearful odds') gives the diaries the form of a synthetic, tabloid commentary. The frequent use of 'we' conflates person with nation in a model ideological transformation into a 'public voice'. 'We sank a German ship in the Kattegat yesterday' (p.31), 'Our air losses are comparatively few, we are very thankful to say', 'But, nevertheless, we shall get over it. We must' (p.146). There is none of the reflection, questioning, or contradictory articulations of Nella Last. The diaries have been marketed because 'they seemed to speak not just of England then but of England now'[25], constructed around a set of assumptions trapped in the myths and rhetorical tropes of the past – a way of sanctioning the present by basing it upon the past.

There is also mixed in with the characteristic understatement (used to displace the emotional) a certain, perhaps understandable, relish – 'This afternoon we heard the good news that 140 aircraft had been destroyed in yesterday's attempt to bomb London' (p.62) unaccompanied, except for the occasional 'humane' reflection, by any perspective on the war, other than this reversal of the understatement, a certain militant, 'macho' feeling: 'Germany . . . had to be paid in her own coin', 'Nevertheless it is a great haul [68,000 prisoners]', 'A very nice surprise for our 'Wop' enemy.' In comments like these it is more than the immediate enemy that is being commented upon, I feel. This is a familiar articulation of, what Barthes calls, 'The other [who] is a scandal which threatens his essence.'[26] In Marx's terms, the diaries are significant because the writer, and her milieu, can be understood in this way: 'What makes them representative of the petit-bourgeois class, is that their minds, their consciousness do not extend beyond the limits which this class has set to its activities.'[27] It is the kind of 'self-party-class-nation' preference which marks the *discursive* limits of the text, its formal, unreflective closures – lexical and ideological. 'Myth' has become 'speech justified *in excess*'[28]: 'When it becomes form, the meaning leaves its contingency behind; it empties itself, it becomes impoverished, history evaporates, only the letter remains.'[29] In this sense, *Mrs. Milburn's Diaries* become like Thatcher's post-Falklands Cheltenham speech – full of form and empty of meaning, dependent entirely on the 'signifiers'.

A final instance of the way in which meaning is evacuated by rhetorical form, pastiche almost, can be seen in the V.E. Day entry:

> This morning's weather seemed symbolic. It was as if in the thunder one heard Nature's roll of drums for the fallen, then the one loud salvo of salute over our heads and the tears of the rain pouring for the sorrow and suffering of the War. And then the end of the orgy of killing and victory symbolized as the sun came out and shed its brightness and warmth on the earth.(p.370)

It is difficult to determine whether the 'public' voice, the parochial 'sovereignty', the rhetorical configurations, and the incorporation of the 'events' of the war into a personal register are all part of a commitment on behalf of a 'unitary subject', or if these represent a *displacement*, a sublimation of the fact that, as a woman, she has no public voice, *is* parochialized and marginalized – powerless, but actively pretending to be the centrepiece of the parade of power. At the fancy dress party, this identification is symbolically completed when she appears as 'Britannia' – the nation as a woman – 'Then the evening came and I went across and did my part with the 'properties' for the entertainment and stood at the end as 'Britannia' with a very sad heart. But it is best to go on, with whatever is one's job at the moment' (p.104). Perhaps the war simply magnified, put into relief, a never articulated 'quiet desperation' – deflected endlessly by roles, parts, performances, linguistic 'bran tubs', rhetorics designed to defer repeatedly the confrontation with the real by the construction of symbolic codes for interpellation. Mrs Milburn is for ever *doing*, never *being* – she is constantly arranging her image, and imagery, for the *public* gaze. There is a latent fragility in all the unity and coherence – kept at bay by the endless myths surrounding her 'trusteeship' – the components of tradition, loyalty, *voluntary* action which substitute for herself a *conscript* Englishwoman serving the 'patrician hegemony'.

This is, admittedly, all very speculative but it does point to a possible deconstructive activity which destabilizes what appears to be an empiricist, essentialist text generalizing and 'speaking for' the unity of the nation, a series of abstract viewpoints authenticating themselves by the 'evidential' chronicle. It may be that the narrative 'voice-over' is only one among many textual voices – not as 'representational' as it would seem. It is 'common sense' which leaves no trace of its inventory, as Gramsci said, but the *Diaries* may, subtextually, contain an inventory which struggles with the completed writing.

The marketing of this generic category of 'women's writings' is, in fact, a means of transforming material social subordination into 'sovereignty' through role – mother, wife, grandmother, writer. All the stress is on the *active* woman, discarding the cultural passivity of gender socialization. At the same time, in its particular inflection here, the war is localized to such an extent that its principal co-ordinates of destruction and death are virtually evacuated by the strategy of over-personalization: the entrepreneurial 'I' which 'blackcloths' the war and diminishes it. In this retrospective genre, there is the danger of a 'portmanteau memory' (in Sartre's phrase) a portmanteau notion of the experience which brings its own interpretation with it.[30] 'Process', 'experience', 'memory' leave no space for analysis, for other than 'subjective' dimensions, a form appropriate to the recent re-discovery of 'neo-liberal individualism'.

In their re-presentation through the medium of radio or television, these autobiographies not only assume, and are constructed as having, a certain *representativeness*, but their *mode* of writing is marketed as an exemplary form of the democratic *subject* – private, local, commonsensically constructed, 'free', de-politicized and de-historicized. These 'representative autobiographies' generate a 'collective representativeness' based upon a romantic ideology of the 'self-produced' subject – a collective, generational 'truth', essentialist in its assumptions. Like popular/popularized songs – e.g. 'Keep Smiling Through' – they are not 'escapist' in that they turn from 'reality' but it is what they turn 'reality' into in the process of popularization: they empty it of its 'inventory', leave only its 'traces'. They drawn upon the stock 'memories' of war in order to *forget* it, rather than remember it. In the name of perspective, everything is put out of any perspective other than the 'personal'.

One Child's War[31] by Victoria Massey, is part of what Susan Briggs[32] has called 'retrospective souvenirs recollected in tranquillity'. The cover description signals its anamnesic function: '*One Child's War* is a brilliant evocation of growing up in the Second World War which will bring back memories for many people.' The structure of the book derives from the 'Life is a Story' metaphor. By operating within a conventional framework, the 'memory' is naturalized. No account is taken of the problematic nature of recall. Signification is a *given* inherent in the temporal, spatial and psychological dimensions of the text. The connectives are neutrally produced, part of the empirical record. The limited dimensionality of the text is prefigured, and validated, by its title – it is *not* a child's war, but much more specific. The question raised by such a structure of sequence and causality is whether the narrative *reflects* the 'experience', or whether the conventional metaphor ('life is a story') conveys the coherence; or, further, whether the coherence is a combination of discursive mode and the post-experience social, cultural and political images of that period's coherence. The book opens with the child's first day at infant school. The memory is partly composed of key 'signifiers' – cold toast, toothbrush, clean face towel – and partly 'written up: 'Yet despite so much industry, our surroundings offered an open and almost rural aspect' (p.7). The text frequently shifts from a formal to an informal register to produce its 'transhistorical' discourse. The formal is stylized and distant, mannered at times in the idiom of the self-taught drawing upon conventions at random. At times, this idiom has the effect of 'past-ing' the autobiography, as does the iconic periodization. Another stock 'trope' of this kind of writing seems to be a form of self-deprecation, particularly in physical terms. This particular text is also intensely visualized, especially in respect of the adults who are seen distorted and deformed into caricature by the reconstruction of the child's perspective, at the same time as the writer as 'historian' records: 'That village nursery class of forty years ago was well equipped' (p.11). Although there are extensive periods when the text is simply 'reconstitutive', it does not attempt to blot out the moment of writing. The discourse is also marked by a euphemistic style. Early memories are invoked in cameo, set-piece fashion – time-stops – so much so that the children 'faced the war fat with memories'. 'As I speak of myself and Joe before the war came, a flash of colour with figures . . . comes to mind' (p.18). This is true also, of course, of the writer as adult 'recalling' the war, and perhaps accounts for the mixed literate/oral mode of telling and the use of the 'flashbulb' technique of memory – the determining contours of biography. The narrative slips in and out of time – pausing to re-enact the 'feel': 'Be careful as you run through the tunnel', and standing back to 'anthropologize' her milieu: 'Nanny, the polite name given to working-class grandmothers who prefer not to sound old' (p.19).

The opening chapter carefully details and situates the central participants – mother, brother, schoolfriend and self. Everything is reduced to the personal reference – 'I clearly remember the day the war started because it was the day Joe and I had our photographs taken' (p.23). Does she remember the day because of the photographs, or do the photographs 'remember' the day? On the same page she demonstrates her own method – 'Later when our own images had been captured and were under development, we would be brought back to stare at the mysterious pictures of ourselves floating in a bowl of liquid' (p.23).

One of the problems of the 'souvenir' or 'scrapbook' mode is that it deals with captured and developed images, retrospectively set into motion as part of an 'already known' (ideologically, historically and personally), preconstructed process which re-arranges it sequentially, causally, and logically (ideologically?). It is the *images* which dominate, hence the privileging of the 'anecdotal' mode in this kind of discourse.

Even though the memory is of *one* child's war, the narrative structure, the shared period signifiers and the familiar codings, generalize the experience and mobilize other people's memories to such a point, that certain *ways* of remembering are privileged and others repressed. The 'autobiography' is constructed in response to a number of 'questions', the forms of which may go beyond the 'person' – how we remember is part of a larger social process bound by dominant empiricist traditions. At the same time, a memory confined by a simulated child-like perception can aestheticize/glamorize certain *shared* memories (e.g. the Anderson shelter) while focusing on the specific distress of the child. It is the generalizing perspective, not the particular one, which tends to reinforce, rather than question, myths of the war: for example, 'suddenly it was like Christmas in reverse' is a dramatic way of characterizing the onset of war, but the almost excessively metaphoric form of the text means that precision is registered through objects and metaphor which *suggest* memories metonymically – they are the *forms* of memory which stand in for memories themselves: tin hat, gas masks, shelters, *Horlicks* tablets, *Ten Green Bottles*, identity discs. These are the anamnesics of this kind of discourse – the war is reduced to iconography, as in the television series *Now and Then* and *How We Used to Live*, in which 'Then' is a full-finished 'memory' and 'used to' is the organizing category of the series. The synchronic orders, and overdetermines, the diachronic: 'I had a quaint dolls' cot made from her wood, peculiarly reminiscent of the thirties' (p.30). The distinctiveness is in the period markers, the 'generic' codes, or, what the text calls, the 'magic moment'.

Like the 'labels flapping in buttonholes' of evacuees, it is not so much the words (details) of memories such as *One Child's War* which register but, by analogy, 'the sound itself' which signifies – images like 'labels', inter-pellant forms. This is not to dispute the memory but to analyse its structuration and potential *use*, particularly the repeated codings of war childhood – pixie hoods, identity labels, and gas mask boxes.

The experience of evacuation in north Wales is poignant and echoes, and is echoed in, other similar memories. There is no attempt to glamorize. Like the initial experiences of school the method used is based upon set-piece 'visuals' and caricatures of adults, mixed with attempts to construct 'memories' of her distant parents captured in vision and smell – metonymic strategies: 'I painted vividly on the walls of my memory cave.' This visual memory-making activity linked with her artistic skills formed the basis of her survival in north Wales. The activity is not unlike the process of reconstruction which characterizes the book, with its emphasis on the way in which the past is *fashioned*. There are several such, conscious or unconscious, metaphors of the retrospective method. It helps to reconstitute the *present* in unitary terms, especially perhaps for a generation 'displaced' by the 1960s and 1970s, or which might perceive itself in these terms. The 'retro mode' is one of many 'voices of the forties' consistently being heard. We do not remember 'narratively'; we recall 'set pieces' under particular stimuli and thread them into a narrative.

When the children return home, the text structures the moment significantly in terms of repetition: 'The same old pictures were on the walls. The little boy above our heads still crawled from the coal scuttle eating coal. The same little boy opposite the window stole jam, as he always had' (p.85). It is significant that this is a return only for a fortnight's holiday – hence the *intensity* of the obser-vation, not for itself but for its potential as memory. The retrospective genre is constructed in a similar way, around an intensity of focus on the repeated, the patterned, the sameness, the 'in and through time' of 'as he always had'. Whatever the differences in emphasis and detail in the genre, it is this *structural feature* which defines and orchestrates the anamnesic codes, it is a way of cutting across an inevitable orientation in time, especially if that time is experienced as in any way ambivalent or in crisis. The retrospective mode is a cultural form of 'crisis-management', a means of preserving equilibrium and reducing anxiety. The 'war' is less important than the way it is handled, remembering also that the 'war metaphor' dominates our own cultural mediations of politics.

The ways in which the family's poverty is coded deflects and deforms it as a *political* experience – it is re-cast in the terms of the child's perception and therefore loses its contextual significance. The childhood memory of war is more important as part of a genre of 'childhood memory': 'I remember the golden days, before the war was over and my body had begun to play tricks on me, when we girls and boys alike were hard and brown and sturdy' (p.113). The war is transformed into a pre-pubescent 'moment', outside of the time of gender differentiation and patriarchal structuring, an illusory 'golden age', an interlude: 'Why in real life were all men horrible?' (p.120). As part of this section (chapter thirteen) there is another insight which illuminates the 'retro' mode:

> Surely there was a real place where you always had the feeling you had at the end of a film, when the music went up, and there were prickles behind your eyes, or as you felt when they played *Jewels of the Madonna* at the beginning of the serial on Children's Hour? It was just this place that was horrible. One day I would leave home and find a place like that. (p.120)

The text both deploys, and distances, this romantic perception drawn from the codes of fiction with *its* coherences. Nostalgia focuses on 'a place like that' and never 'this place' (for place, time can be substituted). The text is constructed as a *rite de passage*, with the war as its ritual form, a transition from child to woman, innocence to experience. What is remembered is not *the* time, but *our* time then – youth. The war is an oblique presence in this mode. The last section of the book confirms my reading in its *overcoding* of VE day with the onset of Victoria's period! Photographs were taken of VE Day and '[I] deliberately glanced away from the cake ... just in case I should appear to all posterity as greedy' (p.123). This stylized self-consciousness, this leaping in and out of the frame, is the most effective feature of the text's method. The stylization is continued in the metonymic 'period' – when Victoria stands in for the whole war experience. The method is an elaborate, almost metaphysical piece of 'wit' – the whole memory is a spatial conceit: 'Then the party was over. . . .'

The whole book is constructed around a series of 'stills'. *One Child's War* is not only a memory of 'how it was', but is constantly seeking to find metaphors, analogues, and formal codes for how it was. More interestingly, it is not one child's war, but war seen *as a child*, an extended 'spatial' moment prior to re-entry into time. The book is capable of variable appropriation – public/national (e.g. *Woman's Hour*) as part of a generic category, or 'oppositional' because of its discursive mode of making visible its processes, marking its *production*. Although it problematizes its representational forms by showing them *as* representational, this doesn't forestall 'readings' within a particular *conformism* as is evidenced by its serialization on *Woman's Hour* and the possibility of 'infantilizing' war and evacuating its death and destruction.

One of the problems with writings such as *One Child's War* is that war simply becomes a metaphor, a set of verbal/visual signifiers. This is particularly so in *popularized* memory, that which is foregrounded and 'marketed' by commercial processes, the repeated generic media constructions of public/national memory. Even if the particular cultural form is structured around the 'private', it is articulated to a public, shared image through its positioning of women and the centrality of familial discourse. The situation is not without contradictions, evidenced by *Nella Last's War* among others but also in a number of television and radio productions such as David Hare's *Licking Hitler* (1978), Dennis Potter's *Blue Remembered Hills* (1979), Ian McEwan's *Imitation Game* (1981), Trevor Griffith's *Country* (1981) and a drama series like *Tenko*. None of these, however, works from within the generic conventions and stereotypes of character, setting and relationships. They interrogate historical stereotypes, interrogate the constructions of women in the popularized retrospective genre, and, above all, they centre upon a problematized narrative (formally and thematically), while deploying visual period signifiers for *secondary* purposes. In the 'generic' retrospectives, the visual signifiers dominate the narrative structure which depends for its motivation, characterization and themes upon the known, the invariable, and the preconstructed cultural significations of 'common sense'.

It is not being argued that recent representations of World War Two evacuate all competing and conflicting ideologies but that, in their popularized forms, they are articulated to a mode of reconciliation, a unity of image and theme. This is a question of cultural and discursive form and does not preclude variable and differential receptions. There is always a risk, admittedly, of memories being 'taken away' and substituted by a bland, shared unitary memory, but cultural mediation does not have the power to erase private, oppositional, 'street' memories – only to marginalize them, cordon off their space either by incorporation or exclusion.

The effects of the war were complex, ranging from a cross-class national unity predicated upon 'British character' to what Andrew Davies has called, 'a democratizing and radicalizing tendency'. Neither one nor the other of these 'extremes' enjoys an uncontested position in current reconstructions of the period, but systematic attempts in the past few years to undercut political and welfare advances of 1945–51, brought about by the democratic and radical presences during the war have meant that the 'leading' ideological representations tend towards the 'pulling together' position. Andrew Davies's *Where Did The Forties Go?*[33], written in 1984, was an attempt to 'recover' those absences from contemporary memory by locating the current dominant imagery in terms of the political developments of the post-war period constructed around cold war rhetoric and American hegemony. It is difficult to 'think' the war in its complexity because so many of its features no longer have a discursive presence in popularized vocabularies. So deep-rooted have so many metaphorical assumptions become, that contrary articulations find it hard to claim any visual or verbal space, only in the margins or the off-peak schedules. Certain alternatives are now, literally, 'unthinkable' in popularized forms because of the dominance of power-full rhetorics and images. 'To go back to the early and mid–1940's calls for a tremendous leap of the imagination because certain attitudes which today are dismissed or ignored were then commonsensical and almost taken for granted.'[34] This, like other arguments in the book, is over-simplified and lacks analytical rigour, but it does suggest that, conversely, many things which in the early and mid–1940s were dismissed or ignored have *today*, through those silenced 'voices of the forties', become 'commonsensical and almost taken for granted'.

Rhetorics of power are actively constructing visual and linguistic spaces in which to 'think' a previously 'unthinkable' post-nuclear 'future'. World War Two emptied of its horrors and destructions (with death being remembered 'statistically') provides a suitable 'back-projection' for such a scenario. 'The War Game' is still, popularly, a 'war game' [publicly spread in the form of endless computerized games and war-gaming societies], while a programme like *Threads* (1985) remains a BBC Two concern.

Part of the problem is the relative nebulousness of the radical/democratic mood; it is difficult to *image*, which in terms of genre reconstructions is deeply problematic, because the 'dominant' memory can call upon an endless number of already existing generic images, drawn from the post-war fictionalizations and the contemporary archival newsreels which were stylized, carefully edited, and 'sanitized' as part of a progaganda strategy. The 'dominant' memory is thus already inscribed in available narratives, the 'radical' has a limited access to its own 'narrativity'. It has neither story nor image in any popular sense, although Jim Allen's *Gathering Seed* (BBC Two, 1983) tried to produce both by showing 1936 to 1948 as a *continuity* in which the war was structured as a 'momentary' interruption. This battle over 'continuities' is not simply a media issue but part of a broader political struggle over where the 'old, familiar landmarks' should really be sited. Allen's drama serial was a relatively isolated attempt to deconstruct the 'popular history' of the 'hungry thirties', war as obliterating all the old structures, and the post-war as 'a new era'. Its BBC Two scheduling limited the impact of its intervention in the face of numberless other re-scriptings which were busy repositioning the 'history' (cf. Cook and Stevenson, *The Slump*) to eliminate '1945' and reclaim the war as the metaphorical basis for the 'new conservatism', a revisionist enterprise which has re-discovered inequality, market forces and non-consensus politics in the form of 'traditionalist populism'. As Davies says 'in present-day Britain . . . the whole consensus which emerged from the war is under attack – the welfare state, full employment and a public sector.'[35]

With a few exceptions, 'alternative' memories of the period have become marginalized and fragmented, confined to localized, 'gala', representations. As Anthony Barnett says, in *The Guardian*, 1985 had become the year of anniversaries, partly due to 'the big official celebration of the Normandy landings, staged last year to try and wrest the legacy of victory in the second world war away from any association with the Soviet Union'.[36] Why the 'fortieth' anniversary should have been celebrated, rather than the more customary moments, it is difficult to establish except that the build-up of Cruise and Trident missiles, and the accompanying proliferation of US bases in Britain, presumably needed cultural legitimations and a set of codes and conventions with which to signify and popularize their presence. The anniversaries of Hiroshima and Nagasaki have been variously 'commemorated', but one 'privileged' interpretation has emerged which quantifies (and legitimizes) the use of the atomic bomb in terms of 'Lives saved'. A hypothetical construction, predicated upon the presence of 'our boys' in Japan, has been used retrospectively to validate those bombs and, such is the power of certain hypotheses, possibly the 'limited' use of other such bombs in our own time. In other words, if nuclear survival has been scripted in terms of Blitz 'memories', then the 'first strike' option has now been effectively *dramatized* (the 62,000 Japanese deaths could have saved how many hundreds of thousands of British?) and entered into 'thinkable' and 'speakable' discourse. The repeated image of the mushroom cloud has now become so familiarized, that it is just another stereotype, almost a period visual signifier – it is an icon, a 'still'. By thus decontextualizing it and removing it from a network of continuities, it is recuperable for a Right interpretation of the 'necessary'.

That the task of re-animating such 'stills' and mobilizing these continuities has been part of a recent cultural/political retrieval is unquestionable, but I should like to conclude by referring to what would seem on the surface to be a parochial piece of writing: Stanley Rothwell's *Lambeth At War*.[36] This was not published 'commercially', but by the SE1 People's History Project in 1981, although written shortly after the war. Rothwell was a Civil Defence rescue worker and PT instructor, and his memoir concentrates upon his activity in the Blitz. The account moves in and out of analysis and in and out of time, but its power lies in its 'over-real' description of the destruction of war, based upon the specifics of one community but capable of wide generalization because of its graphic record of mutilation, death, loss and endless pain: 'they had been tossed there by the blast, heads and limbs missing'; 'he had a hole torn out of his groin by shrapnel from a bomb'; 'but I did not think we would have to shovel them up'; 'The only tangible things were a man's hand, with a bent ring on a finger; a woman's foot in a shoe on the window sill'. This, literal, imagery of 'dismemberment' is an effective way of contesting those remembrances constructed around the royal family and war-time newsreel archives which by their very repetition 'fascinate' as war-time footage. It is a form of *personalization* which challenges the abstractions and false personalizations of popularized memories. It constructs its own signifiers, beyond the 'conventions of remembrance'. The images *disturb* and *unsettle* not just in their immediacy, but because their discursive forms are charged with meanings, contexts and precision. They are memorable because they register what they represent – death, pain, horror – and not for their anamnesic properties. In fact, they are remarkably 'un-periodized' they are liberated from their position as simply visual/verbal signifiers.

The iconography of war is de-territorialized, the *writing* is the nightmare: 'Liquid phosphorus had splashed over him and he kept lighting up. We had to cover him with wet rags to prevent this as he dried out and they had to provide a special casket with wet sawdust lining it for his burial; thank goodness I saw no more of these' (p.29). The imagery of war which is the currency of the 'retrospective genre' is filtered, distanced, aestheticized by its insistent 'periodization', its visual (clothes, faces, black and white, war paraphernalia) and auditory (accents, sounds, songs) *pastness* which are the staple form of its historical displacement – its 'synchronism'. It would be hard to 'aestheticize' Rothwell's account of the liquid phosphorus death, or to consign that out of time. It is this 'in time', continuity aspect of his writing which characterizes its de-constructive mode. It is not simply a matter of *what* he says, but the ways in which *how* he says it takes it out of the grasp of any possible 'generic' recuperation:

On our way back we could hear the *oncoming* doodle bug

behind us *chugging* like a motor-bike, in front of us on a rise to the left we saw two semi-detached houses. A man was *digging* in a garden alongside, a little boy was *running* up the garden path towards the house, his schoolbag slung across his shoulder. At the doorway was a woman *beckoning* him to hurry indoors. The engine of the flying bomb shut off, we crouched *waiting for* the crunch. It glided over and past us and settled on the two houses all in the space of seconds. There was a loud explosion, a mushroom cloud of dust. Everything went up; no houses, no man, no mother and no boy. We picked up three dustbins full of pieces out of the rubble. The only way to identify where they were was the dampening dust and the cloud of flies. (my italics, p.32)

This is an inclusive mode of writing in which 'logically' unrelated signifiers enter into a set of relationships motivated by the use of active, present continuous verbs which dominate the first half of the 'narrative' and by the overarching image of war. With the exception of 'dampening', all the verbs in the second half are in the past tense in terminating and negating, *taking out of time*, the positives of the first half – the animate, living images. The 'we' are implicated onlookers, threatened by the same doodlebug, yet also functional in that they collect the pieces in three dustbins (metonymically suggesting the three people – man, woman, boy: familially coded even if not a family). The homeliness of the images – 'chugging like a motor-bike' and the relatively unmetaphoric writing *focuses* upon/closes up to the situation. There are (with the exception of the doodlebug) no period signifiers – the writing places the event *in time* and *through time*, it is synchronic and diachronic. The determinate absence in this extract is the future tense; the use of the present continuous implies it, but this is negated by the past tense of the second half. Only the functional (because it helps identification) 'dampening dust' is actively coded; interestingly enough, it is placed in a sentence *after* the event which it has facilitated – 'we picked up three dustbins'. So the continuous/causal narrative is not simply structured –

sequentially the last sentence is the penultimate one. The terror of the 'doodle bug' is *enacted* discursively, its effects quantified – 'all in the space of seconds'. The use of the phrase 'mushroom cloud' is drawn from 'Hiroshima' imagery, but here made effective by its translocation from the 'alien' Japan to West Norwood. The 'Englishness' of the imagery underscores this while the rhetorical trope generalizes the 'atomic' effect, as well as grounding it in 'chugging like a motor-bike'.

The visual and temporal/atemporal structures of this writing prevent the 'scene' from becoming a 'still', a period mural. Its impact lies in its *continuity* and its contrasting structures – first half sound and motion, second silence and the absence of motion. The action in the second half is *reported* upon, not 'experienced'. The negative, negating 'dust' becomes 'positive' and 'active' – 'dampening'. It is pictorial, but not a *picture*, with the 'no houses, no man, no mother and no boy' simultaneously domestic, local and actualized, and at the same time symboliz-ing/universalizing the *instant* death of 35,000 people in Nagasaki. The devastation of one becomes the devastation of the other – the *totalizing* effect of war usually forgotten by the overcoded media remembrances. Rothwell's account is both literally and temporally *continuous*: the man is always digging, the boy always running up the garden path, the woman always beckoning.

Many 'memories' of war have separated the human qualities displayed from their specific contexts. Rothwell reconnects these by rhythms which structure life 'in time' and death 'out of time' – war empties the individual of choice; the point, presumably, of the oratorio *Or Shall We Die?* with its syntax of 'choice'. Rothwell reminds us of the only *real* levelling which war brought about, and deploys a language and imagery which cannot be confined to World War Two but open out on to the experience of all and any war – you cannot pin medals on pieces of rubble.

Conclusion: beginning again

'Already a fictitious past occupies in our memories the place of another, a past of which we know nothing with certainty – not even that it is false.'[1]

One important strategy that has been used to maintain power at a symbolic level is to attempt to 'colonize' people's memory of the past, to obliterate dreams and ambitions other than those which correspond with a particular set of ideological definitions. Thatcherism has created an empty space in people's lives, filled it with public images of a privileged national past *and* of people building their own lives in their own way, while actually taking the past away from them in some respects.

As Stanley Rothwell's *Lambeth At War* indicates, however, it is possible to appropriate and make sense of parts of a national memory and national culture in ways which are critical and not reactionary. His work, along with other forms which will be examined in this conclusion, represent another kind of cultural articulation to that found, in what Patrick Wright calls, 'conscripted memories'.[2]

The Second World War has become a particular site for contesting the manufactured images of memory, and a number of television programmes, often with a local inflection, have offered alternative ways of viewing the period as ways of emphasizing that histories, like memories, are *made*. A photographic exhibition (1984) by Hannah Collins in Bethnal Green worked from within a similar perspective, focusing on the *local* and problematizing memory visually and verbally. The immediate postwar period, the basis of the so-called 'settlement' and consensus, has also been subjected to careful analysis and not simply as a way of justifying neo-liberalism. Again, television has been prominent in this process with such programmes as *Now the War is Over* (1985). A novel published in 1982, Ruth Adler's *Beginning Again*, which deals with some of the personal contradictions thrown up by the aftermath of war, particularly takes issue with the constructions of gender which formed the basis of the 'biofictions' examined in Chapter 2.³ As a way of offering another perspective on memory and the making of personal and national pasts, a BFI/BBC programme *For Memory* (1986) will be used as a critical resource.

The third series of LWT's *The Making of Modern London* (1985) focused on the period 1939–45: 'London At War'.⁴ The second programme, 'The Battle for London' sought to de-mystify the Blitz, not to deny its place in popular memory but to offer a more complex account which challenges the selective myths which appropriate it for a particular version of Britishness. Original footage of the time (blue-washed to break with some of the conventions associated with the period) was juxtaposed with voice-over and oral histories constructed from interviews with working people who were living in the East End. The programme shows how many images of war come from the consciously morale-boosting Ministry of Information (MOI) films and British Movietone newsreels, which stressed the heroism and omitted the inefficiency of the defence preparations and the inadequacy of the hastily constructed air raid shelters. Like so many other images of the period, the air raid shelter has been constantly represented in isolation as an *image* without a context. 'The Battle for London' restores the context and shows how the nostalgia for the shelters has to be placed along-side their severe limitations. The programme was not a de-bunking exercise, as it demonstrated the specifics of 'community spirit' (rescued from the nation-as-community myths), but at the same time it restored the blood, destruc-tion and bodies missing from the VE Day anniversary images.

In different forms '1945', as well as the war, is being subjected to a critical revaluation. A simple going back to 1945 in an uncritical fashion would compound a number of errors already made:

> The post-war consensus, built upon full employment and the welfare state, failed to command the support of people because they had seen first that it did not contain within it any element whatsoever of transformation, and, secondly, that even by its own criteria it failed.[5]

The BBC programme, *Now the War is Over* interestingly used the present tense in its title to suggest that many of the issues raised by 1945 are not a matter of nostalgia, or in need of simple re-iteration, but the site of a continuing debate which constantly needs to be engaged.[6] Based upon more than 200 filmed interviews, the eight-part series used a popular format (evidence by the credits and titles drawn from contemporary phrases – 'Making Do', 'From Cradle to Grave,' etc.) and made extensive use of newsreel footage, MOI films and other contemporary documents. The programme covered the whole period from 1945 to 1951 as part of a social history using a mixture of historio-graphic modes. The book of the series written by Paul Addison builds upon his earlier, and very influential, *The Road to 1945*, but is a very different kind of project which he characterizes as 'historical jounalism'. In the preface he argues that the past decade 'has been a great education for us all', a time in which both marxist left and radical right have rejected the 'social democratic legacy' of 1951, commonly seen as the definitive feature of 'consensus politics'.

Addison regards the series, and the book, as a

contribution to a 'radically revised version of the spirit of 1945'.[7] Such a phrase is deeply problematic as is his side-stepping of the issues involved in oral history: 'The interviews have been arranged and conducted according to the rules of television, not according to the rules of social science.'[8] This begs a number of large questions about the accuracy, reliability and over-determined nature of oral historiography which need, at least, to be rehearsed in a book sub-titled 'A Social History of Britain, 1945–51' especially as it is claimed that the interviews 'have flung open many a window on the period'.[9] But despite such qualifications both series and book represented a significant attempt to open up a number of questions about the post-war settlement which have been overlooked by both Left and Right. *Now the War is Over* did attempt to render individual 'stories' intelligible in a way which situated them within certain determinants, whereas the 'Right narratives', discussed in Chapters 1, 2, and 3, were conditioned by an ahistoricity which excized from the 'memories' any perspective from which the past might be questioned.

It is the purpose of this conclusion to focus upon questions of methodology which might transform existing ways of making memories in popularized forms. Recent instances of cultural practice might help to demonstrate potential changes. In July 1984 the community photographer Hannah Collins mounted an exhibition 'Evidence in the Street, War Damage Volumes' at Interim Art in Bethnal Green. Using the 'installation' format she blew up archive photographs of war damage in the community in which she lives and works, London Fields in East London. The exhibition was of three photographs with an accompanying tape presentation focused on war damage, placed alongside recently taken colour photographs. The archive photographs were tinted blue and treated with a fluid which blurred detail, while the current ones were sharply detailed, light, many coloured and neatly framed in glass. The neatness 'screens' the decay and decline of the artist's daily surroundings in Hackney, just out of the frame, so to speak. It is this decay which, apparently, prompted the artist to trace the history of the area back to the blitz. So often in 'periodized' recall it is the *images* of damage which dominate, not the damaged images. In this exhibition, the wall-sized archival materials refused the stock-shot technique and forced a process of *re-witnessing* the devastation without cutting it off from the vantage point of the present. Images of this period have so frequently been annexed to a specific visual code, that actually looking at the photographs was problematic. The 'blue wash' distanced the familiar sepia-tinted iconography. The photograph of the usually 'stock' images of air-raid shelters was effective because these are seldom, if ever, seen (or remembered) as crushed and devastated. The second photograph in which the human images were blurred revealed how the 'personal' was dominated by the gaunt, bare trees, the over-sized verticals. The final photograph looked uncannily like a modern demolition, with the exposed interior cross-section of a bombed house, and here the past-present dialectic was at its most insistent.

The photographs were beautiful, but did not aestheticize their subject to a point where they simply had the 'charm' of old photographs, because the war damage always provoked an active comparison with contemporary forms of damage. The entire exhibition problematized the issue of how 'evidence' in time and space is witnessed. The audio presentation was a series of reflections on the issues raised by the photographs, entitled 'Evidence in the Streets'. Then and now are tangled, their relationship made complex and questioned. The witness is both there and not there, installed in the present and in the archival photographs. The identity of witness and evidence is brought into a problematic interchange. The tape names the roads in the community as reminders of times and places, inhabitants and dwellers, as traces of occupations and provisions, of production and consumption, of participation and belief, and of control. It is an active, lived experience of community, not just a space but a history. The exhibition *made* and produced memories, it did not simply reflect them, but recovered them in an *active process* which shows how memory is always subjected to reconstruction. Images of the past are blurred because images of the past *are* blurred.

Patrick Wright's work, referred to in the introduction and elsewhere, Carolyn Steedman's *Landscape for a Good Woman* (1986) and Ronald Fraser's *In Search of a Past* (1984) have, in their different ways, made it possible to examine the process of making memories as something more than the compilation of linear images, and closer to what Hannah Collins calls 'tangled lines', 'tangled grey routes'. Fraser's 'search' uses both psychoanalytic and historical modes of explanation, yet problematizes both in relocating and recognizing himself in the inter-war world. The mode of writing is hesitant, reflective and uncertain. Class, gender, sexuality and memory are all questioned and 'deconstructed' as the 'subject' (an elusive category for Fraser) is framed in new ways.

In the chapters which have formed the principal 'textual territory' of this study the 'past' is not experienced as problematic or a matter of uncertainty and hesitation but simply as a way of constructing, or, more accurately, deploying a narrative form which will find the 'myth or lie that brings the past into focus'.[10] The past itself is easily disposed of, while an illusory 'past' is installed in its place, 'an *already achieved* and "timeless" historical identity which demands only appropriate reverence and protection in the present'.[11] A 'preferred continuity' is privileged over all other possible contingencies.

Carolyn Steedman's *Landscape for a Good Woman* raises a number of questions about the adequacy of theories of memory, psychoanalysis and cultural criticism for explaining those lives which fall outside certain parameters. The book is concerned with the interactions between herself and the life of her mother — 'lives for which the central interpretive devices of the culture don't quite work'.[12] The book constantly shifts register in a search for a form which will express the complexity of feeling involved in the two lives. By contrast the autobiographies considered in Chapter 1 adopted a prescribed form which homogenized feelings so that the memory was being adjusted to fit the form. Fraser and Steedman both construct an indeterminate, fluid, never completed form to accommodate the personal and collective experiences. The 'sameness' of the commercial autobiographies is treated by Steedman with reference to *The Uses of Literacy* (1957): 'This extraordinary attribution of sameness and the acceptance of sameness to generations of lives arises from several sources. First of all, delineation of emotional and psychological selfhood has been made by and through the testimony of people in a central relationship to the dominant culture.'[13] Up to a point this is true, but she neglects to mention those (like the writers studied in Chapters 1 and 2) whose relationship to the dominant culture is the result of a complex process of mobility from out of the working class, which adds a further inflection to their delineation of experience. In many cases, their own 'complicated psychology' is with-held from others. Nevertheless, the comment about the refusal of a complicated psychology to those living in conditions of material distress is an important one, but it is partly an attribute of prevailing narrative forms, the 'life is a story' metaphor discussed in Chapter 1.

Landscape for a Good Woman is not only about two lives, but about the problems involved in producing adequate metaphors with which to communicate those lives. What Steedman says about the psychoanalytic mode of explanation is also true of a certain kind of commercial autobiography and popular fiction; publishing sanctions (makes public) only specific forms of narrative:

> The narrative holds within itself sets of images that represent the social divisions of a culture, and only with extreme difficulty can it be used to present images of a world that lies outside the framework of its evidential base.[14]

Steedman's work is distinctive because it starts with an autobiographical framework which nevertheless takes explicit account of the difficulties of both writing women's history and of the problematic nature of conflicting and contesting narrative forms. She makes a valuable point, in passing, about Ronald Fraser's *In Search of a Past*, commenting on the positive way in which he allows servants of his childhood a voice, through oral history techniques, yet pointing to a structural limitation: 'But even with this replacement, the narrative continues to work in the same way, telling a story that we know already.'[15]

This 'story that we know already' is a product of a specific narrative imperative based upon *coherence*, a point made repeatedly in my earlier chapters. Steedman quotes Steven Marcus on Freud:

> What we are forced at this juncture to conclude is that a coherent story is in some manner connected with mental health . . . and that this in turn provides assumptions of the broadest and deepest kind about both the nature of coherences and the form and structure of human life. On this reading, human life is, ideally, a connected and coherent story, with all the details in explanatory order and with everything . . . accounted for, in its proper causal or other sequences.[16]

The central theme of this study has been to show how *popularization* depends upon a mode of narrativity which insists upon 'a connected and coherent story'. Arguably, the rhetoric of Thatcherism – especially as deployed in and after the Falklands War – depends for its effectivity precisely upon this same model of coherence. It is class and culture specific, but its success derives from its ability to imply that social (and mental) health is in some way connected with coherence – of nation, person and values ('All these ideas have got saddled as middle class values, but they're eternal'[17]). The interview with Mrs Thatcher quoted in note 17 is a neat summary of the ways in which a 'class narrative' produces explanation, causal sequence, and coherence, while excizing all references to class, except the comment which dismisses claims that the values (the narrative?) are middle class. The dominant discursive mobilizations of the past I have concentrated upon all work within the same narrative parameters, although not without the contradictions which have been noted.

If the past is seen as a constantly renewable and 'rewritable' phenomenon, the writing always operates within the same narrative formula. The challenges to this re-writing of the past, discussed in this conclusion, have all, to some extent, had first to engage with and problematize this formula, before they could construct oppositional ways of making memories.

Finally, I want to discuss one particular television programme, not simply for its content but as a radical methodological resource. *For Memory* (BBC Two, 1986) is a television programme organized into seven sections – 'For Memory', 'Fragile Stories', 'A Memory's Invitation', 'A Walk Through the Strange Museum', 'The Memory Keepers', 'A Historian's Remembrance Speech, Times Lost and Times Regained', and 'Myths, Legends and Lessons: The Battle of Cable Street.'[18] A linking commentary reflects on memory and its processes, with a visual focus on a futuristic city – seen, in some ways, as monolithic, uniform and reducing memory to a single dimension.

The first section concentrates upon the holocaust, linking interviews with British army unit cameramen who filmed and photographed Belsen at the end of the war, with the 1978 fictional melodrama *Holocaust*. 'A traveller once wrote: in our dreams of future cities what frightens us is what we most desire, namely to be free from the tyranny of memory, to be self-sufficient, without sense of past or future.' The future city which recurs in the programme is a space where memory is emptied, past and future evacuated. In the memories examined throughout this study the principal emphasis has been on the ways in which images, objects, and specific visual codes have stood for the past, have *stilled* it, represented it as a set of *givens*, completed and closed. In *For Memory*, it is said that 'for a long time after the second world war the photographs and documents of the German concentration camps have stood for the memory and knowledge of these events'

and it is acknowledged that in the space of a generation
photographs and documents were judged to be no longer
able to carry the weight of the events they once portrayed:

> It was as if a vital memory had been surrendered to guard-
> ians and restorers who could return it to us at will but
> with little trace of its previous existence. As if all that was
> needed to rescue lost histories was to revive them through
> the magical properties of "once upon a time", so that now
> even the most recent and turbulent past could at last be
> turned into another country.

(It is this 'once upon a time' characteristic which dominates the narrative strategies of the autobiographies and
fictions examined in Chapters 1, 2, and 3) The contradictory effect, however, these 'lost histories' are capable of
producing was registered in one response to the *Holocaust*
film which acknowledged that people wept over images
they considered unworthy of their tears. This is the point:
the 'iconic mode' is not corrupt or untrue, in any simple
sense, but unworthy of the complex processes of popular
memory. The mode simulates memory, while freeing it
from any active processes.

Between section two and three the voice over the night
cityscape says:

> Imagine a city which has no place for magicians and
> sorcerers, ju-ju men, or wizards, no belief in ghosts, relics,
> totems, charms or spells. Even in that city it would be
> impossible to silence the dead. It's more a question of how
> they would be allowed to live, how they would breathe
> and move, what stones would carry their spirit and what
> dreams demand their appearance.

This presumes a rational, ordered future which has
expelled the 'irrational', but it also raises questions about
ways in which the past is constructed, versions of it sanc-
tioned, and memories organized. The argument suggests
resistances to the homogenous and the preconstructed,
spaces in which imagination and dream have scope; in
John Berger's words, another way of telling.

The section called 'A Walk through the Strange

Museum' addresses itself to the technical resources which the programme itself is dependent upon – mechanical and electronic means of reproduction: the mediation of images always present because of methods of preservation, retrieval and reproduction. The whole of this section is framed within the larger frame of the screen itself – a metaphor of its own methodology. Image after image is animated within the frame to suggest the randomness of *mediation*. In other words, contesting versions of memory can be eliminated by the dominance of *media memory* – that which is visually reproducible in the 'strange museum'. The programme offers a verbal perspective on its problematic:

> Imagine a city where the past is past and the time is always now, for where the thought of any memory being lost is as much a cause for alarm as a memory being allowed to disrupt the city's daily life . . . in that city which dreams of living in a permanent present but does not let go of its past, freedom is advertised as freedom from history, its promises, its temptations and its demands.

In a situation where any icon of the past is immediately retrievable, then the past ceases to have any historic resonance but is infinitely assimilable to dominant versions of the present. The periodization of the past through visual codes (discussed above in Chapters 1 and 2) and the means whereby a complex historical process of understanding is surrendered to notions of epochal 'spirit' or 'values', has reduced the past to a series of long shots interspersed with a few close-ups of selected icons. The 'strange museum' has evacuated history and replaced it with a discontinuous set of linear images, stored, predictable and the only way in which the past is knowable. For all the specificity of the autobiographies, the biofictions and Delderfield's social romances there is, nevertheless, the feeling that all the detail has been recruited for its use in a permanent present: 'But this strange museum, open all night, with attendants in every room, beams its maps so perfectly that the citizens can dream themselves away from their predicament knowing that nothing has been lost.'

The two sections which follow are designed to question the ways in which an electronically mediated 'past' beams its maps so perfectly that remembering comes close to forgetting – 'the rhythm of the city's headlines', 'a paradise for amnesiacs'. Popular memory is seen as a matter of looking – 'it is not profit to stare at them for too long for a sense of the city's own time might make itself felt.'

Section five, based on the Clay Cross, Derbyshire, museum of 'people's history', shows a number of people looking very closely at photographs – it is the attitude of intense looking which is the key metaphor of this section. It is an *active* process of 'reading', decoding and interpretation in close-up. Cliff Williams, the historian who is interviewed, constantly refers to the 'veneer' of the photographs, 'company' images, which if examined reveal a *class* construction and make possible an alternative form of history. He shows that Clay Cross is far from being without history or memory, but that both have been appropriated in such a way, *acted upon* to an extent designed to induce forgetting. The media 'glance' is contrasted with the close scrutiny which opens up a meaningful distance between what is past and what is present. The programme deliberately introduces two historians – Cliff Williams and E. P. Thompson – as a contrast with the 'newsreel history' of the 'Strange Museum' section.

Section five – 'The Memory Keepers' – is concerned with transmitting a history other than the 'authorized', class one. *This* museum is seen as a means of retrieving and saving working-class history, a vantage-point for looking at the future. Thatcherism sees the future as a projection of the present – everything is recruited to that end – whereas oppositional 'memories' use the past as a resource in the transformation of the present into a different kind of future. The battle over memory is not, therefore, simply a matter of the 'record', but an active and continuing struggle over ways of seeing and recalling.

Power over 'memory' is exercised by the dominant culture as part of its constantly renewed hegemonic strategies.

It is this power which the programme seeks to contest and deconstruct, but it would be illusory to claim that it had a popular reception. It was transmitted on BBC Two on the afternoon of Easter Monday, 1986, with timing and scheduling mitigating against anything but a small audience. It was also a difficult and demanding programme, necessarily complex given its arguments and the burden of 'received memory'.

The second historian focused upon, E. P. Thompson, has a double identity as a leading left-wing academic and a radical activist in the anti-nuclear campaign. The programme concentrated on a speech he gave at the Oxford WEA meeting at Burford on the anniversary of the death of three Levellers buried in the parish church: 'A Historian's Remembrance Speech – Times Lost and Times Regained'. The Levellers are a footnote in 'received' history, *remembered* in Thompson's speech and linked with existing struggles against the late twentieth-century 'kingdom of the beast'. The past event was dwelt upon in its specificity and *its* meanings, not simply there as a medium for the contemporary point to be made. The mode was dialectical.

The concluding section – 'Myths, Legends and Lessons: The Battle of Cable Street' focuses upon one of the key moments of working-class history, but it is not so much the moment but the ways of remembering it which are foregrounded – a combination of oral history with commissioned mural. Neither was privileged over the other. The giant mural – filmed as it was being painted at night – is constructed in a way which makes it close to the linking images of the city of the future. It was as if the mural was the response to the word recurring throughout the commentary – *imagine*.

For Memory attempts to dismantle the dominant narrative codes of memory – the coherent, the connected, and the causal – and displace them with therapy, film, photograph, mural, speech, museum, fiction and history in order to suggest that remembering needs to deploy all these resources, as any one in isolation limits and distorts. It argues that images organized without inventory or contingency constitute a form of forgetting. If *everything* is 'remembered' there is the danger that, in the long run, *nothing* will be remembered: 'Memories no longer have to be held onto, protected and tended; they can be stored, replaced, rejuvenated and if need be made to appear and driven out again without trace.'

Over the past decade, Thatcherism has shed much of its radical rhetoric, modified its more obvious excesses, and successfully constructed an extremely complex, cross-class constituency, or social bloc, of support. In the process it has annexed much of the imagery and discourse of the so-called 'centre' but, more importantly, it has sustained a vocabulary of common sense which has effectively represented Socialism as being of questionable sanity ('the Loony Left') and alien to 'our' nature/nation. The election of 11 June 1987 has made the task of 'beginning again' that much more difficult, yet that much more urgent if a new cultural order is to be inaugurated as a prelude, and accompaniment, to a new political order. Not for forty years or more has it seemed so hard to recreate the verbal symbols, the images and axioms through which the concept of profound social change, rather than a negative rhetoric of adjustment and survival, could be renewed.

I have argued throughout that the interwar and war period have in the past decade become a site for the construction of a version of the national past which articulates it with Conservative ideology.[19] The period has been imaged, condensed, coded and invented. If, as David Lowenthal suggests, 'we cannot now avoid feeling that the past *is* to some extent our creation',[20] and if today's insights can be seen as crucial to the meaning of the past, then, above all, the period has to be *imagined* creatively from a number of alternative perspectives as a means of overcoming the processes of 'organized forgetting'.

'I have to be more careful about my memories, I have to be sure they're my own and not the memories of other people telling me what I felt, how I acted, what I said: if the events are wrong the feelings I remember about them will be wrong too, I'll start inventing them and there will be no way of correcting it, the ones who could help are gone.'

Margaret Atwood, *Surfacing*, 1972, p. 73

Notes

Preface

1 S. Hall, 'Gramsci and Us', *Marxism Today*, June 1987, pp.16–21.
2 The opening section of the 1987 Conservative Manifesto, 'The British Revival', produces an extremely selective one paragraph summary of the late 1970s. At the centre of this sketch are inflation, powerful unions, the Lib-Lab pact, and the 'winter of discontent'. No analysis is offered of any of the possible reasons for these circumstances; instead, in a very interesting phrase, it says 'it seems in retrospect to be the history of another country'. This, as Christopher Lasch says in his introduction to Russell Jacoby's *Social Amnesia*, 1975, is the kind of 'history' that arises from a need to forget rather than that which remembers. Hence I have called the introduction 'Organized forgetting' and have emphasized the ways in which Conservative ideology has constructed a retrospect of the inter-war period which, itself, seems to be the history of another country.

Introduction: organized forgetting

1 M. Kundera, *The Book of Laughter and Forgetting*, 1978; Harmondsworth, Penguin, 1983: 159.
2 R. Johnson *et al.* (eds), *Making Histories*, London, Hutchinson, 1982: 207.
3 Johnson *et al., op. cit.*, p. 211.
4 Interview with Michel Foucault, *Edinburgh '77 Magazine*, pp. 21–2.
5 Q. Hoare and G. Nowell Smith (eds), *Selections from the Prison*

Notebooks of Antonio Gramsci, London, Lawrence & Wishart, 1971.

6   A. Heller, *Everyday Life*, 1970; London, Routledge & Kegan Paul, 1984.

7   P. Wright, *On Living in An Old Country*, London, Verso, 1985.

8   Johnson *et al., op. cit.*, p. 256.

9   Wright *op. cit.*, pp. 135–60.

10 See Wright's treatment of the Mary Rose, *op. cit.*, pp. 162–92.

11 A. Gamble, *Britain in Decline*, London, Macmillan, Second Edition, 1985:206.

12 P. Derbyshire, 'George is Dead', *Z/G* London, ZG Magazine, 1983:116.

13 R. Levitas, 'New Right Utopias', *Radical Philosophy*, 1985:6.

14 P. Jenkins, 'Mrs Thatcher's Vision of Good', *The Guardian*, 14 November 1984.

15 In P. Golding and S. Middleton, *Images of Welfare*, Oxford, Martin Robertson, 1982.

16 *Shebbear*, Channel 4, 1984.

17 S. Sontag, quoted in J. Berger, *About Looking*, London, Writers and Readers Cooperative, 1980:50.

18 Quoted in P. Fussell, *The Great War and Modern Memory*, New York, Oxford University Press, 1975:334.

19 J. Stevenson and C. Cook, *The Slump*, London, Jonathan Cape, 1977.

20 R. Barthes, *Mythologies* 1957; London, Paladin, 1973. The discussion of Myth and History takes place on pp.129–59.

21 D. Lowenthal, *The Past is a Foreign Country*, Cambridge, Cambridge University Press, 1985:194.

22 R. Williams, *Politics and Letters*, London, Verso, 1979:391.

23 P. Townsend, *Poverty in the United Kingdom*, Harmondsworth, Penguin, 1979:239.

24 C. McArthur, *Television and History*, London, BFI, 1980.

25 S. Yeo, 'The Politics of Community Publications', in R. Samuel (ed.), *People's History and Socialist Theory*, London, Routledge & Kegan Paul, 1981:32–8.

26 Berger, *op. cit.*, p. 62.

27 S. Sontag, *On Photography*, Harmondsworth, Penguin, 1979:71.

28 Sontag, *op. cit.* p. 21.

29 J. Williamson, *Decoding Advertisements*, London, Marion Boyars, 1978.

30 Williamson, *op. cit.*, p. 164.

31 Williamson, *op. cit.*, p. 160.

32 Williamson, *op. cit.*, p. 160.

33 F. A. Hayek. *A Tiger By The Tail*, London, Institute for Economic Affairs, 1972:87–8.

34 S. Hall and M. Jacques (eds), *The Politics of Thatcherism*, London, Lawrence & Wishart, 1983.

35 By David Held in G. McLennan *et al.* (eds), *State and Society in Contemporary Britain*, Cambridge, Polity Press, 1984:306–10.

36 Gamble, *op. cit.*, p. 145.

37 R. Eccleshall *et al.*, *Political Ideologies*, London, Hutchinson, 1984:110.

38 S. Hall, *Drifting into a Law and Order Society*, London, Cobden Trust pamphlet, 1980.

39 See R. W. Johnson, *The Politics of Recession*, London, Macmillan, 1985.

40 G. Pearson, *Hooligan: A History of Respectable Fears*, London, Macmillan, 1983:4

41 B. Jessop *et al.*, 'Authoritarian Populism, Two Nations, and Thatcherism', *New Left Review*, No. 147, September/October, 1984:32–60.

42 S. Hall, 'Authoritarian Populism: A Reply to Jessop *et al.*', *New Left Review*, No. 151 May/June, 1985:115–24.

43 J. H. Plumb, *The Death of the Past*, London, Macmillan, 1969: 50

44 Quoted in A. Barnett, *Iron Britannia*, London, Allison and Busby, 1982:151. The whole speech is reproduced on pages 149–53.

45 S. Hall, *New Socialist*, 5 July/August 1982.

46 One of the most valuable analyses of 'Thatcherism' may be found in Bill Schwarz, 'The Thatcher Years', in R. Miliband, L. Panitch, and J. Saville (eds) *Socialist Register 1987*, London, Merlin Press, 1987.

1 In those days

1 F. Harrison, *Strange Land*, London, Sidgwick & Jackson, 1981:110.

2 Harrison, *op. cit.*, p. 101.

3 F. Bartlett, *Remembering*, 1932; Cambridge, Cambridge University Press, 1967.

4 Golding and Middleton, *Images of Welfare*, Oxford, Martin Robertson, 1982:226.

5 Golding and Middleton, *op. cit.*, p. 226.

6 The term 'schemata' is used by Bartlett, *op. cit.*

7 Foreword, W. Foley, *No Pipe Dreams for Father*, London, Futura, 1978:11.

8 Introduction, S. Shears, *Tapioca for Tea*, London, Elek, 1971.

9 R. Williams, *The Country and the City*, St. Albans, Paladin, 1975:61.

10 F. Thompson, *Lark Rise to Candleford*, Harmondsworth, Penguin, 1973.

11 Introduction, F. Thompson, *Lark Rise*, London, Folio society, 1979.
12 Thompson, *op. cit.*, p. 10.
13 H. Casson in Thompson, *op. cit.*, 1979:16.
14 J. Berger, *About Looking*, London, Writers and Readers Publishing Cooperative, 1980:88.
15 R. Gamble, *Chelsea Child* London, Ariel Books, BBC, 1979, pb 1982; W. Foley, *A Child in the Forest* 1974, Futura pb, 1977; Helen Forrester, *Twopence to Cross the Mersey*, London, Jonathan Cape, 1974, Futura pb, 1981; *Liverpool Miss*, London, the Bodley Head, 1979, Futura pb, 1982; *By the Waters of Liverpool*, London, The Bodley Head, 1981, Futura pb, 1983; Mollie Harris, *A Kind of Magic*, London, Chatto and Windus, 1969, Oxford University Press pb, 1983.
16 J.-N. Pelen quoted in P. Joutard 'Ethnotexts', *Oral History Journal*, 9, 1, 1981.
17 G. Lakoff and M. Johnson, *Metaphors We Live By*, London, University of Chicago Press, 1980:172.
18 In *Oral History Journal*, 9, 1, 1981:41–45.
19 C. McArthur, *Television and History*, London, BFI, 1980:16.
20 Lakoff and Johnson 1980:175.
21 J. White *History Workshop Journal*, 15 1983:186.
22 S. Sontag, *On Photography*, London, Penguin, 1979:22–3.
23 Berger, *op. cit.*, p. 50.
24 Berger, *op. cit.*, p. 55.
25 R. Gamble, *op. cit.*, pb 1982:8. All further references will be to this edition and will be included in the text.
26 K. Worpole, 'A Ghostly Pavement: The Political Implications of Local Working-Class History', in R. Samuel (ed.), *People's History and Socialist Theory*, London, Routledge & Kegan Paul, 1981:27.
27 Worpole, *op. cit.*, p. 28.
28 J. White, review, *Oral History Journal* 10, 1, 1981:74.
29 A. Calder, *The People's War*, London, Panther, 1971:20.
30 Golding and Middleton, *op. cit.*
31 J. McCrindle and S. Rowbotham, *Dutiful Daughters*, Harmondsworth, Penguin, 1983.
32 Forrester, *op. cit.*, 1981, 1982, 1983. The first volume was dramatized for radio on Radio Four, Monday, 14 April 1986.
33 H. Forrester, *By the Waters of Liverpool*, p. 104. All further references to this text, and the other two volumes in the autobiography, will be to the paperback editions cited in note 15 and will be included in the text as LM, TCM, BWL.
34 Golding and Middleton *op. cit.*, p. 5
35 Golding and Middleton *op. cit.*, p. 37.
36 Golding and Middleton *op. cit.*, p. 48.
37 Golding and Middleton (1982:195).

38 W. Benjamin, *Illuminations*, 1955; London, Fontana, 1973:259.
39 Benjamin, 1973:258.
40 W. Foley, 1977 pb. All further references will be to this edition and will be included in the text.
41 M. Harris 1983. All further references will be to this edition and will be included in the text.
42 J. Neuenschwander, 'Remembrance of Things Past', *Oral History Review*, 1978:43–54.
43 A supplement to the *Oxford English Dictionary*, Vol. 11, H-N Oxford, 1976:1254.

2 A temporary thing

1 J. Stevenson and C. Cook, *The Slump*, London, Jonathan Cape, 1977; Quartet Books, pb 1979:1.
2 Stevenson and Cook, *op. cit.*, p. 3
3 R. Barthes, *S/Z*, trans. R. Miller, London, Cape, 1975:19.
4 In my discussion of the semic code I have drawn extensively on the valuable treatment of this in K. Silverman, *The Subject of Semiotics*, Oxford, Oxford University Press, 1983.
5 The texts chosen are those based upon certain formulaic conventions found in the 'feminine romance', a term which I first introduced in 'Natural Boundaries: The Social Function of Popular Fiction', *Red Letters*, 7, 1978:34–60.
6 F. Jameson, 'Reification and Utopia in Mass Culture', *Social Text* I, 1979:132.
7 F. Jameson, 'Magical Narratives: Romance as Genre', *New Literary History*, 7, No. 1, Autumn 1976:159.
8 Jameson, *op. cit.*, p. 143.
9 M. M. Bakhtin, *The Dialogic Imagination*, trans. Caryl Emerson and Michael Holquist, Texas, University of Texas Press, 1981.
10 E. Rhodes, *Opal*, London, Corgi, 1984. All references will be to this edition and will be included in the text.
11 H. Kanter, S. Lefanu, S. Shah and C. Spedding, (eds) *Sweeping Statements*, London, The Women's Press, 1984:127.
12 Kanter *et. al., op.cit.*, p. 128.
13 Kanter *et al.*, op.cit., p. 157.
14 M. Joseph, *Polly Pilgrim*, London, Arrow Books, 1984. All references will be to this edition and will be included in the text.
15 E. Blair, *Nellie Wildchild*, London, Arrow Books, 1983:170.
16 C. Heilbrun, 'Hers', *The New York Times*, 26 February, 1981:C2.
17 J. Winship, 'Fantasies of Liberation', *Marxism Today*, November, 1984.
18 L. Kennedy, *Nelly Kelly*, London, Futura, 1981. All references will be to this edition and will be included in the text.
19 In some ways, this 'already known discourse' is based upon certain

images of the working class developed by Richard Hoggart in *The Uses of Literacy* (1957) and, earlier, by George Orwell in *The Road to Wigan Pier* (1937); images which, by frequent repetition, have become stereotypes and clichés. Much of Jeremy Seabrook's work on the working class is based upon a similar set of sentimental and stylized assumptions.

20 Quoted in P. Golding and S. Middleton, *Images of Welfare*, Oxford, Martin Robertson, 1982:227.

21 E. Wilson, *Only Halfway to Paradise*, London, Tavistock Publications, 1980:16.

22 P. Jenkin on *Man Alive*, 1979 quoted in A. Coote and B. Campbell, *Sweet Freedom*, Picador, London, 1982:87.

23 A book like Ferdinand Mount's *The Subversive Family*, London, Unwin, 1982, with its emphasis on the 'natural' superiority of the private, the 'feminine', the domestic and the familial indicates how much of a threat this kind of choice poses to the current disposition of ideological hegemony.

24 M. Barrett, *Women's Oppression Today*, London, Verso, 1980:111.

25 R. Barthes, *Camera Lucida*, 1980; London, Fontana, 1984:76.

26 F. Bechhofer and B. Elliott, (eds) *The Petite Bourgeoisie*, London, Macmillan, 1981:191.

27 Bechhofer and Elliott, *op.cit.*, p. 193.

28 Bechhofer and Elliott, *op.cit.*, p. 193.

29 Bechhofer and Elliott, *op.cit.*, p. 192.

30 A. Foreman, *Femininity as Alienation*, London, Pluto Press, 1977:92.

31 Barrett, *op. cit.*, p. 111.

32 A. Gamble and P. Walton, *Capitalism in Crisis*, London, Macmillan, 1976:145.

33 Coote and Campbell, *op.cit.*, p. 197.

3 People like us

1 A. Schutz, *The Phenomenology of the Social World*, trans. G. Walsh and F. Lehnert, Evanston, Illinois, Northwestern University Press, 1967.

2 K. Kosik, *Dialectics of the Concrete; A Study of Problems of Man and World*, Dordrecht, 1976:42–3.

3 S. Hall, 'Variants of Liberalism', in J. Donald and S. Hall (eds), *Politics and Ideology*, Milton Keynes, Open University Press, 1986:55.

4 R. Eccleshall *et al. Political Ideologies: An Introduction*, London, Hutchinson, 1984:70.

5 D. Howell makes this distinction in *British Social Democracy* London, Croom Helm, 1976.

6 I would not wish to over-stress the link between the SDP and the cultural expression of consensual values based upon 'decency', 'Britishness', 'citizenship' and 'social responsibility', because although the party appropriated many of these features at the emotional level of rhetoric and symbol, its 'Atlantic' perspective, equivocal commitment to welfare, very cautious reformism and 1950s subscription to a 'mixed economy', all suggest that its appeal to the 'centre' based on a nebulous popular radicalism was a short-term political strategy designed to *dramatize* the break with the Labour Party; a piece of theatre and little more than an acknowledgement of the 'dreaming suburbs'. The Alliance went into the June 1987 election with a 'vision of a Britain united', with a stress on unity and 'drawing Britain together again' (phrases taken from the manifesto). The manifesto title 'Britain United' had a hollow ring as the SDP and Liberal Party revealed several disagreements during the campaign, and the post-election 'merger' battle left the SDP looking very much a spent force. With predicted economic problems likely to modify Thatcherism and the Labour Party's 'new realism' shaping an appeal to 'comfortable Britain' based upon a modernized version of 'Gaitskellism', it is doubtful whether the SDP as a separate political entity will continue to have a meaningful presence in British politics.

7 L. Althusser, 'The "Piccolo Teatro": Bertolazzi and Brecht', in *For Marx*, trans. B Brewster, 1966; Harmondsworth, Penguin, 1969:129–52.

8 Althusser, *op.cit.*, p. 135.

9 Althusser, *op.cit.*, p. 139.

10 Althusser, *op.cit.*, p. 139.

11 E. Laclau, *Politics and Ideology in Marxist Theory*, London, NLB, 1977.

12 S. Heath quoted in R. Coward and J. Ellis, *Language and Materialism*, London, Routledge & Kegan Paul, 1977:49.

13 Coward and Ellis, *op.cit.*, p.50. As Coward and Ellis note: 'The narration calls upon the subject to regard the process of the narrative as a provisional openness, dependent upon the closure which the subject expects as the very precondition of its pleasure. In order that the narrative is intelligible at all, it is necessary that the subject regards the discourse of narration as the discourse of the unfolding of truth.' Coward and Ellis, *op.cit.*, p. 50.

14 As Laclau argues: 'The more separated is a social sector from the dominant relations of production, and the more diffuse are its 'objective interests' – the more the evolution and resolution of the crisis will tend to take place on the ideological level.' Laclau, *op.cit.*, p. 104.

15 This can be linked with Laclau's suggestion that, 'Not the least of the bourgeoisie's successes in asserting its ideological hegemony is

the consensus it has achieved ... that many of the constitutive elements of democratic and popular culture in a country are irrevocably linked to its class ideology.' Laclau, *op.cit.*, pp.110–11.

16   R. F. Delderfield, *The Dreaming Suburb*, 1964; London, Coronet, 1971, prefatory note.

17   See B. Anderson, *Imagined Communities*, London, Verso, 1983 for an important discussion of 'nation making' as a cultural process.

18   As a way of constructing the past, Delderfield's fictions come close to providing a cultural popularization of a tendency which Martin Wiener identifies in *English Culture and the Decline of the Industrial Spirit 1850–1980*, Harmondsworth, Penguin, 1985 (first published in the USA in 1981). Wiener's 'thesis' is that British middle- and upper-class culture has a suspicion of material and technological development which has led it to the symbolic exclusion of industrialism in favour of 'a softly rustic and nostalgic cast' (Preface, p. ix, Wiener, *op.cit.*, 1985) which can be linked with 'the modern fading of national economic dynamism' (Preface, p. ix). This is a complex cultural issue which Wiener reduces and over-simplifies. Whatever its limitations, Delderfield's work however, could also be understood as a sustained effort to reorganize culture from a point of view which gives power and aauthority to those traditionally excluded from the élite centres of British society. The fictions belong to the genre of sentimental writing, conventional and emotional, but (and this is particularly true of *People Like Us*) designed to construct a set of moral values which challenge both the exclusiveness of the 'softly rustic and nostalgic cast' (Esmé's dream of the Manor, and of its chivalric values, is placed critically) and the acquisitive self-interest of 'economic dynamism'. A reading of Delderfield from the viewpoint of the 'canonical' common sense of literary criticism, a reading which sees the texts themselves simply as expressions of 'common sense', misses the complexity of this particular genre and its relation to common sense as a cultural form (see note 48 below). In the face of the State, industrialization, and a rhetoric which is almost exclusively national, Delderfield's fictions can be seenn as part of a cultural process which gives power to the local and the 'nuclear' community (school, or neighbourhood) to change the world in which they are situated.

19   These distinctions are made by J. Ellis in *Visible Fictions* London, Routledge & Kegan Paul, 1983.

20   J. Berger, *Another Way of Telling*, London, Writers and Readers Publishing Co-operative, 1982.

21   Whyte, *The Organisation Man*, 1957; Harmondsworth, Penguin, 1961:11–12.

22 J. P. Faye, 'The Critique of Language and Its Economy', *Economy and Society*, 5, 1976:59.

23 Faye, *op.cit.*, p.63.

24 Claus Offe and Helmut Wiesenthal, 'Two Logics of Collective Action: theoretical notes on social class and organizational form', in M. Zeitlin (ed.), *Political Power and Social Theory*, Vol. 1, Jai, Greenwich, Connecticut, 1980:69.

25 Offe and Wiesenthal, *op.cit.*, p.92.

26 Offe and Wiesenthal, *op.cit.*, p.102.

27 N. Poulantzas, *Classes in Contemporary Capitalism*, London, New Left Books, 1975.

28 Poulantzas, *op.cit.*

29 R. F. Delderfield, *To Serve Them All My Days*, 1972; London, Coronet, 1980:566. All further references will be to this edition and will be included in the text.

30 G. Dangerfield, *The Strange Death of Liberal England*, 1935; St. Albans, Paladin, 1970.

31 J. B. Priestley, *English Journey*, 1934; Harmondsworth, Penguin, 1977:389, 390.

32 Margaret Thatcher quoted in R. Brunt and G. Bridges (eds) *Silver Linings*, London, Lawrence & Wishart, 1984.

33 Poulantzas, *op.cit.*, p. 289.

34 Offe and Wiesenthal, *op.cit.*

35 N. Abercrombie and J. Urry, *Capital, Labour and the Middle Classes*, London, Allen & Unwin, 1983:135–6.

36 Laclau, *op.cit.*, p. 167.

37 Barnett, *op.cit.*

38 J.H. Plumb, *The Death of the Past*, London, Macmillan, 1969:86.

39 F. S. Northedge, *Descent From Power*, London, Allen & Unwin, 1974:357–62.

40 Laclau, *op.cit.*, p. 167.

41 Laclau, *op.cit.*, p. 167.

42 A. Gramsci, *Prison Notebooks*, eds Q. Hoare and G. Nowell-Smith London, Lawrence and Wishart, 1971:197.

43 Gramsci, *op.cit.*, p. 323.

44 Gramsci, *op.cit.*, p. 326.

45 Gramsci, *op.cit.*, p. 324.

46 See R. Barthes, *S/Z*, trans. R. Miller, London, Cape, 1975 for this notion of reading.

47 A distinctive contribution to the debate on 'common sense' may be found in Clifford Geertz's *Local Knowledge*, New York, Basic Books, 1983, especially the chapter, 'Common Sense as a Cultural System', pp. 73–93. Geertz treats common sense as a relatively organized body of considered thought, *in spite of its also being* a tangle of received practices, accepted beliefs, habitual judgments and untaught emotions – the components of 'colloquial culture'.

According to Geertz, common sense's claim to represent 'how it is' is, in fact, an interpretation or re-presentation of 'how it is', an historically constructed gloss on, or mediation of, the immediacies of 'experience'. Common sense has become a central category of vernacular 'philosophy' and of the sentimental genre of writing, and is the conceptual root and paradigm, not only of Delderfield's fiction, but of much else in British cultural life. It is part of the need, and desire, to render the world distinct and habitable cultur-ally. As a cultural system, in Geertz's analysis, common sense is an elaboration and defence of the claims to truth of 'popular', colloquial reason; it certifies a seen order, momentarily freed of all traces of societal structuration – hierarchy, organization, differ-entiation and inequality. I have developed the links between common sense and popular cultural forms further in an essay, 'Dreaming the Local', in Peter Brooker and Peter Humm (eds), *Dialogue and Difference*, London, Methuen, 1989.

48   G. Stedman-Jones, 'The Poverty of Empiricism', in R. Blackburn (ed.), *Ideology and the Social Sciences*, London, Panther, 1972: 96–115.

49   N. Abercrombie, S. Hill and B. S. Turner (eds), *The Penguin Dictionary of Sociology*, Harmondsworth, Penguin, 1984:17.

50   F. Bechhofer and B. Elliot, *The Petite-Bourgeoisie*, London Macmillan, 1981:193.

51   Margaret Thatcher, *Sunday Times Colour Supplement*, 20 August 1978.

52   Plumb, *op.cit.*

53   M. Wood, 'You Can't go Home Again', in P. Barker (ed.) *Arts in Society*, 1974: Fontana, London, 1977:21–30.

54   R. F. Delderfield, *The Avenue Goes to War*, 1964; London, Coronet, 1971:441.

55   Delderfield, *op.cit.*, p.629.

56   H. M. Drucker, *Doctrine and Ethos in the Labour Party*, London, Allen & Unwin, 1979:32. A lot of my discussion in this section is indebted to Drucker's analysis in his chapter 'The Uses of the Past', pp.23–43.

57   A point made by M. Oakeshott, in R. Kirk (ed.) *The Portable Conservative Reader*, Harmondsworth, Penguin, 1982:571.

58   Wood, *op.cit.*, p. 21.

59   Wood, *op.cit.*, p. 23.

60   See especially Barnett, *op.cit.* and S. Hall, 'Thatcher's War', *New Socialist*, 6, July/August 1982:5–7.

61   Wood, *op.cit.*, p. 29.

62   Wood, *op.cit.*, p.29–30.

63   N. Deakin, 'Looking for a Feasible Socialism', *New Society*, 8 March 1984:357.

64   H. Wainwright, *New Statesman*, 30 January 1981:13.

65 B. Crick, *New Statesman*, 26 March 1982:19–20.
66 B. Crick, *New Socialist*, 5 May/June 1982:46–9.
67 H. Young, *Sunday Times*, March 1984.
68 S. Hall, *Marxism Today*, December 1982:18.
69 P. Jenkins, *Marxism Today*, December 1982:16.
70 Hall, *op.cit.*, p. 15.
71 The ideological territory described in this paragraph has been usefully summarized by Arthur Marwick in the notion of 'secular Anglicanism' as a description of the dominant Conservative position for several decades now.
72 Edward Heath recalls, however, that he made eighty speeches in the EEC referendum of 1975, while Margaret Thatcher, as newly elected leader, made one. (Information from Northedge, *op.cit.*).
73 Northedge, *op.cit.*
74 Northedge, *op.cit.*, p. 352.
75 By July 1973 only 42 per cent of the British people approved of the Common Market as compared with 48 per cent who disapproved. Northedge, *op.cit.*, p. 352.
76 Quoted in full in Barnett, *op.cit.*, p. 149–53.
77 Barnett, *op.cit.*, p. 150.
78 Northedge, *op.cit.*, p. 360.
79 Plumb, *op.cit.*, p. 30.
80 Plumb, *op.cit.*, p. 32.
81 The phrase is used by Hall, *op.cit.*, p. 18.
82 R. Samuel, 'The SDP and the New Political Class', *New Society*, 22 April 1982:124–7.
83 S. Williams, *Politics is for People*, Harmondsworth, Penguin, 1981:28.
84 S. Williams, *op.cit.*, p. 52.
85 R. Williams, *The Country and the City*, St Albans, Paladin, 1975:49–50.
86 S. Williams, *op.cit.*, p. 209.
87 It has been difficult to decide whether to use past or present tense when referring to the Social Democratic Party. At the time of writing (August 1987) the party has voted to negotiate a merger with the Liberal party, and David Owen has resigned as leader. It is possible, but unlikely, that the SDP will continue in some form or other. Some disputes over the use of the name will probably take place, but by March/April 1988 a Liberal Democratic party looks like being formed by the bulk of the existing alliance. David Owen will either gravitate towards the Conservative Party or disappear from politics.

4 Everything British

1 E. Hobsbawm and T. Ranger (eds), *The Invention of Tradition*, Cambridge, Cambridge University Press, 1983:13.
2 See especially T. Harrisson, *Living Through the Blitz*, Harmondsworth, Penguin, 1978.
3 T.V. a.m., 'Good Morning Britain', 8 May 1985.
4 R. Williams, *Problems in Materialism and Culture*, London, Verso, 1980:39.
5 R. Barthes, *Mythologies*, trans. A. Lavers, 1957; London, Paladin, 1973:143.
6 S. Hall, 'Thatcher's War', *New Socialist*, 6 July/Aguust 1982:7.
7 Barthes, *op.cit.*, p. 157.
8 G. Dawson and B. West, 'Our Finest Hour? The Popular Memory of World War II and the Struggle over National Identity', in G. Hurd (ed.), *National Fictions*, London, BFI, 1984:10.
9 J. Ranciere, quoted in Stephen Heath, 'Contexts', *Edinburgh '77 Magazine*, 1977:37.
10 M. Foucault in 'Film and Popular Memory: Cahiers du Cinéma/Extracts', *Edinburgh '77 Magazine*, 1977:22.
11 Freud quoted in Heath, *op.cit.*, p. 39.
12 Ranciere in *Edinburgh '77 Magazine*, 1977:28.
13 Heath, *op.cit.*, pp.37–42.
14 Heath, *op.cit.*, p.39.
15 See C. McArthur, *Television and History*, London, BFI, 1980.
16 Heath, *op.cit.*, p.41.
17 Heath, *op.cit.*, p.42.
18 *Nella Last's War: A Mother's Diary 1939–45*, edited by R. Broad and S. Fleming, 1981; London, Sphere, 1983. All further references will be to this edition and will be incorporated in the text.
19 N. Last, *op.cit.*, p.viii.
20 *Mrs Milburn's Diaries:* An Englishwoman's Day-to-Day Reflections 1939–45, edited by Peter Donnelly, 1979; London, Fontana, 1981. All references will be to this edition and will be incorporated in the text.
21 M.L. Settle, *All the Brave Promises*, 1966; London, Pandora, 1984:83.
22 Mass Observation, *Britain*, London, Penguin, 1939:200.
23 M. Foot, *The Guardian*, 6 December 1982:13.
24 L. Harris, 'State and Economy in the Second World War', in G. McLennan *et al.* (eds), *State and Society in Contemporary Britain*, Cambridge, Polity Press, 1984:75.
25 David Hare, Introduction, *The History Plays*, London, Faber, 1984:13.
26 Barthes, *op.cit.*, p. 151.
27 Marx, quoted in Barthes, *op.cit.*, p. 151.
28 Barthes, *op.cit.*, p. 130.

29 Barthes, *op.cit.*, p. 117.
30 Quoted in P. Anderson, *Arguments Within English Marxism*, London, Verso, 1980:29. This book contains an excellent discussion of the concept of 'experience' which I have drawn upon extensively.
31 V. Massey, *One Child's War*, 1978; London, Ariel Books, BBC, pb 1983. All references will be to this edition and will be incorporated in the text.
32 S. Briggs, *Keep Smiling Through*, London, Weidenfeld and Nicholson, 1975:11.
33 A. Davies, *Where Did the Forties Go?*, London, Pluto Press, 1984.
34 Davies, op.cit., p.107.
35 Davies, op.cit., p. 107.
36 A. Barnett, *The Guardian*, 6 August 1985:17.
37 S. Rothwell, *Lambeth At War*, London, SE1 People's History Project, 1981. All references will be to this edition and will be incorporated in the text.

Conclusion: beginning again

1 J. L. Borges, 'Tlön, Uqbar, Orbis Tertius', 1961:42–3.
2 P. Wright, *On Living in an Old Country*, London, Verso, 1985:188.
3 R. Adler, *Beginning Again*, London, Hodder & Stoughton, 1983. This novel won the Woman of the Eighties Book Award in 1982, and covers the period 1945 to 1949. The central family in the text is Jewish and the husband and wife are both members of the Communist Party. Conflict over education, health and generation occur in the novel, but the central theme is based upon the complex relationship of Rebecca and Morris Lederman. Morris is a shopkeeper and a very active member of a Jewish Welfare Association and the local CP branch. His life is public and political, Rebecca's private, domestic and secondary. Politics almost obliterate his personal life, while Rebecca's personal life almost obliterates her politics. It is a subtle and sensitive novel in which Rebecca struggles for space for her writing and her politics. What the novel emphasizes is that the private and the public, the familial and the political are not (as the fictions examined in Chapter 2 suggest) incompatible. The epigraph to Part Two is from Storm Jameson, *Journey to the North*, Vol. II:

> A woman who wishes to be a creator of anything except children should be content to be a nun or a wanderer on the face of the earth. She cannot be a writer and woman in the way a male writer can also be husband and father. The demands made on her as a woman are destructive in a peculiarly disintegrating way – if she considers them. And if she does not consent, if she

cheats . . . a sharp grain of guilt lodges itself within her, guilt, self-condemnation, regret. . . .

This dilemma is rooted in the confusing and contradictory experience of the postwar 'settlement' and is unusual in the way in which it foregrounds gender issues in a popular format, suggesting that the popular is not inaccessible to radical possibilities.

4 *The Making of Modern London*, London Weekend Television, 1985.
5 Tony Benn, interview with Eric Hobsbawm, *Marxism Today*, October 1980:6.
6 *Now the War is Over*, BBC1, eight-part series, 1985.
7 P. Addison, *Now the War is Over*, London, BBC and Jonathan Cape, 1985:vi.
8 Addison, op. cit., p. vii.
9 Addison, op. cit., p. viii.
10 R. Fraser, *In Search of a Past*, London, Verso, 1984:6.
11 P. Wright, 'Misguided Tours', *New Socialist*, July/August, 1986:34.
12 C. Steedman, *Landscape for a Good Woman*, London, Virago, 1986:6.
13 Steedman, op. cit., p.11.
14 Steedman, op. cit., p.77.
15 Steedman, op. cit., p. 138.
16 S. Marcus quoted in Steedman, op. cit., p.131.
17 Interview with Margaret Thatcher, *The Sunday Times* colour supplement, 20 August 1978:

I want decent, fair, honest, citizen values, all the principles you were brought up with. You don't live up to the hilt of your income; if someone gets the bills wrong you tell them, you don't keep the extra change; you respect other people's property; you save; you believe in right and wrong; you support the police. . . . We were taught to help people in need ourselves, not stand about saying what the government should do. Personal initiative was pretty strong. You were actually taught to be clean and tidy, that cleanliness was next to Godliness. All these ideas have got saddled as middle class values, but they're eternal.

18 *For Memory*, BBC-BFI co-production, directed by Marc Karlin, 1983, transmitted on 31 March 1986. All further quotations in my text are taken from this programme unless otherwise specified.
19 A recent, and quite remarkable, instance of this form of consciousness (the 'social amnesia' cited in the Preface) was the introduction to 'Vision 2010', a report by the CBI's London Region Council Education and Training Committee. The report by a team of 'high flying executives' stated:

We are all under 35. What has struck many of us is the contrast between the state of mind of the nation now, and the state of mind *we have been told* existed years ago. It seems that you have to go back to the War to find a time when everyone pulled together and backed the same ideal.

During the War people knew what they and their fellow countrymen stood for; there was a common goal or purpose. To that, everyone surrendered their petty greed, their selfishness, their moaning. They became personally responsible for their part in the war, and they bit on the hardship it entailed.

Funnily enough, some of that generation will tell you that it was the best time of their life.

(My italics) quoted in *City Limits*, 30 July – 6 August 1987:6

The report is explicitly nationalist (it speaks of 'developing our national character') and the rhetoric very familiar now as part of that re-writing of the 'historical narrative' which has formed the basis of much of this book. It draws upon those 'preferred memories' analysed in chapter 4, and takes no account of the deep contradictions in the experience of war. Instead, myth and 'Image-banks' are allowed to stand in for historical analysis and explanation. While many in the past decade ('the state of mind of the nation now') have esteemed petty greed and selfishness, they are still anxious to construct a narrative in which possible hardship is given a specific national (not individual) inflection. The report calls this a 'national context for action'. Most people experience contradictions at *local* and *personal* levels; this is their existential reality. Those without power only experience the *national* in rhetorical/iconic terms, hence the use by the report, and by Thatcherism generally, of a 'national past' generated ideologically out of antagonism to region, gender, class, ethnicity, period-specificity – all those historical and individual *particularities* which deterritorialize the coherences of the 'national allegory'.

The CBI report's representation of the national past, like its construction of 'the mind of the nation', is not history, but deliberately crafted, accessible and habitable, mythology. Like the 'New Right' narrative it is effective because, like so much of our media experience, it 'moves rhetorically back and forth between fiction and the real world'. This phrase is quoted from Paul Erickson (writing about Reagan) by Harvey Kaye in, what is to date, the most illuminating discussion of this whole issue. The discussion may be found in *Socialist Register 1987*, ed. R. Miliband, L. Panitch and J. Saville, London, The Merlin Press 1987:332–64; 'The Use and Abuse of the Past: The New Right and the Crisis of History'.

20 D. Lowenthal, *The Past is a Foreign Country*, Cambridge, Cambridge University Press, 1985:410.

Bibliography

Place of publication London unless otherwise specified.

Primary Sources

Where applicable, the second date cited is that of the paperback
edition.

(a) *Novels*

Adler, R., *Beginning Again*, Hodder & Stoughton, 1983;
Coronet, 1985.

Blair, E., *Nellie Wildchild*, Arrow Books, 1983.

Cookson, C., *Pure as the Lily*, MacDonald, 1973.

Delderfield, R.F., *The Dreaming Suburb*, Hodder & Stoughton,
1964; Coronet, 1971.

Delderfield, R.F., *The Avenue goes to War*, Hodder &
Stoughton, 1964; Coronet, 1971.

Delderfield, R.F., *To Serve Them All My Days*, Hodder &
Stoughton, 1972; Coronet, 1980.

Joseph, M., *Molly Pilgrim*, Arrow Books, 1984.

Kennedy, L., *Nelly Kelly, MacDonald, 1981; Futura, 1981.*

Rhodes, E., Opal, Corgi, 1984.

(b) *Autobiographies, Diaries, Letters*

Beechey, W., *The Rich Mrs Robinson*, Oxford, Oxford University Press, 1984; Futura, 1985.

Foley, W., *A Child in the Forest*, MacDonald, 1974; Futura, 1977.

Foley, W., *No Pipe Dreams for Father*, Douglas McLean, 1977; Futura, 1978.

Forrester, H., *Twopence to Cross the Mersey*, Jonathan Cape, 1974; Futura, 1981.

Forrester, H., *Liverpool Miss*, The Bodley Head, 1979; Futura, 1982.

Forrester, H., *By the Waters of Liverpool*, The Bodley Head, 1981; Futura, 1983.

Gamble, R., *Chelsea Child*, Ariel Books, 1979, 1982.

Harris, M., *A Kind of Magic*, Chatto & Windus, 1969; Oxford, Oxford University Press, 1983.

Holden, E., *The Country Diary of an Edwardian Lady*, Michael Joseph with Webb & Bower, 1977; Sphere Books, 1982.

Last, N., *Nella Last's War: A Mother's Diary 1939–45* edited by Richard Broad and Susie Fleming, Falling Wall Press, 1981; Sphere Books, 1983.

McCrindle, J., and Rowbotham S., (eds), *Dutiful Daughters*, Harmondsworth, Penguin, 1979.

Massey, V., *One Child's War*, Ariel Books, BBC, 1978, 1983.

Mrs Milburn's Diaries, An English Woman's Day-to-Day Reflections 1939–45, edited by P. Donnelly, Harrap, 1979; Fontana, 1980.

Rothwell, S., *Lambeth at War*, SE1 People's History Project, 1981.

Scannell, D., *Dolly's War*, Macmillan, 1975.

Settle, M.L., *All the Brave Promises*, 1966; Pandora Press, 1984.

Thompson, F., *Lard Rise to Candleford*, 1945; Harmondsworth, Penguin 1973.

(c) *Television Programmes*

BBC 1, *Dunkirk: The story behind the legend*, May 1980.

Channel Four, *Shebbear*, 1984.

TV-AM, *Good Morning Britain*, 8 May 1985.

ITN, *Victory Remembered*, 8 May 1985.

LWT, *The Making of Modern London*, 1985.

BBC1, *The Promised Land*, 1985.

BBC 1, *Now the War is Over*, 1985.

BBC-BFI, *For Memory*, 1983, 1986.

Yorkshire Television, *How We Used to Live*, 1976, repeated on May 8 1985.

Secondary Sources

Books
[Where appropriate the original date of publication is the first item given after the title in parenthesis]
Abercrombie, N., and Urry, J., *Capital, Labour and the Middle Classes*, Allen & Unwin, 1985.
Abercrombie, N., Hill, S., and Turner, B.S., *The Penguin Dictionary of Sociology*, Harmondsworth, Penguin, 1984.
Addison, P., *Now the War is Over*, BBC and Jonathan Cape, 1985.
Age Exchange, *What Did You Do in the War, Mum?*, Age Exchange, 1985.
Althusser, L., *For Marx*, trans. B. Brewster, Harmondsworth, Penguin, 1969.
Anderson, B., *Imagined Communities*, Verso Editions and NLB, 1983.
Anderson, P., *Arguments Within English Marxism*, Verso Editions and NLB, 1980.
Armstrong, P., Glyn, A., and Harrison, J., *Capitalism since World War Two*, Fontana, 1984.
Baddeley, A.D., *The Psychology of Memory*, New York, Basic Books, 1976.
Bakhtin, M.M., *The Dialogic Imagination*, trans. C. Emerson and M. Holquist, Texas, University of Texas Press, 1981.
Barker, P., (ed.), *Arts in Society*, Fontana, 1977.
Barker, R., *Political Ideas in Modern Britain*, Methuen, 1978.
Barnett, A., *Iron Britannia*, Allison & Busby, 1982.
Barrett, M., *Women's Oppression Today*, Verso editions and NLB 1980.
Barthes, R., *Mythologies*, trans. A. Lavers [1957] Paladin, 1973.
Barthes, R., *S/Z*, trans. R. Miller [1970] Cape, 1975.
Barthes, R., *The Pleasure of the Text*, trans. R. Miller, 1975; Cape, 1976.
Barthes, R., *Camera Lucida*, trans. R. Howard [1980] Fontana, 1984.
Bartlett, F.C., *Remembering: A Study in Experimental and Social Psychology* [1932] Cambridge, Cambridge University Press, 1967.
Bechhofer, F., and Elliott, B., *The Petite-Bourgeoisie*, Macmillan, 1981.
Benjamin, W., *Illuminations* [1955] Fontana, 1973.

Berger, J., *About Looking*, Writers and Readers Co-operative Society Ltd., 1980.

Berger, J., *Another Way of Telling*, Writers and Readers Co-operative Society Ltd., 1982.

Briggs, S., *Keep Smiling Through*, Weidenfeld & Nicolson, 1975.

Brittain, V., *England's Hour* [1942] Futura, 1981.

Brunt, R., and Bridges, G., (eds), *Silver Linings*, Lawrence & Wishart, 1984.

Bryant, A., *Protestant Island*, Collins, 1967.

Bryant, A., *Spirit of England*, Collins, 1982.

Calder, A., *The People's War*, Panther, 1971.

Campbell, B., *Wigan Pier Revisited: Poverty and Politics in the Eighties*, Virago Press, 1984.

Coote A., and Campbell, B., *Sweet Freedom, The Struggle for Women's Liberation*, Pan, 1982.

Corrigan P., and Sayer, D., *The Great Arch: English State Formation as Cultural Revolution*, Oxford, Basil Blackwell, 1985.

Coward, R., and Ellis, J., *Language and Materialism*, Routledge & Kegan Paul, 1977.

Coward, R., *Female Desire*, Paladin, 1984.

Dangerfield, G.M., *The Strange Death of Liberal England* [1935] St Albans, Paladin, 1970.

Davies, A., *Where Did the Forties Go?*, Pluto Press, 1984.

Donald, J., and Hall, S., (ed), *Politics and Ideology*, Milton Keynes, Open University Press, 1986.

Drucker, H.M., *Doctrine and Ethos in the Labour Party*, Allen & Unwin, 1979.

Eccleshall, R., Geoghegan, V., Jay, R., and Wilford, R., (eds), *Political Ideologies*, Hutchinson, 1984.

Ellis, J., *Visible Fictions*, Routledge and Kegan Paul, 1982.

Foreman, A., *Femininity as Alienation*, Pluto Press, 1977.

Formation of Nation and People, Routledge & Kegan Paul, 1984.

Foster, H., (ed.), *Post-Modern Culture*, Pluto Press, 1985.

Fraser, R., *In Search of a Past*, Verso Editions and NLB, 1984.

Fussell, P., *The Great War and Modern Memory*, New York, Oxford University Press, 1975.

Gamble, A., *Britain in Decline*, Macmillan, 1981; 2nd edn, 1985.

Gamble, A., and Walton, P., *Capitalism in Crisis*, Macmillan, 1976.

Golding, P., and Elliot, P., *Making the News*, Leicester, University of Leicester Centre for Mass Communication Research, 1976.

Golding, P., and Middleton, S., *Images of Welfare: Press and Public Attitudes to Welfare*, Oxford, Martin Robertson, 1982.

Grafton, P., *You, You and You*, Pluto Press, 1981.

Gramsci, A., *Selections from the Prison Notebooks*, eds Q. Hoare and G. Nowell Smith, Lawrence & Wishart, 1971.

Gurevitch, M., Bennett, T., Curran, J., and Wollacott, J., *Culture, Society and the Media*, Methuen, 1982.

Hall, S., Critcher, C., Jefferson, T., Clarke J., and Roberts, B., *Policing the Crisis: Mugging, the State and Law and Order*, Macmillan, 1978.

Hall, S., Hobson, D., Lowe A., and Willis P., (eds), *Culture, Media, Language*, Hutchinson, 1980.

Hall, S., and Jacques, M., (eds), *The Politics of Thatcherism*, Lawrence & Wishart, 1983.

Halsey, A.H., *Change in British Society*, Oxford, Oxford University Press, 3rd edition, 1986.

Hare, D., *The History Plays*, Faber, 1984.

Harrisson, T., *Living Through the Blitz*, Harmondsworth, Penguin, 1978.

Hayek, F.A., *A Tiger by the Tail*, Institute for Economic Affairs, 1972.

Held, D., Anderson, J., Gieben, B., Hall, S., Harris, L., Lewis, P., Parker, N., Turok, B., (eds), *States and Societies*, Oxford, Basil Blackwell in association with the Open University Press, 1983.

Heller, A., *Everyday Life* [1970] Routledge & Kegan Paul, 1984.

Henige, D., *Oral Historiography*, Longmans, 1982.

Hobsbawm, E., and Ranger, T., (eds), *The Invention of Tradition*, Cambridge University Press, 1983.

Howell, D., *British Social Democracy*, Croom Helm, 1976.

Hurd, G., (ed.), *National Fictions*, BFI, 1984.

Johnson, R.W., *The Politics of Recession*, Macmillan, 1985.

Johnson, R., McLennan, G., Schwarz, W., and Sutton, D., (eds), *Making Histories; studies in history-wrting and politics*, Hutchinson, 1982.

Kanter, H., Lefanu, S., Shah, S., and Spedding, C., (eds), *Sweeping Statements, Writings from the Women's Liberation Movement*, 1981–1983, The Women's Press, 1984.

Kirk, R., (ed.), *The Portable Conservative Reader*, Harmondsworth, Penguin, 1982.

Kosik, K., *Dialectics of the Concrete; A Study on Problems of Man and World*, Dordrecht, publisher not known, 1976.

Laclau, E., *Politics and Ideology in Marxist Theory*, NLB, 1977.

Lakoff, G., and Johnson, M., *Metaphors We Live By*, Chicago, University of Chicago Press, 1980.

Lowenthal, D., *The Past is a Foreign Country*, Cambridge, Cambridge University Press, 1985.

Marwick, A., *The Home Front*, Thames & Hudson, 1976.

Mass Observation, *Britain*, Penguin Special, 1939.

Memory Lane: A Photographic Album of Daily Life in Britain 1930–53, Dent, 1980.

Middlemass, K., *Politics in Industrial Society*, Andre Deutsch, 1979.

Morley, D., and Worpole, K., (eds), *The Republic of Letters: Working Class Writing and Local Publishing*, Comedia Publishing Group, 1982.

Mount, F., *The Subversive Family*, Hemel Hempstead, Counterpoint, Unwin Paperbacks, 1982.

McArthur, C., *Television and History*, BFI, 1980.

McLennan, G., Held, D., and Hall, S., (eds), *State and Society in Contemporary Britain; A Critical Introduction*, Cambridge, Polity Press in association with Basil Blackwell, Oxford, 1984.

Northedge, F.S., *Descent from Power*, Allen and Unwin, 1974.

Ong, W.J., *Orality and Literacy: The Technologizing of the Word*, Methuen, 1982.

Pearson, G., *Hooligan: A History of Respectable Fears*, Macmillan, 1983.

Pecheux, M., *Language, Semantics and Ideology* [1970] Macmillan, 1982.

Plumb, J.H., *The Death of the Past*, Macmillan, 1969.

Poulantzas, N., *Classes in Contemporary Capitalism*, NLB, 1975.

Priestley, J.B., *English Journey* [1934] Harmondsworth, Penguin, 1977.

Samuel, R., (ed.), *People's History and Socialist Theory*, Routledge & Kegan Paul, 1981.

Schlesinger, P., *Putting Reality Together*, Constable, 1978.

Schutz, A., *The Phenomenology of the Social World*, trans. G. Walsh and F. Lehnert, Evanston, Illinois, Northwestern University Press, 1967.

Shrapnel, N., *The Seventies: Britain's Inward March*, Constable, 1980.

Silverman, K., *The Subject of Semiotics*, Oxford, Oxford University Press, 1983.

Sontag, S., *On Photography*, Harmondsworth, Penguin, 1979.

Steedman, C., *The Tidy House: Little Girls Writing*, Virago Press, 1982.

Steedman, C., *Landscape for a Good Woman*, Virago Press, 1986.

Stevenson, J., and Cook, C., *The Slump: Society and Politics during the Depression*, Quartet Books, 1979.

Thompson, E.P., *Writing by Candlelight*, Merlin Press, 1980.

Thorns, D., *Suburbia*, St Albans, Paladin, 1973.

Those Were the Days, 1919–1939: A Photographic Album of Daily Life in Britain, Dent, 1983.

Townsend, P., *Poverty in the United Kingdom*, Harmondsworth, Penguin, 1979.

Whyte, W.H., *The Organisation Man*, Harmondsworth, Penguin, 1961.

Williams, R., *The Country and the City*, St Albans, Paladin, 1975.

Williams, R., *Keywords*, Fontana, 1976.

Williams, R., *Problems in Materialism and Culture*, NLB, 1980.

Williams, R., *Politics and Letters*, Verso Editions and NLB, 1981.

Williams, S., *Politics is for People*, Harmondsworth, Penguin, 1981.

Williamson, J., *Decoding Advertisements*, Marion Boyars, 1978.

Wilson, E., *Only Halfway to Paradise: Women in Postwar Britain – 1945–1968*, Tavistock Publications, 1980.

Wright, P., *On Living in an Old Country: The National Past in Contemporary Britain*, Verso, 1985.

INDEX